Migration for Employment

BILATERAL AGREEMENTS
AT A CROSSROADS

OECD

ORGANISATION FOR ECONOMIC CO-OPERATION AND DEVELOPMENT

ORGANISATION FOR ECONOMIC CO-OPERATION AND DEVELOPMENT

Pursuant to Article 1 of the Convention signed in Paris on 14th December 1960, and which came into force on 30th September 1961, the Organisation for Economic Co-operation and Development (OECD) shall promote policies designed:

- to achieve the highest sustainable economic growth and employment and a rising standard of living in member countries, while maintaining financial stability, and thus to contribute to the development of the world economy;

- to contribute to sound economic expansion in member as well as non-member countries in the process of economic development; and

- to contribute to the expansion of world trade on a multilateral, non-discriminatory basis in accordance with international obligations.

The original member countries of the OECD are Austria, Belgium, Canada, Denmark, France, Germany, Greece, Iceland, Ireland, Italy, Luxembourg, the Netherlands, Norway, Portugal, Spain, Sweden, Switzerland, Turkey, the United Kingdom and the United States. The following countries became members subsequently through accession at the dates indicated hereafter: Japan (28th April 1964), Finland (28th January 1969), Australia (7th June 1971), New Zealand (29th May 1973), Mexico (18th May 1994), the Czech Republic (21st December 1995), Hungary (7th May 1996), Poland (22nd November 1996), Korea (12th December 1996) and the Slovak Republic (14th December 2000). The Commission of the European Communities takes part in the work of the OECD (Article 13 of the OECD Convention).

Publié en français sous le titre :
Migration et emploi
LES ACCORDS BILATÉRAUX À LA CROISÉE DES CHEMINS

FOREWORD

In a world that requires constant policy adaptation, meeting places in which to exchange our views enable us to reflect on our daily actions and practices. They are all the more crucial in that migration is a sensitive and complex area of study. It is in this spirit that, as the host country, we had the great pleasure of welcoming to Montreux the seminar, the proceedings of which are reproduced in this publication. This seminar on bilateral agreements and other forms of recruitment of foreign workers provided a wonderful opportunity for us to exchange views and experiences on migration policies.

Switzerland is not a stranger to the phenomenon of migration movements. Indeed, the country's past and recent history is made up of both emigration and immigration. Let us bear in mind that the current share of foreigners in the population of Switzerland reaches nearly 20%, accounting for a significant proportion of 21st century Swiss society. Such a proportion constitutes a constant challenge for the Swiss authorities in terms of integration policies, as these migrants are undoubtedly one of the keys to a future boom in our national economy.

Taking these elements into account, we are certain that within the framework of the OECD, the Swiss experience in the field of migration policies – especially as regards foreign workers – can pave the way forward or raise interesting questions for partner countries. We are as eager to share our experiences as to learn from other countries, especially when our partner's responses are innovative. In thanking the contributors to the Montreux seminar, I hope this publication will find an echo in the process of elaboration of our various present and future migration policies.

The OECD provides us with a much-needed forum on migration, a sort of agora of modern times. Indeed, the reflections and exchanges that such a seminar makes possible are the two sources that nourish political action, with the aim of better preparing for the future. In a world that is evolving faster and faster, and becoming increasingly complex, any action that can help anticipate proves to be a necessity. Let us remember this phrase of Denis de Rougemont : « *Toute politique est autorisation de l'avenir* ».

Let us take the pulse of our times in order to better prepare for our future.

Ruth Metzler-Arnold
Former Swiss Federal Councillor

This book is published under the responsibility of the Secretary-General of the OECD.

TABLE OF CONTENTS

Part I
A RENEWED INTEREST IN BILATERAL LABOUR AGREEMENTS

Part II
ALTERNATIVES IN FOREIGN LABOUR RECRUITMENT

Part III
ASSESSING NEW OPPORTUNITIES FOR LABOUR MIGRATION

EXECUTIVE SUMMARY

This publication brings to light the diversity of situations found in OECD member countries. The background papers and the debates were centred on three questions: What exactly are the objectives of bilateral labour agreements? Are such agreements effective in achieving those objectives? Are there other ways of achieving the objectives? Bilateral labour agreements are part of a long tradition in some member countries such as Germany and Switzerland. In others countries, they are more limited and cover only a small share of labour-related migration. Finally, some countries such as Australia, Canada and New Zealand have little experience with bilateral agreements, while others like the United States or the United Kingdom have opted to develop other labour-related migration programmes.

From the receiving country standpoint, the primary aim is to meet labour market needs by facilitating short-term or medium to long-term adjustment. In the short term, agreements concern temporary migrants (including seasonal workers) and demand for low-skilled labour in particular. In the medium to long term, however, the agreements focus more on skilled workers to tackle more structural labour shortages (*e.g.* in information and communication technology and health care). Host countries use bilateral agreements to manage migration by asking sending countries to sign in exchange readmission agreements for migrants in an irregular situation. This is the case of agreements signed between Italy and Romania, and by Spain with Morocco and Ecuador. Receiving countries may also wish to promote specific economic ties or wider regional economic integration. Examples include bilateral agreements that Germany has signed with some central and eastern European countries. One final objective is aimed more specifically at strengthening cultural ties between partner countries, as does Australia's working holidaymaker programme. The objectives of sending countries are to ensure better living conditions and increased earning capacity for migrant workers, and to promote the acquisition or enhancement of their professional skills and qualifications. In addition to remittances, technology transfers and building human capital foster the development of sending countries. Finally, sending countries now place greater emphasis on the rights and welfare of their nationals working abroad.

Are bilateral agreements effective in achieving the above objectives? The effectiveness of these agreements is not easy to assess because of the multitude of objectives. To achieve short-term labour market objectives, the key to success lies in flexibility. Agreements that are too bureaucratic, complex and costly, risk failure. It is important to take into account the salient features of the agreements and the countries concerned, for example those between Germany and Poland. Also of interest are the procedures introduced by the United Kingdom, and in particular those leading to the delivery of a work and residence permit within 24 hours. For longer-term adjustment, as in the case of workers in the information and communication technology or health care sectors, migration alone cannot alleviate labour shortages. For the most part, the solution rests on conducting structural reform in the host country, involving labour markets, and education and training systems. Better human capital management is a precursor to the reforms, and is important in meeting the challenges of an ageing population.

Having multiple objectives makes it challenging to assess whether agreements are effective and inevitably creates trade-offs among goals. Some objectives may actually conflict. Thus, the effectiveness of agreements will depend on the weight assigned to each goal. For instance, if the aim is to promote rapid labour market adjustment, security problems may appear, due to the lack of information on new arrivals. At the same time, attempts to tackle labour shortages may raise ethical concerns such as "brain drain", and undermine the objective of promoting economic development in sending countries. Thus, it is necessary to promote social dialogue by involving social partners in drafting and monitoring migration agreements, to ensure that all stakeholders benefit from these agreements.

Are there other ways of achieving these objectives? Some countries have experimented with schemes other than bilateral agreements. To meet labour market needs, the United States and Canada, for example, have promoted transparency in the regimes governing migration, namely within temporary migration – with specific stay duration and precise rules on limited renewal – and permanent migration, also subject to precise criteria. These systems create the environment for improved migration flow management and are, thus, effective in terms of that objective. They are probably effective also in meeting medium-term needs on the labour market. Yet, the systems require the introduction of new, lengthy procedures and prove less effective in meeting the short-term needs of the labour market. In the longer term and for skilled labour in particular, a comprehensive approach (based on selective policies as in Australia, Canada and New Zealand or special visas, as in the United States) is probably more effective than bilateral agreements.

INTRODUCTION

The OECD Secretariat and the Swiss Federal Office of Immigration, Integration and Emigration (IMES) organised a joint seminar on bilateral labour agreements and other forms of recruitment of foreign workers in Montreux, Switzerland, on 19 and 20 June 2003. The main aim was to offer participants an opportunity to exchange experiences and obtain information on labour recruitment policies among OECD member and non-member countries. The Montreux seminar brought together numerous policy makers and experts from OECD member countries and sending countries, as well as observers from the European Commission (EC), the Council of Europe (CE), the International Labour Organization (ILO) and the International Organization for Migration (IOM). Experts represented employee groups, employers associations, trade unions, government officials and international migration research institutions.

The seminar comprised three sessions (see Annex 2A) beginning with an overview of labour recruitment practices in OECD member countries. The second session focused on the implementation of these practices within certain sectors (new technologies, health care) and the viewpoint of sending countries, employers and the social partners. During the third session, the challenges and limits to the negotiation of labour recruitment agreements were discussed, as well as the prospects for potential co-operation on development issues in sending countries. In preparation, numerous background missions and interviews were conducted, centred on three questions: What exactly are the objectives of bilateral labour agreements? Are such agreements effective in achieving those objectives? Are there other ways of achieving the objectives? The results of this research are presented in detail in the case studies prepared for the seminar and are summarised in this volume, which presents a synthesis of the interviews, room documents and seminar discussions.

The overview provides a description of the types of agreements covered, with a focus on the reasons behind the creation of these agreements. The management and implementation of these agreements are reviewed in Part I, with specific attention given to the perspective of the social partners. Part II covers the lessons learned by sending and receiving countries in terms of the impact of the agreements on their labour markets, economic development and migration policies. Finally, Part III examines prospects for, and possible improvements in, the recruitment of foreign labour for sending and receiving countries.

Additional information on the variety of bilateral agreements and other forms of labour recruitment are given by country in Annex 1.A. The annex lists the principal agreements signed by OECD member countries, by type of recruitment scheme (*e.g.* seasonal workers, contract workers, guest workers, trainees, cross-border workers and working holidaymakers).

OVERVIEW OF BILATERAL AGREEMENTS AND OTHER FORMS OF LABOUR RECRUITMENT[1]

by

Daniela Bobeva

Director, International Relations and EU Integration, Bulgarian National Bank

and

Jean-Pierre Garson

Head, Non-Member Economies and International Migration Division
Directorate for Employment, Labour and Social Affairs, OECD

Diversity of labour recruitment schemes

This report covers all forms of arrangements between countries, regions and public institutions that provide for the recruitment and employment of foreign workers. A variety of labels are given to these agreements by different countries (employment treaties, labour agreements, recruitment treaties, migration agreements, agreements for exchange of labour). The legal status of such agreements may vary (intergovernmental agreements, protocols of agreements, memoranda of understanding, memoranda of agreement, national policy regulations), reflecting the broadening of the content and aims of foreign labour recruitment. Since World War II, OECD member countries have resorted to a wide variety of labour recruitment schemes to help address labour shortage problems. Despite the mass migration of ethnic groups and displaced persons immediately after the war, the reconstruction of post-war Europe generated significant labour shortages. In response, the government authorities of the countries concerned, along with firms and private agencies, actively recruited migrant workers. Western European countries, including Belgium, France, Germany, the Netherlands and Switzerland, concluded a series of bilateral agreements with Ireland, southern Europe (Greece, Italy, Portugal, Spain), Turkey, the former Yugoslavia and North Africa (Algeria, Morocco, Tunisia).

In Asia, bilateral agreements were concluded mainly by the Philippines, Thailand and Vietnam. During the late 1970s and 1980s, the Philippines, now considered to be the largest labour exporting country in the Asian region, signed agreements concerning its expatriate workers with numerous countries in the Asia-Pacific region (Bangladesh, Papua New Guinea), the Middle East (Jordan, Iran, Iraq, Qatar), Europe (Austria, Belgium, Cyprus, Greece, United Kingdom) and Africa (Liberia, Libya). Limited labour mobility within North America was formalised with the signature and ratification of the

---

1.   The authors would like to thank Anaïs Loizillon, Consultant, for her help in finalising this overview, and for her contribution to the editing of this publication.

North Atlantic Free Trade Agreement (NAFTA), but this trilateral agreement did not lead to the expected decrease in irregular migration flows from Mexico to the United States.

Although the largest labour movements between countries take place outside the channel of bilateral agreements, more than 176 bilateral agreements and other forms of labour recruitment are currently in force in OECD countries. These schemes are found throughout all the regions of the world. As a consequence of the newly opened borders of Central and Eastern European countries (CEECs), the number of bilateral investment treaties quintupled at the beginning of the 1990s. In some former sending countries (*e.g.* Italy, Portugal, Spain), there has been a new wave of agreements since the late 1990s, reflecting labour shortages in these countries. More recently, many OECD member countries have amended legislation or developed new migration policies to facilitate the entry of skilled foreign workers. The diversity of labour recruitment schemes among OECD member countries reflects the different economic environments, specific labour market conditions, nature of labour shortages and current and projected economic conditions, as well as political concerns. By definition, recruitment schemes are labour market oriented and take into account knowledge of current labour market conditions within receiving countries.

For both bilateral labour agreements and other forms of labour recruitment, the permitted length of stay given to migrant workers is a central feature of the various schemes. While some forms are clearly more temporary than others (*e.g.* seasonal workers), labour recruitment is generally considered to be a short or medium-term policy goal to meet significant labour shortages. However, some schemes can lead to permanent settlement through changes in status to permanent residence or even naturalisation. In some countries there is the possibility, in particular circumstances, of converting a temporary permit into a permanent residence or settlement permit at the end of a period of employment. One current recruitment scheme with permanent settlement was introduced by the Czech Republic to recruit young qualified workers and their families from three test countries (Bulgaria, Croatia and Kazakhstan) during a five-year pilot project (2003-2007), but it is still too early to evaluate the results of this scheme. In Germany, a draft law proposed several systems (point-based, or for highly qualified specialists) that would grant eligible labour migrants permanent residence permits under certain conditions. While active recruitment schemes differ across OECD member countries, they can be grouped into two main categories: bilateral labour agreements (strictly defined as a labour mobility agreement between two countries), and other forms of labour recruitment.

Bilateral labour agreements

Bilateral labour agreements are by far the most widespread method of recruiting labour in terms of the variety of existing schemes, but not of the number of people involved. A list is presented in Annex 1.A by country and by type of labour recruited (*e.g.* seasonal workers, contract workers, guest workers, trainees, cross-border workers and working holidaymakers). The most common categories of bilateral labour agreements are described below.

Seasonal worker agreements concern stays ranging from three months to a year, and are usually limited to sectors with a high variation of employment over the year, such as hospitality, catering, agriculture or construction. Most seasonal worker agreements use quotas to limit the number of entries, while attempting to meet employer demand. Employment services or other intermediaries in the sending or receiving country facilitate recruitment. The largest supplier of seasonal labour through bilateral agreements is Poland, with nearly 300 000 workers in other OECD member countries in 2002. In North America, Canada's Seasonal Agricultural Worker Programme, begun in 1966 with Caribbean nations and extended to Mexico in 1974, has recently admitted more than 15 000 workers per year.

Contract worker and project-linked worker agreements cover foreign workers who are directly employed, either by a foreign-based company or by a domestic firm carrying out work abroad. Such agreements facilitate access to work permits. Quotas under these provisions usually limit the number of contract workers, while the sending country distributes the quotas among firms. For example, in Germany, agreements dating from 1989 have allowed foreign workers to be sent by their employers to work in Germany for a maximum period of three years under a contract for work and services. In 2002, 45 400 contract workers were employed in Germany.

Guest worker agreements have regressed in scope and scale since their widespread use for the reconstruction of Western Europe after World War II. Germany, for example, signed eight bilateral agreements between 1955 (Italy) and 1968 (former Yugoslavia) to hire 2.6 million *Gastarbeiter* (guest workers). Currently, these schemes are smaller and have shifted from general recruitment mechanisms to skilled professional training schemes. Most guest worker programmes are limited to one year, with a possible extension for another year. In 2001, Germany hosted less than 6 000 foreigners under this scheme.

Trainee agreements, or other short-term training programmes, similar to modern guest worker schemes, aim to enhance the professional training of young workers or help students complete their studies through work experience abroad. Agreements allow the visit to vary from 12 to 18 months and require that applicants secure their own training. Eligibility for recruitment can be made subject to entry requirements based on language and skill qualifications (for Czech nationals in Germany) or be generalised to the entire labour market (for Romanians in Hungary). However, in this last example, even though the bilateral agreement grants access to all Romanians, in effect, the language requirements mean that only ethnic Hungarians may participate. Recruitment schemes for professional trainees are popular in Germany and Luxembourg, and especially in Switzerland, which has signed 28 agreements with foreign countries to allow graduates to work in occupations related to their field of study. Co-operation and development play an important role in such agreements, all of which include the critical element of reciprocity among signatory countries.

Cross-border worker agreements exist in European OECD countries and are mostly between EU and non-EU member countries. These agreements are based on the geographical proximity or regionalism of labour markets. They often set quotas according to domestic labour conditions and require migrant workers to maintain their primary residence in their own country. In 2001, Switzerland and Luxembourg respectively hosted 168 000 and 99 000 cross-border workers. Austria signed agreements allowing residents of the Czech Republic and Hungary to work in the Austrian border regions.

Working Holidaymaker Schemes allow young adults who are travelling to take up limited incidental employment to supplement their travel funds. The basis of these schemes is to promote cultural ties and international exchanges between young people for a short period of time (ranging from six months in Italy, to two years in the United Kingdom). The criteria for eligibility set limits on age and require a minimum level of funds to guarantee return to the home country. The United Kingdom restricted its working holidaymaker scheme to the 53 other Commonwealth countries, while Australia recently extended its programme eligibility to a total of 17 countries in Asia, Europe and North America. The number of such agreements has increased, as has their flexibility in terms of the type and length of employment.

Other forms of labour recruitment

Some OECD member countries are reluctant to sign bilateral agreements and have implemented other means of recruiting foreign labour. In some cases, other countries have decided to abandon labour recruitment entirely (Henri de Lary, Chapter 2). At a regional level, governments have facilitated the recruitment of foreign labour, with schemes that are responsive to the labour market. While these schemes are mostly country-specific in their characteristics and administration, most can be categorised in terms of their primary goal, which is to relieve sector-based or skill-based shortages.

Sector-based schemes are created to fill shortages within particular sectors, depending on local labour market conditions. Schemes recently developed by receiving countries recruit foreign workers for temporary employment in the following sectors: agriculture (Italy, United Kingdom, United States), information technology and other new technologies (Germany), health and medical care professions (Canada, Italy, Norway, United States) and hospitality (Italy, United Kingdom). The primary difference between sector-based schemes and bilateral agreements which recruit within the same sectors is that sector-based schemes focus on meeting labour market needs regardless of the applicant's nationality, at least in theory. Administrative limits, however, can be placed on specific nationalities for security, language or other reasons. Sector-based agreements are economically more efficient since, by definition, they recruit for the specified occupational need and nationality is not a factor.

Skill-based schemes focus on recruiting individuals who are highly skilled or skilled to enter the country as a job-seeker, an entrepreneur or a recruited employee. In using permanent migration routes to meet labour market needs, Australia, Canada and New Zealand each have their own points system, a formula quantifying the worker's credentials (*e.g.* former salary, profession, education level, years of professional experience and language ability and, in some cases, age). Bonus points are usually given for the partner or applicant's qualifications. The United Kingdom has used the points system to create a temporary migration programme based on skills. The highly skilled migrant programme allows highly-skilled foreigners to enter the United Kingdom in search of employment.

In some cases, skills criteria also are linked to sectors with labour shortages. Ireland's working visa scheme targets specific shortages in skilled and qualified labour across the construction, information technology, health, medical and social care sectors. The United States runs two sector-based visa schemes for skilled workers including H-1B (speciality occupations) and H-1C (nurses). Sector-based schemes that recruit low-wage workers are rarer. Following consultations with employers, the United Kingdom created the sectors based scheme in 2003 to admit low-skilled labour for acute shortages faced in the food processing and hospitality sectors. These forms of labour recruitment are characterised by the fact that qualified candidates are not limited to specific sending countries (*e.g.* as in a bilateral agreement); applications are open to all nationalities. Required qualifications reflect labour market conditions, and acceptable candidates must match criteria such as skill level, age, nationality, recognised qualifications or professional experience. Access to the public sector remains limited to foreign workers in most OECD member countries. Some countries, such as Australia, Canada, the United Kingdom and the United States provide examples of countries making use of alternative forms of labour recruitment.

Labour recruitment in this framework is conditional on creating sufficient flexibility within existing administrative immigration systems in order to adapt quickly to labour market needs. The combination of such flexible and rapid responses limits the delay between the market's stated need for additional labour and the entry of migrant workers to fill those vacancies. Similarly, the administrative process can be lengthened or expedited as needed, reflecting labour market conditions. In the United Kingdom, for example, Work Permits UK currently functions without quotas, and processes complete applications within 24 hours. Although the scheme does place limits on skill levels, these were eased recently to increase the applicant pool. The United Kingdom has revised other selective recruitment schemes for the same purpose (*e.g.* the highly skilled migrant programme), but retains the ability to tighten conditions to respond to a downturn in the economy (Nicolas Rollason, Chapter 8). Flexible recruitment schemes generally operate through employers, that is, the burden of recruiting and identifying international candidates is borne by the employer. For example, for both work permits in the United Kingdom and working visas in Ireland, applications for non-European Economic Area (EEA) candidates are made by employers, and subsequently reviewed for approval by the government. In addition, in some of the recruitment schemes, qualified candidates in specific occupational categories are prioritised in the permit application system (*e.g.* the UK work permit shortage occupation list).

Beyond labour objectives: additional factors behind recruitment schemes

The nature of bilateral agreements has evolved rapidly, through a broadening of their scope, implementation and institutional frameworks, to become a powerful tool for international co-operation. They have the potential of helping to better regulate migration flows, to combat illegal employment and to protect human rights. They thus address a broad spectrum of economic and political issues. Some labour recruitment agreements between sending and receiving countries, for example, have been introduced as an incentive for sending countries to improve the management of migration outflow pressures.

In addition to responding to labour shortages, labour recruitment schemes were developed in response to other concerns of an institutional, economic or social nature. Among these are:

Protecting special post-colonial or political relationships. For example, this was the case for France with Algeria until the early 1970s (Henri de Lary, Chapter 2), or for the United Kingdom with the working holidaymaker scheme signed with the other 53 Commonwealth countries. For historical and economic reasons, the Czech Republic and the Slovak Republic agreed to the mutual employment of their citizens since the creation of these two independent states in 1993.

Promoting cultural ties and exchanges. The programme of working holidaymakers was developed to maintain youth cultural exchanges between countries, mostly with reciprocity clauses. The main countries running such programmes include Australia, New Zealand and the United Kingdom, as well as Japan and Canada.

Protection of workers' rights. For example, Filipino labour recruitment agreements focus on the terms and conditions of employment of Filipino workers abroad (Stella Go, Chapter 11).

Combating unemployment in the sending country. For example, in Romania, with its worsening employment situation as a result of economic restructuring, temporary emigration is viewed as a means of relieving the country of the socio-economic consequences of unemployment.

Easing labour mobility and integration into regional economies. This is the case for many Central and Eastern European countries which signed special transition agreements in preparation for accession to the European Union in May 2004.

Increasing the training of migrants. Switzerland stands out as a clear example, with programmes that allow migrants to enter for the purpose of either increasing their skill levels as young professionals, or completing their education with temporary access to the labour market.

Managing migration flows is a common concern in labour agreements. Increasingly, many OECD member countries are turning to labour recruitment schemes to help regulate both labour emigration and immigration flows. The last decade has witnessed a proliferation of bilateral agreements between sending and receiving countries as an incentive for sending countries to improve the management of migration movements. For both low-skilled and high-skilled workers, the factors determining international mobility derive from a combination of push and pull factors. While sending countries wish to decrease the supply pressure (push factors), receiving countries hope to fill significant labour shortages (pull factors). In both groups of countries, there are additional social and economic reasons that might precipitate individual labour migration decisions (*e.g.* high unemployment and low security on the push side, compared to improved education and economic opportunities on the pull side). Bilateral agreements and other forms of labour recruitment increase push and pull factors by providing a legitimate relationship between labour supply and demand. For example, Romanian nurses recruited for general nursing posts in Italy receive an average monthly wage ten times that of a specialised nursing post in Bucharest (or EUR 150) (Jean-Gabriel Barbin, Chapter 13).

Recruitment schemes can be adapted to improve the framework of labour migration so that both sending and receiving countries can share the burden of monitoring and administration. For example, ensuring adequate travelling, living and working conditions, or creating a system to avoid the dual payment of social security taxes, can create incentives for potential employers and migrants to participate in the agreement. In some cases, labour recruitment schemes were developed for the purpose of combating irregular migration and the illegal employment of foreigners. Italy, for example, has become an immigration country in the past decade, with an increasing role for foreign workers in the labour force, and a growing concern about irregular immigration and the illegal employment of foreign workers. In response, Italy signed readmission agreements with 28 countries to facilitate the repatriation of their citizens found in an irregular situation in Italy. In the case of Albania (1997) and Tunisia (2000), Italy also signed "second generation" agreements (*i.e.* after the signing of an initial readmission agreement with a specific country) related to labour recruitment and limited to seasonal work. Recently, Portugal (with Bulgaria and Romania) and Spain (with Colombia, Dominican Republic, Ecuador, Morocco, Poland and Romania) also signed bilateral agreements for the purposes of combating irregular immigration, regulating labour migration flows and selecting foreign workers for temporary migration in accordance with labour market needs.

Implementation and management

Bilateral agreements and other forms of labour recruitment involve the participation not only of government agencies, migrant workers and employers, but also of an increasing range of private and nongovernmental organisations. Their aim is to make the process beneficial for all, reduce any negative consequences and increase the positive impact. This section examines the implementation and management of bilateral agreements and other forms of labour recruitment, with a special emphasis on the role of private recruitment organisations and other nongovernmental groups. The recruitment arrangements that function best in practice appear to be those with a formal structure in place, ensuring that all the key players were engaged and fully committed to the process.

Defining labour shortages and recruitment

Since the demand for labour is the key driving force behind bilateral labour agreements and other forms of recruitment, the main challenges for government administrations are: to assess labour market needs; to complete intergovernmental negotiations; to design appropriate policies; and to manage the recruitment or permit approval process. These responsibilities need to be implemented as quickly as possible.

There is no general consensus among OECD countries concerning the definition of labour shortages and the way in which these should be measured (see "Labour Shortages and the Need for Immigrants" in *Trends in International Migration*, OECD, 2003a). Some countries carry out formal or informal surveys of employers, but unbiased responses are difficult to obtain. National employment offices and private agencies are responsible for vacancy postings only within certain economic sectors and do so with varying degrees of efficiency. For example, vacancies for domestic work or other household services are frequently advertised informally. Moreover, economic actors within a country can disagree on what constitutes labour market tightness in a particular sector or for particular skill levels. The role of governments in identifying labour shortages is therefore crucial for the development of recruitment strategies. In some countries, employers and employer representatives communicate their difficulty in filling advertised vacancies to appropriate government agencies (usually labour and employment ministries) and exert pressure, with the expectation that the hiring of foreign workers will be expedited to ease labour market pressures. For example, in the United Kingdom, the government has created quarterly sector-based panels to receive updates from employers on the labour market situation. Other countries (*e.g.* the Netherlands, Portugal) carry out various forms of employment projections, based on flows in and out of the labour market, and on expectations of labour demand, to assess potential future shortages within occupations and sectors. Local authorities (*e.g.* in France, Germany, Italy, Spain, Switzerland) also play a part in identifying labour shortages.

In most OECD member countries, the process of negotiation is not carried out by those responsible for the implementation of the recruitment schemes. Usually, senior staff in employment, labour or immigration ministries conduct the negotiations with other governments. In a few cases however, national employment offices develop and implement the recruitment procedure with sending countries. This is the case with Germany's Federal Employment Agency, which hires seasonal workers directly in the sending countries through their respective local employment services, without the need for ministerial agreement. In some cases, the negotiation process between countries can take several years. The national ratification process and the establishment of the implementation framework can further lengthen the procedure. Finally, certain agreements have not been implemented after signature because the receiving country no longer sees the need for foreign workers. Policy development and design of recruitment schemes can occur within the same ministries. Often, these schemes are designed with the assistance or consultation of representatives of employers, trade unions, foreign workers or other groups that might also be affected by the schemes. In most Asian bilateral labour agreements, the selection and transfer of workers is administered by private recruitment agencies (as stipulated in the agreements). In other regions, the public administration controls the process. There is evidence in Romania that the involvement of government authorities in the administration of the recruitment process guarantees better protection of workers, lower cost for the beneficiaries and greater control over the performance of employers (Dana Diminescu, Chapter 4).

Recruitment by government can be centralised at the national level (*e.g.* through national labour offices) or devolved to local or regional authorities. In France and Italy, recruitment occurs in regional employment offices that monitor labour shortages in their areas. Some countries have also found it effective to recruit directly in sending countries, through the creation of representative offices abroad. For example, France's International Migration Office (*Office des migrations internationales*) has offices in Morocco, Poland, Tunisia and Turkey to run recruitment services and expedite permit applications. Recruitment can also be managed by employers facing labour shortages. They sometimes recruit directly in sending countries where no bilateral agreements exist, as is the case for Irish and UK employers. In other cases, employers can use intermediaries, such as private recruitment agencies in sending or receiving countries.

Once established, bilateral agreements and other forms of recruitment of foreign labour require specific administrative procedures to ensure their smooth operation. The desire to better manage the process in most cases leads to the creation of an excessive number of procedures and restrictions. Experience suggests that the best-managed recruitment schemes are those that are less bureaucratic, *i.e.* they require less administration and have fewer entry conditions. The successful administration of foreign labour recruitment is based on free access to information about the rules, procedures and opportunities in both sending and receiving countries. Those interviewed in sending countries (public administrations, employers, workers) stated that participation in the recruitment schemes is highly competitive. This is the case in all countries observed, including those where there is less incentive to emigrate (*e.g.* Czech Republic, Hungary). Despite burdensome administrative procedures, the prospect of employment abroad organised by public authorities remains attractive. While most of the employers interviewed confirm that they are informed about the opportunities from the media and by government agencies, migrant workers stated that their main source of information consisted of friends and relatives.

Public/private partnerships

Employers and their organisations play an important role in the overall process, the success of which depends on balancing the interests of all parties. The involvement of employers, nongovernmental organisations (NGOs), trade unions and other related groups in the design and implementation of labour recruitment schemes contributes significantly to their efficiency and, in some cases, lowers administrative costs. For example, NGOs are often involved in organising language training and selection procedures, as well as providing migrants with information on the destination country (*e.g.* culture, labour market, migrants' rights). The contribution of nongovernmental actors, however, is mostly found within receiving countries. The involvement of employer organisations within sending countries remains limited. The Slovak Republic was one of the few countries that allowed a review of draft agreements by trade unions and employer organisations. In sending countries, nongovernmental organisations have a greater role than employers (*e.g.* Bulgaria, Hungary, the Philippines, Poland, Romania). These advocacy organisations protect the interests of migrant workers and provide information to recruitment agencies, foreign employers and migrant workers. Some organisations have opened offices in the receiving country (mainly in Germany). In Hungary, organisations assist national companies engaged in contract work abroad in verifying that they operate in a fair competitive environment in the receiving country.

In receiving countries, on the other hand, employers, trade unions and other nongovernmental organisations are involved throughout the recruitment process, from the definition of labour shortages to the monitoring of recruitment schemes. In Ireland, Portugal and the United Kingdom, employers and their representatives are actively engaged in identifying labour shortages and communicating these to the government. In Ireland, employer organisations exert pressure on the government to adapt the number of work permits issued to the prevailing economic conditions (*i.e.* by increasing or decreasing the number of permits granted). Conversely, relaxation of certain conditions for permit applications has occurred, following pressure from employers facing hiring difficulties (*e.g.* United Kingdom, United States). Employers are often responsible for ensuring that candidates meet the required entry criteria for the recruitment scheme. In some countries, employers or their intermediaries must also verify credentials and, in some cases, apply language proficiency tests (*e.g.* Canada, Italy) before requesting permits. Labour market testing often remains the responsibility of the employer. For example, in Ireland and the United Kingdom, employers must show that vacancies remained unfilled, despite advertisement, registry with the local employment office or unsuccessful interviews, over a period of time specified in the scheme. In Canada, however, labour market testing is performed by a national government ministry, Human Resources Development Canada (HDRC), through its local offices.

In recent years, employer organisations have begun supporting and conducting training programmes in sending countries, in order to better prepare migrant workers for overseas employment. In Italy, for example, employers were involved in funding vocational training for specific industries in source countries (*e.g.* nursing training in Romania). The Canadian Province of Ontario funded several innovative projects to help foreign-trained nurses and pharmacists acquire the additional skills and education necessary to help fill significant labour shortages in the region. Trade associations also play a key role in organising training courses and facilitating the admission of groups of trained foreign workers. The knowledge of these interested parties helps to formulate a migration policy which reacts to changes in the economy or in the labour force. Not only can programmes be adjusted quickly (*i.e.* quotas increased, application delays reduced, conditions eased), but also new schemes can be developed in response to specific needs (*e.g.* the sector-based scheme in the United Kingdom). By engaging the private sector and NGOs in migration policy, the Home Office has succeeded in providing a base for public support and in creating an image of consensus around migration issues (Anaïs Loizillon, Chapter 7).

Private recruitment agencies

Recruitment with private fee-charging agencies has become commonplace, to assist employers in obtaining an adequate labour supply. Private agencies exist in both sending and receiving countries, and contribute to the growing exchange of labour between these groups of countries (ILO, 1997). The role of private agencies can vary from a simple matching function to a comprehensive hiring package consisting of recruitment, skills testing, travel, visa and living arrangements. In several European sending countries (*e.g.* Bulgaria, Czech Republic, Hungary, Poland, Romania), public labour offices recruit and fill more vacancies abroad than private agencies. In some countries, for example Romania, competition among these recruitment agencies exists even though they operate in different segments of the labour market. In Asia, private recruitment agencies are more visible, as they supplement the limited capacity of public labour offices, particularly concerning large labour emigration flows. For example, Thailand supported the establishment of an independent nongovernmental body to handle the recruitment of Thai migrants for work abroad on the government's behalf.

Other types of intermediaries can also provide recruitment assistance. In the United Kingdom, under the seasonal agricultural workers scheme, a number of non-profitmaking organisations (known as "charities" in the United Kingdom) are responsible for linking local farmers with foreign agricultural students who, in turn, are selected by the sending country universities. These programme operators are not allowed to charge participants recruitment or application fees. In many cases, though, operators ask for payments to cover the cost of the work permit, accommodation, medical insurance or cultural activities. Employers cover the charity's administrative fees for each migrant worker. Furthermore, the government has mandated that charities also monitor the living and working conditions of scheme participants. Criticism of private recruitment agencies occurs mainly when there is evidence of corruption in some agencies that do not provide socially protected jobs. Such agencies have been accused of requiring excessively high commission, providing unsafe and unsanitary work and living conditions, and fuelling new trafficking networks into receiving countries (Dana Diminescu, Chapter 4; Stella Go, Chapter 11). Romania created a new Office for Labour Migration in December 2001, whose responsibilities include the protection of Romanian workers abroad and the monitoring of private recruitment agencies. The high fees charged by Romanian recruitment agencies to migrant workers are now prohibited, in line with an ILO Convention stipulating that this cost should be covered by the recruiting company.

Regional approaches

Regions in OECD countries play an important role in the implementation of bilateral labour agreements as well as the other forms of recruitment of foreign labour. Several regions or national governments are very proactive in recruiting foreign workers to areas with specific labour needs. Although several countries allow regions to become involved in recruitment (*e.g.* through local employment offices), Australia, Canada and Italy are leading innovators within OECD member countries in merging regional and rural development with immigration goals (see "Regional Aspects of Migration" in *Trends in International Migration*, OECD, 2004). Regional bilateral incentives in recruiting foreign labour seem to be successful in both meeting labour market needs and gaining public support for labour migration.

In the early 2000s, the province of Ontario, Canada faced severe skill shortages in several manufacturing trades, such as mould-makers, foundry pattern-makers and tool and die-makers. The sectoral agreement created in 2001 for a period of two years, in partnership with a consortium of employer and training representatives, facilitated and expedited the permit application process for qualified foreign workers. Under the agreement, employers are exempt from the national labour market test, which requires proof that adequate efforts were made to attempt to recruit Canadians. Australia developed state specific and regional migration initiatives as part of a broader agenda for regional economic development. State and territorial governments, as well as regional authorities, play an increased role in determining the volume and characteristics of migrant workers. Applications receive priority processing at the national level and enable skilled migrants to fill vacancies more rapidly. Recent amendments to the schemes have facilitated further regional migration.

In Italy, the devolution of certain administrative and legislative powers to the regions has created a favourable framework for the regions to pass laws on international recruitment and co-operation (Jonathan Chaloff, Chapter 3). In some Italian regions, these laws address the need for foreign labour in the context of international co-operation projects. The Friuli-Venezia-Giulia region has been extremely active in Romania and has opened its third international desk in Bucharest. Some Italian regions have also worked with the Romanian government to provide language and professional training for Romanian workers to migrate temporarily to Italy (Jean-Gabriel Barbin, Chapter 13). In some cases, regionally facilitated recruitment exists, in the absence of international agreements. For example, to ensure support of its regional tourist industry, the Trento-Alto-Adige region posted its staff in Italian consulates in central Europe to monitor and streamline administrative procedures in distributing seasonal work permits. Innovative programmes have also been developed within the nongovernmental sector. The Agricultural Workers Solidarity Foundation based in Barcelona recruits seasonal workers directly in the sending country (*e.g.* Colombia, Morocco, Romania) for selected employers in Spain. In addition, the organisation promotes development in the sending country by educating seasonal workers on entrepreneurship and management and, in some cases, by supporting development-oriented work upon their return.

Quotas

Many bilateral agreements have quotas to limit the number of candidates accepted under the scheme. Although quotas are usually applied to labour agreements to protect the internal workforce from an excessive supply of foreign labour, they can also be construed as recruitment goals. For example in Germany, of the 20 000 information technology slots allocated initially to the Green Card programme, out of 14 000 accepted applications, only 10 000 were used as of December 2002. The United States uses quotas for non-immigrant programmes as a way of ensuring some protection of its internal work force. Quotas are usually adjusted every year in response to economic and political changes. Governments can also use quotas to fine-tune bilateral agreements or other forms of labour recruitment by creating sub-quotas according to sector (United Kingdom), occupation (Italy), receiving region (Australia, Italy, Switzerland), sending country (Poland) or firm size (Germany). Italy's quota system, introduced in 1998, with annual revisions, applies at least four sub-categories. The scheme limits the number of foreign workers allowed into the country every year by: regional quota (further divided into provincial quotas); labour type (*e.g.* seasonal, contract work); occupation; and nationality. Spain applies its quota for recruited workers by sector and by province.

Impact and benefits

This section examines the question of how recruitment schemes affect labour markets in sending and receiving countries, employers, migrant workers, economic development and migration policy. There are few studies which assess the impact of the policies, or which provide information about the implementation of bilateral labour agreements.

Studies on the social and economic impact of foreign labour migration, however, are numerous. Most studies suggest that immigration grants small net gains to the receiving country in terms of per capita output and that migration inflows have contributed to wage moderation (Coppel *et al.*, 2001).

It is important to note that most recruitment efforts are of a temporary nature, especially in the European countries of the OECD, Japan and Korea. Switzerland, for example, makes a clear distinction between those who qualify for short-term or long-term residence permits (Manuela Florez, Chapter 1). Labour recruitment schemes for specific occupations tend to be created to alleviate short-term imbalances in the labour market, until further training and education can produce new workers with the required qualifications. Generally, low-skilled employment is the most temporary (*e.g.* seasonal) and longer stays are given to the highly skilled. Contract-based work which can involve any skill level, is usually limited to two to three years. The permanent recruitment of migrants in selected settlement countries (*e.g.* Australia, Canada, New Zealand) is mostly limited to skilled workers. The length of time defined as temporary also varies by country and can be difficult to categorise. For example, temporary H-1B work permits in the United States can be granted for up to six years and even longer in certain cases (Jacquelyn Bednarz and Roger Kramer, Chapter 6). By contrast, even annual permit holders in Switzerland are expected to meet several prerequisites regarding their ability for economic and social integration (Thomas Liebig, Chapter 10).

Labour market impact

The impact of employment agreements on the labour markets in most sending countries remains small. In 2002, about 300 000 Polish workers were employed abroad through bilateral agreements, but they represented only a small fraction of the domestic labour force (which amounted to approximately 17.2 million in 2002). The majority of this employment abroad (around 80%) represents contracts for seasonal work in Germany, a number that has been increasing in recent years. The preference for short-term labour emigration over long-term settlement is evident among many migrant workers. In certain Asian countries, however, there is considerable labour-related migration. In these cases, for example in the Philippines and Thailand, the impact on the sending country's labour market can be significant. Overseas Filipino workers constitute about 2.5% of the domestic labour force, and between 1994 and 2001, more Filipinos found jobs overseas each year than the total of new entrants into the local labour market. Assuming that these workers would not have been employed if they had remained in the domestic market, the unemployment rate in the Philippines would have increased and remained in double-digit figures in recent years. Generally, recruitment schemes cannot be expected significantly to alter unemployment rates in sending countries, given the rather small numbers emigrating, mostly on a seasonal or temporary basis. There is evidence, however, that migrant workers who return to their home country at the end of the work period abroad do not enter the local labour market, but instead wait for another foreign employment contract. Thus, their long-term attachment to the domestic labour market decreases over time and their competitiveness on the local labour market is no longer guaranteed.

The effect on the receiving country's labour market varies according to the characteristics of the agreement or recruiting scheme. Sectoral agreements, for example, significantly reduce employment shortages in those sectors, allowing them to remain viable and, in some cases, become more competitive. This is the case, for example, for agriculture in Germany, horticulture in the United Kingdom and catering and tourism in Italy. In 2002, migrant workers under the seasonal agricultural workers scheme in the

United Kingdom were estimated to represent nearly 30% of all agricultural seasonal workers that same year and farmers requested a higher quota for the following years. Finally, some schemes are significant components of labour migration flows. Australia's temporary entry programme is dominated by working holidaymakers (88 758 in 2002-2003), who represented more than double the number of skilled entries in the permanent migration programme the same year.

From the domestic labour market perspective, recruitment schemes that are sensitive to labour market fluctuations and amenable to changes in the face of changing economic conditions are preferred. These recruitment schemes are characterised by elements of flexibility and responsiveness, allowing a rapid reaction to employment conditions. Finally, recruitment schemes also have the potential benefit of moving workers from an irregular employment situation into the regular labour force, as observed after the signature of the Poland-Germany bilateral agreement in 1990. Critics of the vast recruitment of foreign workers cite the threat of displacement of the indigenous workforce. In most recruitment schemes, labour market testing remains common in both individual recruitment efforts and work permit approvals. Testing usually requires verification that there is no one in the domestic workforce to fill the vacancy advertised by the employer. Consequently, the domestic workforce is not displaced and foreign workers are subject, in principle, to the same working conditions and protection as domestic workers.

Impact on employers

Bilateral labour agreements contribute to the economic and employment growth of receiving countries. Employers have access to the labour needed and this encourages them to expand their business. Nearly 50 interviews with employers and employer organisations were carried out in sending and receiving countries (Bulgaria, Czech Republic, Germany, Italy, Poland, Romania, Switzerland and the United Kingdom). The responses revealed that bilateral agreements had a very strong positive impact on bilateral business relations. From the perspective of the sending countries, companies performed better and were more competitive in the domestic market after gaining experience in more developed markets. In some cases, firms were enriched with new capital equipment or with increased technological expertise from abroad. Agreements also facilitated the expansion of small and medium-sized companies from sending countries within Europe and eased their integration into the European Union single market. Revenue from projects abroad had a real impact on the sending country economy, but did not compensate for the foregone foreign direct investment. Another added benefit was that companies gained information on foreign working conditions, including legal standards, accommodation conditions, food distribution, social security and safety in the workplace.

In receiving countries, companies obtained the labour they needed, in most cases at a cheaper price and at a satisfactory professional standard. Interviews revealed that companies often create their contacts directly in the sending country, through public or private intermediaries, and obtain better access to those labour markets (particularly in the case of project-linked employment). Several OECD member countries mandate conditions for temporary employment. For example, employers have to provide seasonal workers with adequate housing or assistance in obtaining suitable accommodation at a reasonable price (*e.g.* Germany, Italy, United Kingdom) or, in the case of the United States, with rent-free government-approved housing under the H-2A agricultural worker programme.

Impact on migrant workers

This section derives its information from interviews conducted with Bulgarian, Polish and Romanian workers who obtained employment through bilateral agreements, as well as from special surveys of Polish seasonal workers in bilateral schemes (Marek Okólski, Chapter 12). Firm conclusions based on evidence from these sources cannot be offered, due to limited data. Employment under bilateral agreements often was limited to young workers, since many agreements incorporate age limitations. The work experience obtained tended to be short and concentrated in a number of sectors (*e.g.* agriculture, hotel and catering, medical and healthcare), as many bilateral agreements did not concern information technology or other highly-skilled personnel. Migrants' skills and education levels were often below the level of upper secondary education. Workers participating in bilateral agreements were more mobile than the remainder of the labour force, with respect to their employment situation in the home country, and changed employer often or remained out of work before returning abroad. Nonetheless, nearly half of all seasonal workers in Poland had permanent jobs, but worked in Germany to supplement their household income.

Workers participating in bilateral programmes obtained information about foreign employment opportunities through personal networks which often relied on those who had some experience abroad. At the same time, these networks played an important role in selecting applicants, due to the intense competition for the limited work opportunities in receiving countries. In some cases, workers returning to work abroad are allowed to choose or help select their own team for the next project or seasonal contract. In the case of Polish seasonal workers, the organisation of the work abroad is so culturally homogenous (*e.g.* with Polish team-leaders) that there is no need to learn German. Migrant workers view their experiences with bilateral agreements positively. They see work abroad as a means of improving their standard of living. In Poland, earnings from abroad contributed 19% to average household incomes. Some bilateral agreements include provisions to guarantee the free transfer of migrants' earnings. Although employment abroad was seen to improve workers' labour market competitiveness, re-entry into the local labour market was often difficult. The impact of migrants' earnings (both cash and in kind) on the sending country's balance of payments is not easy to assess. The volume of remittance flows depends on numerous factors, including the size of labour flows, migrants' earning potential, the duration of employment abroad, and their ability to save and send remittances. For example, Romania received the equivalent of about 3% of its GDP in remittances in 2002.

In terms of professional development, available research does not conclude that migrants develop strong entrepreneurial attitudes or plans. Their labour mobility does not reflect an increased preference for risk. Instead, the rewards of employment abroad are simply better than those offered by starting a business in their home country. The only bilateral agreement which encourages more business start-ups is project-linked employment, because an employee can see the immediate benefits of owning a contracting company. The attractiveness of receiving country markets and the contacts developed, contribute to entrepreneurship.

Impact on migration and development policies

The impact of recruitment schemes on migration flows is difficult to establish, and to separate out from other factors. In some OECD countries, bilateral agreements, in particular, seem to have led to improved management of migration flows (*e.g.* Germany, Switzerland). In these cases, improved migration management strongly influences the behaviour of employers. If it is in their interests that their workers return home, the control of the public authorities is more successful and the agreements do not open the door to irregular migration (via scheme overstayers). Other countries have had less success so far in reducing the illegal employment of foreigners or irregular migration flows through labour recruitment schemes (*e.g.* United States). The United Kingdom's managed migration policy has broken, at least temporarily, the association in the public mind between irregular and labour migration, despite an 18% increase in asylum applications between 2001 and 2002. With respect to the illegal employment of migrant workers, effective migration control can best be achieved through the development of policies which recognise and respond to legitimate labour shortages in the economy. Bilateral agreements and other forms of labour recruitment are important tools for such policies. French and German employers found that their respective seasonal agreements with Poland were highly successful in terms of obtaining the labour supply needed and reducing irregular migration flows. Employers attributed this success to the hiring mechanisms they developed through informal networks rather than to the implementation of the agreement (Marek Okólski, Chapter 12). Yet, easing German bureaucratic obligations and time restrictions was linked to the employment of an additional 100-150 000 Polish seasonal workers.

Bilateral agreements have a strong influence on the attitudes of migrants. In all cases, there is a clear wish for a longer-term contract or easier access to a new one. The desire for permanent residence abroad, however, is marginal. This is substantiated by the fact that most workers invest in real estate in their home countries, improve their houses and buy property (Marek Okólski, Chapter 12). These outcomes depend greatly on the type of employment provided by the agreement. Project-linked employment creates strong ties between employers and workers, and the latter rely on the home company to employ them in their own country as well as abroad. Employers, workers and public authorities believe that the mutual dependence of workers and employers has tended to attenuate the desire for long-term migration. Bilateral labour agreements have the added benefit of promoting negotiation on other migration issues. Italy's use of readmission agreements as a prerequisite for the signing of bilateral labour agreements signifies a new direction in international co-operation. Bilateral agreements also play an important political role in initiating or maintaining co-operation between the countries concerned. For example, they are still used to encourage CEECs to develop migration policies, train the administration and learn about practices in contracting countries.

In the context of development policies, the role of labour recruitment mechanisms in balancing the labour market needs of sending and receiving countries needs to be considered. In particular, labour imports and outgoing foreign direct investment could potentially represent a trade-off. The recruitment of cheaper foreign labour by receiving countries in lieu of outsourcing production abroad could be a factor limiting their foreign direct investment in sending countries. Finally, the rapid outflow of skilled workers, with the risks of a brain drain in some developing countries, raises the issue of policy coherence between migration and development policies in sending countries. Human resource management, as well as the recognition of benefits from labour mobility to both parties, must be taken into consideration to understand this issue.

Prospects and improvements

Prospects

The interested parties are generally satisfied with the outcomes and operation of bilateral agreements. There is a clear intention to continue efforts at improving these schemes. Sending countries in particular would like more countries to sign agreements. For example, after signing the Association Agreement with the European Union (effective 2 February 1995), the Slovak Republic pursued negotiations with 13 EU member states that they had not yet approached. They successfully signed reciprocal trainee agreements with Finland and Luxembourg (both in 1998). In Europe, two main factors will change the landscape of bilateral labour agreements and other forms of labour recruitment. First, slow economic growth in Germany has raised concerns that demand for foreign labour will fall, and that quotas will be further reduced. Second, the main sources of labour migration under bilateral labour agreements have been nationals from CEECs. With the first accessions taking place in May 2004 and more expected in 2007, a large number of bilateral agreements will eventually become redundant. The ten countries acceding in 2004 (Cyprus, Czech Republic, Estonia, Hungary, Latvia, Lithuania, Malta, Poland, Slovak Republic and Slovenia) agreed to a transitional period for establishing the free movement of workers, which effectively prolongs many bilateral agreements with European Union countries. The Association Agreements for applicant countries recommended that current EU member states improve the access of applicant country nationals to the EU labour markets. Several member states announced that they planned to lift limits to immigration, either by sector or generally, immediately upon accession in May 2004. Ireland passed the Employment Permits Act in 2003, which facilitates the entrance of nationals from these countries, but allows restrictions, if warranted by the economic situation (Jerry J. Sexton, Chapter 9). Nonetheless, no major new agreements were developed, conditions modified or quotas increased.

Some of the agreements for project-linked employment will become redundant from the date when access to a specific sector is liberalised. The activities of companies in the new member countries, with the exception of the construction sector, will be regulated in the European Union, based on the rules for free movement of services. The current plan is to maintain the validity of bilateral agreements concluded between EU member states and candidate countries once the transition period is terminated. Candidate countries also plan to keep agreements with non-EU member states (Michal Meduna, Chapter 5). The prospects of bilateral labour agreements in Europe will partly be influenced by the new agreements developed by the countries of southern Europe (Italy, Portugal and Spain). Once these bilateral agreements become operational and expand, they will constitute a test of the policy of return migration, and reintegration of return migrants.

In Asia, there is a growing view that the protection of migrants' rights cannot be achieved bilaterally, but rather on a multilateral level. The Philippines took the initiative to bring together several sending countries in Asia to co-ordinate their policies on bilateral agreements and to work together with receiving country governments. An agreement signed with Indonesia in 2003 is a joint attempt to promote workers' rights, train and certify migrant workers, and provide them with legal aid. Mexico has been enthusiastic about negotiating new bilateral arrangements with the United States, but discussions stalled following 11 September 2001. Prospects did not seem promising until January 2004, when the US government announced a proposal for new legislation that would enable undocumented foreign workers and their families to gain temporary residence status in the United States for a period of three years. An estimated five to eight million undocumented people could be affected, if the new legislation is implemented. In addition, on 1 January 2004, the cap established for certain categories of skilled Mexican professionals (*e.g.* medical and health care, scientist, teacher) under NAFTA was lifted (Jacquelyn Bednarz and Roger Kramer, Chapter 6).

On the path to improvement

Most sending countries do not have specific policies in place for returning migrants. If such measures are envisaged, they are usually implemented by the receiving countries (*e.g.* France or Spain *vis-à-vis* Romanian migrants). Two problems limit the expansion of such policies: budgetary constraints in sending countries and the view of policy makers that protecting and further investing in migrant workers who have gained experience and skills abroad (and hence should be more competitive upon their return) makes little sense. Benefits for the sending countries may increase if certain policies are implemented. Sending countries could enhance the return of workers by increasing their competitiveness in the local labour market (*e.g.* certification of skills gained abroad, recognition of foreign diplomas) or by encouraging their entrepreneurship (financial and technical assistance regarding business opportunities). In addition, receiving countries could set up support systems for the families who remain behind, and improve public information on work opportunities and conditions abroad. For example, by integrating national agencies into more regional and global networks, sending countries could develop an adequate institutional capacity to form productive partnerships with receiving countries.

Demand in the international labour market for skilled and highly-skilled workers is intensifying. Sending countries could envisage the development of training programmes to prepare migrants for specific labour markets in need. Some countries have recently developed pre-migration training (*i.e.* cultural background and language training) to impart practical knowledge to migrant workers about their living and working environment abroad. This training could also incorporate elements which would prepare migrants for socio-economic reintegration when they return to their country of origin. The development of bilateral and multilateral co-operation will further facilitate the labour migration process for the mutual benefit of sending and receiving countries. Eventually, agreements will meet labour market demand more effectively and improve the protection of migrants' rights.

From bilateral to multilateral agreements

A fundamental issue raised is whether bilateral approaches are the most appropriate means for foreign labour recruitment. The grounds for a multilateral approach in the recruitment of foreign labour are based on the growing number of labour shortages in receiving countries, particularly in specific sectors and occupations (*e.g.* health personnel, information technology specialists, domestic workers, social services). The scale of these shortages has led some OECD member countries to develop multilateral recruitment schemes that target a large group of sending countries (*e.g.* Switzerland's experience with trainee agreements, or the United Kingdom with the new working holidaymakers scheme). Other countries have instituted programmes and policies that are open to all applicants who qualify, regardless of their nationality. The similarities in labour demand across receiving countries, as well as the emerging competition for labour from sending countries, may support a multilateral approach or at least co-ordinated policies among receiving countries (OECD, 2003b).

Recent experiences in several OECD countries suggest that multilateral schemes (including those open to all nationalities) can help meet domestic labour market needs successfully. As a general rule, each receiving country offers the same terms and conditions for recruiting foreign labour from different countries (*e.g.* Germany with all European countries). This framework supports the need for multilateral protection for the rights of migrant workers, which could be stronger than that achieved under bilateral labour agreements. Additional efforts have been made in sending countries to co-ordinate policies with respect to the protection of workers (*e.g.* the Philippines initiative) and this should also create a favourable environment for multilateral approaches. Multilateral regulation of private recruitment agencies is needed, in order to set up international rules and prevent trafficking. The multilateral approach was introduced mainly to protect migrant workers' rights. Countries can go beyond national measures and bilateral negotiations, to set up a framework that better meets the interests of participating countries. At an international level, the International Labour Organization (ILO) was joined in its efforts to protect migrant workers rights by the United Nations General Assembly which adopted the International Convention on the Protection of the Rights of all Migrant Workers and Members of their Families in 1990. Another benefit gained from multilateral approaches is the reduction of the time-consuming and laborious process often involved in the negotiation of separate agreements between countries, or among regions. Notwithstanding this, there needs to be an adjustment, in the creation of multilateral agreements or other forms of labour recruitment in order for these to match existing schemes governing migration, and to benefit from increased flexibility and transparency in recruitment and labour market demand.

Concluding remarks

Four main lessons emerged from the above:

First, the diversity of labour recruitment schemes employed underscores the options available to meet the economic and political conditions of the sending and receiving countries. In some cases, countries follow a free market recruitment approach that allows employers to directly recruit labour abroad, within the framework of a migration policy. Other countries have chosen a co-operative recruitment approach, where countries jointly organise and manage recruitment, training, preparation for emigration, or re-integration into the home labour market.

Second, while there are clear differences in the design and implementation of labour recruitment schemes, it can also be observed that there is a convergence of recruitment goals. For example, the German and UK systems for the recruitment of seasonal agricultural workers are very close in their implementation. Both recruit workers mostly from the CEECs for similar employment posts and under similar conditions. The UK employers and intermediaries recruit through universities in the CEECs, while in Germany, the respective labour offices usually are involved both in Germany and in the sending country.

Third, many countries are increasing the participation of nongovernmental actors in nearly all phases of the design and implementation of recruitment schemes. In addition to assisting in the identification of labour shortages, employers, trade unions or NGOs are contributing to training and preparing migrants for work abroad (*e.g.* Romania, Poland), managing the recruitment process (*e.g.* United States) and even supporting the development of new schemes (*e.g.* United Kingdom, Italy).

Finally, there is a gap in the knowledge of whether bilateral agreements and other forms of labour recruitment actually meet their initial goals. There are currently no evaluations or other scientific studies in place to analyse the impact of these schemes.

What role could the OECD play with respect to bilateral and multilateral labour agreements or other forms of labour recruitment? This volume provides a first step for the exchange of information on migration for employers, policy makers and experts, and for them to gain a better understanding of the wide range of scheme options available. The efficient and rapid implementation of these programmes is of critical importance.

The OECD could further examine labour market outcomes related to all forms of recruitment of foreign labour by studying to what extent they effectively relieve short-term labour shortages. From another angle, the future work of the OECD could focus on enhancing the discussion around regional economic integration and labour migration, especially in the context of European Union enlargement and the on-going development of the Free Trade Area of the Americas. Finally, the OECD could further analyse international co-operation through labour-related migration, to reinforce the links between migration and the development of the sending countries.

BIBLIOGRAPHY

Coppel, J., J.C. Dumont and I. Visco (2001), "Trends in Immigration and Economic Consequences", OECD Economic Department Working Papers, No. 284, OECD, Paris.

ILO (International Labour Organization) (1997), "Protecting the Most Vulnerable of Today's Workers", Tripartite Meeting of Experts on Future ILO Activities in the Field of Migration, ILO, Geneva.

OECD (2003a), *Trends in International Migration*, OECD, Paris.

OECD (2003b), *Employment Outlook*, OECD, Paris.

OECD (2004), *Trends in International Migration*, OECD, Paris.

PART I

A RENEWED INTEREST IN BILATERAL LABOUR AGREEMENTS

PART I

Chapter 1

MIGRATION FOR EMPLOYMENT POLICY IN SWITZERLAND:

An Overview of the Current Situation and Future Challenges[1]

by
Manuela Florez[2]

Introduction

Since the end of World War II, Switzerland has recorded an unprecedented influx of foreign workers, in response to the labour shortages generated by strong economic expansion. Because of this demand for workers, Switzerland signed foreign labour recruitment agreements in the second half of the 1960s with three European countries: Italy, Portugal and Spain. Initially, workers came from the European countries sharing borders with Switzerland, but the trend has gradually been reversed over the years. Although the majority of foreign workers or workers of foreign origin still come from European countries, the migration balance for these countries has been negative for several years. This explains the arrival on the Swiss labour market of a large number of workers from countries outside the European Union.

Today, Switzerland is still facing local labour shortages in some sectors of the economy. Highly-skilled human capital, for instance, is increasingly sought throughout much of the OECD area. Developed countries are now looking for specialists worldwide, while at the same time trying to retain those they already have. Therefore, understanding the challenges facing Swiss migration policy means gaining more insight into Switzerland's migration system, the foreign population, global economic needs and labour market requirements. Switzerland is now seeking to adjust its migration policy, so as to keep its economy competitive and maintain labour market equilibrium. The purpose of this chapter is to provide an insight into Switzerland's current migration policy and the kind of challenges the country will be facing in the future. It sets out the basic principles governing the admission of foreign workers and provides a profile of these workers. The chapter then goes on to focus on skilled workers and issues relating to brain circulation.

---

1. This text is a revised and expanded version of a contribution by the author to the seminar papers of the *Institut de Sociologie de l'Université de Neuchâtel* on "The International Mobility of Skills: Flight or Circulation?" (7-8 November 2002).

2. At the time of writing, Ms Florez was scientific consultant to the Federal Office of Immigration, Integration and Emigration (IMES), Switzerland.

Overview of the admission system for foreign workers

Current Swiss migration policy on foreigners is based on the federal law on the residence and settlement of foreigners, *Loi fédérale sur le séjour et l'établissement des étrangers* (LSEE), dating from 1931 and currently in the process of revision, and on an order limiting the number of foreigners, *Ordonnance limitant le nombre des étrangers* (OLE). The OLE seeks to strike a numerical balance between the Swiss population and the resident foreign population, and to enhance the structure of the labour market and simultaneously achieve an optimal balance in employment. In addition to these two statutory instruments, on 1 June 2002, an agreement between Switzerland and the European Union entered into force, an order on the free movement of persons, *Ordonnance sur la libre circulation des personnes* (OLCP). This order applies solely to nationals from EU member states or the European Free Trade Association (EFTA). The status of other nationals is governed by the OLE.

Access to the Swiss labour market therefore differs according to whether or not a worker is an EU national. Although the law provides for a transitional period of 12 years until full freedom of movement is achieved for workers from EU member states, citizens of the EU already have facilitated access to the Swiss labour market. In anticipation of Switzerland's membership of the European Economic Area (EEA), a recruitment policy based on the three-circle model was introduced in 1991. Workers were recruited first from the European Union or the European Free Trade Association, second from other traditional labour recruiting countries (Australia, Canada, New Zealand, United States) and third from any other country. Nationals from countries in the third circle were exempt from labour market testing only if they had special skills, or if they provided training as part of Swiss development assistance and co-operation projects.

On 1 November 1998, the Federal Council decided to replace the three-circle model with a binary recruitment system. Although several neighbouring countries, members of the EU, were operating along similar lines at that time, it was vital for Switzerland to introduce a binary recruitment system before signing bilateral agreements with the European Union, in particular on the free movement of persons. Under the new system, priority goes to workers from EU member states, while there are restrictions on the admission of non-EU workers; access is confined to specialists and skilled workers. The recent entry into force of the agreement with the European Union on the free movement of persons has bolstered the system. It is important to note that, while controlling supply and demand on the labour market is one of the main constants in any migration policy, Switzerland has not signed any bilateral agreements on foreign labour recruitment in specific fields for the past 30 years.

The draft revision of the federal law on the residence and settlement of foreigners gives priority, as before, to the EEA labour force. For nationals of other countries, the emphasis will be on their vocational skills and capacity for long-term social and economic integration, subject to the obligations of international public law. The draft legislation provides for improvements to the legal status of foreigners, by simplifying the formalities required for professional and geographical mobility. It also introduces the possibility of family reunion for workers with short-stay residence permits. Any foreign national seeking admission to Switzerland for gainful employment must first obtain a work and residence permit from the cantonal authorities. Residence permits exceeding four months are now, with some exceptions, subject to a quota set by the Federal Council. Furthermore, before granting a permit, the labour market authorities must also consider the economic situation and the labour market, as well as other conditions governing paid work. For example, they must check to see whether the pay and working conditions are in line with those prevailing locally in the industry concerned, and whether a resident worker is able and willing to fill the vacancy under the same conditions.

This priority does not apply to the international transfer of managers within the same company, or to persons awarded residence permits under the category of family reunion. Exceptions to this rule are also possible for anyone residing in the country for training or development assistance and co-operation. The rule also differs according to the industry concerned. Exceptions may be made, for instance, for an industry experiencing labour shortages in both the Swiss and European labour markets. Currently, labour demand is so high in some sectors, such as health or information technology, that it cannot be met by the labour supply available in the Swiss or the European labour markets. In these sectors, recourse to skilled labour from countries outside the European Union may be authorised by the Swiss labour market authorities, following close scrutiny of the company's application and within the bounds of the statutory framework mentioned above.

Foreign workers: main characteristics

Switzerland has a large number of permanent foreign residents. Foreign workers residing on Swiss soil share a number of common characteristics which have facilitated their admission into the national labour market. A profile of this particular group in 2001 and 2002 is given below. It draws on data from the Central Aliens Register drawn up by the Federal Foreign Office and, in some data categories, on statistics from the Federal Statistical Office (OFS). Owing to changes in the legislation on 1 June 2002, it was no longer possible to obtain specific figures on the foreign labour force in Switzerland from the Central Register, as of late December 2002. Accordingly, the figures used here relate to data from the Central Aliens Register at the end of December 2001. Chart 1.1 shows that the number of foreign workers resident on an annual basis, or permanently settled in the country, was 738 840 at the end of December 2001, approximately one-quarter of the total labour force. Over half, in fact 60%, were foreigners who had settled permanently in the country, while 20% held annual residence permits. The number of seasonal workers[3] amounted to 14 990, and cross-border commuters to 168 090. It is worth noting that these four categories together accounted for 921 560 foreigners in gainful employment, 4% up on the end of the previous year.

Despite significant return flows over the past few years, EU nationals still account for 46% of the foreign working population. Moreover, foreign workers are generally younger than their Swiss counterparts. In 2001, for instance, almost 60% of foreigners in gainful employment were under 40 years of age, whereas only 47.5% of the Swiss labour force fell into that age group. The number of foreigners in paid employment in Switzerland peaked in 1994 at 911 630. From 1995 to 1998, this number declined in line with economic developments, before rising again in 1999. In 2000 and 2001, the upturn continued and became even more marked. The unemployment rate at the end of December 2001 stood at 2.4% of the total number of permanent residents in Switzerland, which meant that unemployment was up on the year 2000 (from 1.9% at the end of December 2000). While 1.7% of Swiss nationals were out of work, the corresponding figure for the foreign population was 4.8%.

---

3.   As the number of seasonal workers is at its lowest in December, any study of this category of worker must use the figures for August.

According to the figures for the end of December 2001 (Chart 1.2), the highest number of foreign workers were in the areas of commerce, banking and insurance[4] (221 990, 24.1%), followed by metalwork and machinery (145 562, 15.8%), the hotel and catering industry (106 136, or 11.5%) and construction and civil engineering (86 331, 9.4%). Compared with the year 2000, the number of foreign workers rose in all of the above industries. However, it fell in other sectors, such as textiles, agriculture and livestock farming. By and large, these are the declining industries in the Swiss economy, and they employ fewer and fewer people, be they of Swiss or foreign origin.

As for foreign worker status, the findings of a survey on the foreign population in Switzerland in 2001 (*La population étrangère en Suisse*, 2002, Federal Statistical Office, Neuchâtel) show that foreigners who are self-employed (5.8%) or have private incomes (10.7%) were on average half as numerous as their Swiss counterparts (10.3% and 23%, respectively) in 2002 (Table 1.1). One possible explanation for this trend could be that many foreign nationals reaching retirement age return to their country of origin, where their old-age pension provides them with a better standard of living than in Switzerland. Furthermore, unemployment in the foreign labour force appeared to be four times higher than that for Swiss nationals (4.28% as against 1.44%) in 2002.

The lack of useable statistics makes it hard to assess the skills of foreign workers in Switzerland. Analysis of the small number of statistics listed in Table 1.2, however, does give some information on the overall level of achievement among the foreign labour force resident in Switzerland in 2002. The evidence shows that 41% of Swiss nationals have completed apprenticeships, only 18% left school after completing compulsory education and 12% have higher vocational qualifications. In addition, 7.5% have obtained their upper secondary certificate and 8% hold university degrees. In the case of foreigners, only 28% have completed apprenticeships, 7% have attended a higher vocational college, 7.5% have obtained their upper secondary certificate and 11.3% have attended university. Finally, 36% of foreigners left school after completing compulsory education. There are fewer foreigners than Swiss nationals with average educational attainments. On the other hand, more of them hold university degrees, which is to some extent due to a liberal entry policy for foreign nationals seeking a Swiss education. In short, most foreign workers in Switzerland are EU nationals. Half of them are less than 40 years of age and hold permanent or annual residence permits (80%). A majority work in the service sector. As for labour market integration, almost half of foreign men from northern or western Europe are employed at managerial level. They are generally less educated than Swiss nationals and more likely to be unemployed during an economic recession.

The labour market and a new direction for migration policy

Like other OECD member countries, Switzerland has been affected by two developments that have tended to influence its policies on employment-related migration in recent years. The first is the growing demand for relatively unskilled labour. To meet that demand in industries such as agriculture, the hotel industry or healthcare, several European countries signed bilateral labour recruitment agreements with countries in North Africa or Central and Eastern Europe. Switzerland, however, has not amended its tight admission policy for this category of worker. The second development relates to the recent increase in international migration by highly-skilled workers in new information technologies, research, science and other cutting-edge industries. This trend

---

4.   Including real estate agents and brokers.

has prompted several of Switzerland's neighbours to take special steps to facilitate the recruitment of such workers. The authorities have simplified entry procedures, for instance, or introduced work permits that give these workers more rights than do the ordinary rules governing the employment of foreigners.

In Switzerland, skilled and highly-skilled workers are given priority in migration policy. Highly-skilled foreign workers account for a relatively small percentage of the foreign labour force. However, the characteristics of this category of foreign worker are hard to identify. This is because the lack of detailed data on permanent and temporary flows of migrants by socio-professional category makes it difficult to assess their actual size and how they are evolving. Yet the presence of such workers is crucial to Swiss enterprises. Table 1.3 shows the share of foreign workers in corporate management posts and in other professional occupations.

This table and the findings of the survey on the foreign population in Switzerland in 2001 (*La population étrangère en Suisse*, 2002, Federal Statistical Office, Neuchâtel) show that there are proportionally more northern and western European workers than Swiss nationals in managerial posts, whereas southern European and non-EU workers are under-represented in these socio-economic categories. Slightly more than 13% of non-EU workers are unskilled, compared with 5% among Swiss nationals and just under 1% among foreigners from northern and western Europe.

Chart 1.3 depicts the share of the Swiss population, EU nationals and non-EU nationals in category 1 (corporate managers), category 2 (professionals) and category 3 (the remainder, *i.e.* those employed in all of the occupational categories listed in Table 1.3). Northern and western Europeans in this context clearly have more high-level skills than Swiss nationals. According to survey findings on the foreign population in Switzerland, foreigners with settlement or annual residence permits working in highly-skilled posts and high-paid industries are better paid than Swiss nationals with the same type of job in similar industries. One reason for this is that the work of highly-skilled migrants is valued in the host country. Employers bringing in skilled workers from abroad are willing to shoulder certain migration-related costs and this will be reflected in their pay.

The widely-held idea that the recruitment of staff from abroad gives rise to wage dumping, for instance, needs to be qualified. The fear is only warranted in specific industry sectors (excluding service provision), where workers can easily be replaced and do not have special skills. In those sectors, foreigners who are willing to work come from countries with a lower national income than Switzerland, as well as poorer labour standards. However, the more integrated these workers become. *i.e.* the longer they stay in Switzerland, the greater their demands will be for the same pay and working conditions as those offered to workers who have settled there permanently. The fact that when they apply for residence permits for gainful employment, the relevant government department formally checks their working conditions, means that Switzerland can guarantee that their pay will be in line with local pay levels, thereby avoiding wage dumping. There is evidence, however, that foreign workers with seasonal permits are paid less than their Swiss counterparts or those who are permanent residents in Switzerland. There is no evidence that this applies to highly-skilled workers, whose decision to migrate is a matter of choice rather than of economic necessity. These workers are more demanding in terms of working conditions and are in a position of power when negotiating with their employers. In addition, they demand the kind of working conditions that will make emigration worthwhile. What is at stake for them is the financial benefit gained from their decision to emigrate, rather than the need to find a job, even one with poor working conditions, in the host country.

Regarding highly-skilled workers from countries outside the European Union, it is interesting to note that they are subject to the requirement on prior consideration of the employment situation. There are several legal provisions in the OLE, however, that still permit the inflow of highly-skilled workers from non-EU countries such as, for example, the transfer of managers as provided for under the General Agreement on Trade in Services (GATS), signed by many members of the World Trade Organization (WTO). Workers who benefit from these arrangements are provisionally transferred to a Swiss subsidiary of the parent company. To benefit from this option, they must be highly skilled and employed in corporate management posts. This kind of transfer is possible for four years at the most, and facilitates brain circulation between OECD member countries. The transfers concern migrant workers who, for the most part, come from or are going to European countries or to the United States.

Conclusion

The majority of foreign workers in Switzerland are permanent residents, mostly from EU member states. Their impact on the Swiss economy is similar to that of the Swiss labour force. This is a clear sign that foreign workers, or workers of foreign origin, are becoming integrated into the labour market and into Swiss society at large. Swiss migration policy *vis-à-vis* this category of foreigners is governed by the rationale behind the bilateral agreement on the free movement of persons signed with the European Union. Thus, eventually, migration flows between Switzerland and EU member states will have to be fully liberalised, with no labour restrictions whatsoever. In practice, the process is not simple to put into place, and the transition phase may be quite long, depending on the circumstances.

In any event, the future challenges of immigration lie elsewhere, and concern more specifically non-EU nationals who are not covered by the freedom of movement provisions. A strict policy has been adopted with regard to this group, and only the most highly-skilled workers in specific industries may theoretically enter the Swiss labour market. This policy is aimed at actively managing these migration flows which Switzerland could not absorb into its labour market. Allowing non-EU nationals into the country to offset labour shortages in Switzerland and other European countries is an economic, but also a social and cultural, approach, that is currently being used throughout the European Union and in other OECD countries.

At the present time, Switzerland has a labour market imbalance due to a lack of highly-skilled and low-skilled staff in certain industries. But unlike other European countries, and in spite of strong demand from employers, Switzerland has not adjusted its policy to admit non-EU nationals into some industries. Only highly-skilled workers are still being allowed in, within the strict limits set by the order limiting the number of foreigners. This situation must be viewed against the background of the current poor economic climate. Given European Union enlargement in 2004, however, Switzerland has new challenges to meet in the near future, and may have to adjust its migration policy to some extent. It remains to be seen whether a consensus on migration policy can be achieved, as in the past, between all those concerned by the issue of foreign labour.

Table 1.1. **Swiss and foreign permanent residents by occupational status, 2002**

Permanent residents aged 15 and over (thousands)

Occupational status	Swiss	Foreigners*	Total
Self-employed	500	68	569
Family workers	93	8	101
Salaried staff	2 373	708	3 081
Apprentices	163	45	208
Unemployed	70	50	120
In training	213	52	265
Housewives/husbands	253	73	326
Retired, private income	1 115	125	1 240
Other persons outside the labour market	71	36	107
Total	**4 852**	**1 166**	**6 018**

* With residence or settlement permits.

Source: Swiss Survey of the Labour Force (*Enquête suisse sur la population active ESPA/SAKE*), 2002.

Table 1.2. **Swiss and foreign permanent residents by educational attainment, 2002**

Permanent residents aged 15 and over (thousands)

Level of attainment	Swiss	Foreigners*	Total
Compulsory schooling	907	419	1 326
Elementary school or learning on the job	111	29	140
General education schools and others**	210	21	230
Apprenticeship	1 970	329	2 299
Full-time vocational education	286	53	339
Upper secondary certificate	401	90	491
Higher vocational education	591	84	676
University or equivalent	363	132	495
Unspecified/don't know	13	9	22
Total	**4 852**	**1 166**	**6 018**

* With residence or settlement permits.
** Business course (one to two years), domestic science course, diploma courses.

Source: Swiss Survey of the Labour Force (*Enquête suisse sur la population active ESPA/SAKE*), 2002.

Table 1.3. **Persons in work by occupation [ISCO 88 (COM)] and by nationality, 2002**

Percentages

Occupation	Total	Swiss	Western and northern EU nationals	Southern EU nationals	Non-EU nationals
1. Corporate managers	6.1	6.2	10.9	3.8	4.1
2. Professionals	16.0	16.9	32.5	6.5	7.4
3. Technicians and associate professionals	19.9	21.6	22.8	11.8	10.7
4. Clerks	13.7	14.6	8.5	11.9	9.9
5. Service workers and shop/market sales workers	13.7	12.7	8.8	16.7	23.3
6. Skilled agricultural workers	4.4	5.3	2.2	1.1	0.5
7. Crafts and related trades workers	15.1	13.6	8.1	26.9	22.3
8. Plant operators and assemblers	5.0	4.0	3.0	9.7	10.2
9. Elementary occupations	5.5	4.4	2.7	11.4	11.1
10. Unspecified	0.5	0.6	0.5	0.1	0.4
Total	**100**	**100**	**100**	**100**	**100**

Source: Swiss Survey of the Labour Force (*Enquête suisse sur la population active ESPA/SAKE*), 2002.

Chart 1.1. **Foreign workers by residence category, 2001**

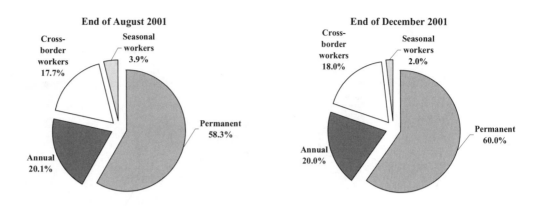

Source: Federal Foreign Office.

Chart 1.2. **Foreign workers by industry, 2001**

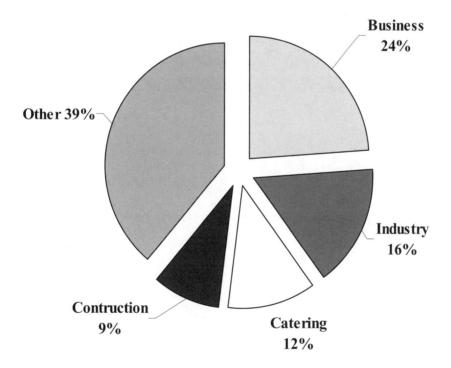

Source: Federal Foreign Office.

Chart 1.3. **Working population by occupation in 2002**

Percentages

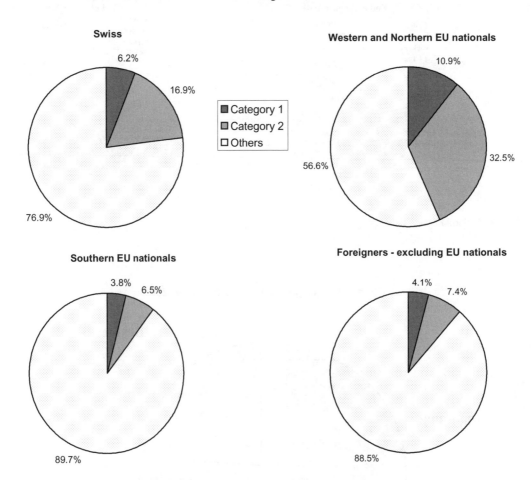

Category 1: corporate managers.
Category 2: professionals.
Others: remainder, *i.e.* those employed in all of the occupational categories listed in Table 1.3.

Source: Federal Foreign Office.

Chapter 2

BILATERAL LABOUR AGREEMENTS CONCLUDED BY FRANCE

by
Henri de Lary[1]

Consultant to the OECD

Overview of foreign labour recruitment in France

In the context of post-war reconstruction and as early as the 1950s, the French government began to introduce measures aimed at attracting foreign labour to regions and economic activities where the need for such labour was felt. This constituted a break with practice between the wars, when the recruitment of foreign labour had been left very largely to the initiative of private associations linked to large industrial employers and to those with interests in the agricultural sector. The creation of the *Office national d'immigration* in 1945 had the aim of bringing migration flows under control. Once the stream of prisoners and displaced persons became employed, the latent domestic labour supply had dried up. The aim of managing migration flows was achieved for several decades, thanks in large part to the negotiation and implementation of bilateral labour agreements.

The first such agreement was signed with Italy as early as 1947 and was followed by agreements with Spain (1956), Morocco (1963), Portugal (1964), the former Yugoslavia (1965), Tunisia and Turkey (agreements which were signed in 1964 and came into force in 1969). A special type of agreement, with a supposedly preferential status, was signed with Algeria on 27 December 1968. This agreement will be discussed later in this chapter, but not first without having stressed the fact that the 15 October 1968 marked the adoption of Council Regulation (EEC) No. 1412/68 on freedom of movement for workers between the six founding countries of the European Community. More than 20 years passed before the next and final labour agreement on seasonal work, which was concluded between France and Poland in 1992. With the exception of the agreement with Poland, for the past 25 years France's migration environment has been governed by these bilateral agreements. The substantial needs of the economy for labour, and the real fear of running short of workers which seemed characteristic of some policy makers, were answered by a good neighbour policy with Italy, by taking advantage of the first signs of relaxation by the authoritarian regimes in Spain and Portugal, and by the decolonisation in Algeria, Morocco and Tunisia. France signed another important agreement with the former Yugoslavia. Germany also signed an agreement with the former Yugoslavia, after

1.   Henri de Lary wishes to thank the Population and Migration Directorate of the Ministry for Social Affairs, Labour and Solidarity, and the *Office des migrations internationales* for their valuable assistance.

France, but soon caught up with, and even surpassed, France in terms of the scale of their agreement. France's 1969 agreement with Turkey, though, was a precautionary measure, as Germany was already solidly established there for labour recruitment.

With the introduction of freedom of movement of persons under the Treaty of Rome, France's agreements lapsed with Italy in 1969, and with Spain and Portugal in 1993. Other agreements were seriously affected by France's unilateral decision to suspend permanent immigration in July 1974. Nonetheless, except for the agreement with the former Yugoslavia, which was suspended in 1995, the other agreements survived, and continue to affect the management of seasonal and family flows. They also are used as references in defining, maintaining or improving the legal provisions applying to certain foreign populations living in France. In this respect, the management of labour agreements was truly central to the migration debate; it could almost be called the "migration controversy". On the one hand, as a host country, France wanted to have an appropriate labour force readily available, with the option of not committing to that resource if the economic situation deteriorated. After some time, it became clear that France also wanted to integrate these foreigners and see them assimilate into the domestic population. On the other hand, the authorities of sending countries were eager that their surplus labour in the domestic market move abroad. Ideally, expatriated workers would keep their jobs or work entitlement after the end of the first contract, but would return as often as possible to their country of origin, where they maintained all their contacts, especially family ties.

The fact that foreign workers also wanted to remain employed after the first one-year contract was encouraged by French national legislation. At that time, it was possible to obtain a three-year work permit after only one year of employment. Yet, with the break in immigration as of 1974, it became impossible to keep the work permit in the event of a prolonged absence from France, or to obtain a new one. This policy had serious consequences that have been highlighted for some time. In many cases, workers who hitherto wanted to come and go as they pleased and sometimes remained outside France for long periods, decided to have their families join them. This possibility was expressly provided for in labour agreements, albeit within the strict framework of French legislation. As foreign workers were now accompanied by their families and settling in France, the signatory countries of the bilateral agreements were obliged to give long-term consideration to the condition and future of the foreign populations concerned, in particular in terms of legislation on employment, stay and mobility. In fact, a number of sending countries were eager to negotiate new bilateral agreements in the form of amendments to the original agreements, either out of a concern that their nationals in France maintain their preferential status compared to other foreigners, or simply to guard against a major shift in French immigration policy

Origin of the bilateral agreements

Before examining how these agreements evolved during the past 20 years from the point of view of their overall legal status and the labour movements they helped manage, this section deals briefly with the environment in which the agreements were signed, and their content.

Environment

For the sending country

The agreements were a matter of the sending country lending its labour to France on the basis of a privileged relationship, that is, within a framework of co-operation, progress and improved training for workers. This aspect is particularly visible in the case of the Franco-Moroccan agreement, but also is apparent in the Franco-Tunisian and Franco-Algerian agreements.

For the receiving country

From France's perspective, the question was to host labour from a particular country and establish a special relationship, with consequences to be felt over the long run. In the short term, the existence of a labour agreement would attempt to discourage irregular immigration.

For the worker

Migrant workers did not really have a choice as to their destination country, but the labour agreement enabled them to:

- Leave their own country carrying a free passport or one obtained very cheaply.

- Enter the country of employment without a visa, but with a work contract and no travel costs.

- Enjoy the social benefits that accompanied the job as soon as they arrived, and obtain employment and residence papers.

It is worth noting that in the 1960s, countries of origin issued few or no passports to tourists, air travel was still fairly rare and land borders were significant obstacles, *e.g.* for Moroccans wanting to cross Spain, and Turks wanting to reach France. Unlike today, these factors did not encourage the spread of trafficking networks. Even though irregular migration was often the prelude to the signing of agreements, it continued to increase despite the stated strict attitude of the countries of origin. In fact, it was encouraged by the benevolence of the French authorities, who were prepared to regularise irregular immigrants outside the scope of bilateral agreements. The case of Portugal is illustrative in this respect. The Portuguese authorities refused to allow their workers to emigrate, because they were needed for the Portuguese economy, even though they were sought after by France under the bilateral agreement.

Table 2.1 summarises the main original provisions of the four bilateral agreements still in force. Table 2.2 describes the flows into France from Spain and Portugal before the introduction of freedom of movement for workers in 1992. It is worth observing that even before 1986, when Spain and Portugal joined the European Economic Community (EEC), these countries had been keen to claim in advance special provisions for their nationals in France, particularly regarding social protection and equal treatment, *e.g.* regarding handicapped adults, which they would only obtain upon joining the EEC. This experience highlighted the fact that the prospect of benefiting from the protective system based on EEC membership made it pointless for countries to seek protection by any other means. This was not the case of the three Maghreb countries and Turkey, which are linked to the European Union (EU) by association agreements containing clauses on migrants. Their bilateral agreements with France continue to have a major impact in terms of the legal status of these countries, as well as their migration flow management. The case of Poland concerns only seasonal workers and thus does not have any effect on the status of the Polish population in France.

Changes made in the clauses in bilateral agreements take into consideration the origin of the agreements, and the character of the relationships that gradually developed between France and its partners. When considering whether bilateral agreements created a special status for the foreigners in question, a distinction can be made between the Franco-Algerian and the Franco-Tunisian agreements on one hand, and the agreements signed with Morocco and Turkey on the other.

The Franco-Algerian agreements

Table 2.1 clearly illustrates the singular nature of the 1968 Franco-Algerian agreement, compared with those concluded earlier with other countries. It is important, of course, to bear in mind that this agreement, more than the others, was concluded within a particular environment of decolonisation. As Algeria was no longer part of France in 1968, the object was to change the situation of Algerians from the freedom of movement they had enjoyed before and after independence (1962), to controlled mobility. At the same time, the new status had to balance respect for the rights of the population already settled in France with that of the population still to come. Moreover, the changes had to take into consideration the Algerian authorities, since they were empowered to choose who would be part of the quota of 35 000 people admitted into France every year, and who would be entitled to look freely for employment during a nine-month period. The 1968 Franco-Algerian agreement thus had multiple traits: a labour agreement (although the annual quota was not renewed after 1971); an agreement on the legal system applying to Algerians in France; an agreement on the movement of people and, to a certain extent, an agreement on settlement. The agreement was the only legal document governing in detail the situation of the Algerian population in France, despite the French legislation which applied to other foreigners. The general regime for foreigners gradually evolved towards more favourable terms, due to changes made nearly every five years.

Conversely, any changes in French immigration policy, for example regarding visas, did not apply to Algerians, unless the Franco-Algerian agreement was amended. This is why the 1968 agreement was the subject of at least three amendments during a 15-year period. Following the request of the Algerian and the French authorities, the amendments updated the agreement *vis-à-vis* the general regime applying to foreigners in France. For example, the most recent amendment signed in July 2001 aligned the rules on family reunification for Algerians with the French law on foreigners. It also extended to Algerian nationals most of the provisions contained in the French law of 11 May 1998 regarding the entry and stay of foreigners in France, and asylum rights, also known as the RESEDA Act (*Loi relative à l'entrée et au séjour des étrangers en France et au droit d'asile)*.

The Franco-Tunisian agreements

In 1964, Tunisia concluded a standard labour agreement with France. From 1988, Tunisia began to seek to amend its bilateral agreement to incorporate some elements of the 9 September 1986 Act (*Loi Pasqua*), which were more favourable to all foreigners. At the same time, France required that Tunisians be subject to a visa system, from which they had been hitherto exempt. France also had secured the same status for its nationals working in Tunisia as that enjoyed by Tunisians in France (a one-year residence permit, which after three years can become a 10-year residence permit). Therefore, the two series of agreements with Algeria and Tunisia, and their respective amendments, responded to changes in the general regime for foreigners. When conditions could or did become more or less favourable to all foreigners, Algeria and Tunisia separately attempted to ensure that the system applicable to their respective nationals was not disadvantageous, compared to the general regime (admittedly at the cost of certain concessions).

The Franco-Moroccan agreements

There are far fewer changes in the 1963 Franco-Moroccan agreement, because the Moroccan authorities did not request any amendments to take into account French legislative changes. All alterations in the general regime for foreigners were applied in their entirety and with immediate effect to all Moroccan nationals, regardless of the positive or negative impacts. The 1983 and 1986 amendments to the 1963 agreement, however, are two exceptions. They introduced short-term and long-term residence visas, as well as a reciprocal status for French nationals working in Morocco. The idea of negotiating a bilateral readmission agreement was briefly envisaged, but never concluded. The European Commission proposed the draft of a readmission agreement to Morocco in 2002.

The Franco-Turkish agreement

This agreement still applies mainly to families of Turkish workers residing in France, and has not been amended regarding the status of Turkish nationals in France.

The Franco-Polish agreement

This agreement enabled the regularisation of an irregular flow of seasonal grape-pickers in the Burgundy and Champagne regions in the early 1990s.

Changes in flows managed under the labour agreements

The 1974 decision to suspend the immigration of permanent workers and to award work permits to all foreigners, including Algerians as of 1984, was taken by authorities related to the Ministry of Labour, based on the employment situation. It is therefore difficult to claim that these foreign workers were regularised as a result of bilateral labour agreements with their country of origin. However, the migration scheme established by bilateral labour agreements continues to apply to two types of flows: seasonal workers and family members. This is true, at the very least, with regards to Morocco, Tunisia and Turkey (in this last case, families only) and includes Polish seasonal immigration governed by the 1990 Franco-Polish agreement. In all of these four countries, the French government agency *Office des migrations internationales* (OMI) runs a recruitment service for which the status and operating methods are defined in the original bilateral agreement. The recruitment staff work in close co-operation with national authorities, and are responsible for overseeing the travel of workers and their families who have received prior authorisation to enter France.

Seasonal workers

Tables 2.3 and 2.4 summarise the activity of recruitment services for seasonal workers in 2000 and 2001. Seasonal migration from the former Yugoslavia persisted at a very low level, despite the absence of an OMI service and the suspension of the bilateral agreement. Overall, seasonal flows remained relatively modest, and concerned workers who entered legally and regularly returned every year. The return of Moroccan and Tunisian workers to their respective countries of origin was monitored. Family immigration within the framework of, or in parallel with, labour agreements, concerned 9 433 families, or 15 562 persons in 2001, out of a total (all nationalities combined) of 14 046 families, or 23 081 persons (Table 2.5). In short, more than 67% of family immigration into France in 2001 was related to labour agreements concluded by France. It is noteworthy that the absolute figures given are on the rise compared to previous years. Yet, the following ratios have remained relatively constant for the last five years: families to number of persons; admitted to regularised families; and families under the agreements to other foreign families.

Other bilateral agreements accompanying labour agreements

Due importance should be attached to the numerous agreements France concluded with countries of origin to provide workers and their families with protection against short-term concerns, *e.g.* sickness, maternity; long-term factors, *e.g.* disability, pensions, and in the area of family allowances. It is also important to stress that all the sending countries which are party to agreements with France have signed association agreements with the European Union (or an accession treaty in the case of Poland) which contain numerous provisions on equal treatment, non-discrimination, social security and the accumulation of contributed insurance periods. The process of extending the number of beneficiaries of Regulation 1608-71 on immigrant social security contributions is nearly completed. Agreements on occupational training, which were annexes of some labour agreements, were very important in the past. It is interesting to consider whether it might be useful to return to this practice.

General observations

Two series of observations come to mind following this brief overview of policies on bilateral worker agreements between France and its partners. The first concerns the recruitment of highly-skilled permanent or temporary labour. In 1974, the French authorities suspended the provisions in labour agreements which allowed this type of labour to enter France. Since then, France has not wished to restore the relevant provisions, even during the recent period of shortages of highly-skilled labour. This policy was put to the test in 1998, when it was necessary to adjust for a major shortage of computer analysts in the labour market, coinciding with the advent of the year 2000 and the arrival of the euro. French domestic regulations were amended to facilitate the recruitment of foreign personnel from all parts of the world and the recruitment objective was achieved. Yet, it transpired that a large proportion of specialists came from Morocco, and that they had recourse to visa applications and entry procedures which were practically independent of the Franco-Moroccan labour agreement. The second observation relates to unskilled or low-skilled labour in France, which has been in surplus for many years. The level of unemployment amongst such workers is of great concern. France appears to have little reason to implement agreements which favour this sort of recruitment (apart from seasonal workers) because every year thousands of Algerian, Moroccan, Tunisian and Turkish nationals enter France under the family reunification scheme. The majority are entitled to employment immediately.

Furthermore, over the past 25 years, France has developed a process to decompartmentalise the administrative control of foreigners. In many cases, this has prompted the French authorities to do away with constraints that are difficult to enforce, or simply counter-productive in reducing unemployment. For example, the removal of geographical restrictions regarding employment made labour shortages less acute and reduced the need to resort to recruitment via bilateral labour agreements.

Agreements on exchange of young professionals

For many years, and in fact since before World War II, France has concluded bilateral agreements with a number of countries regarding the exchange of young professionals (Table 2.6).

A multi-purpose instrument

Depending on whether France is signing these agreements with developed or developing countries, these agreements can serve:

- To increase the expatriation of French nationals to developed countries (Canada, Switzerland, United States); or

- To encourage young professionals to work in France on a temporary basis, with the aim of co-operating with countries that have embarked on a process of economic restructuring (*e.g.* Hungary, Poland) or with countries seeking occupational and professional training schemes (*e.g* Argentina, Morocco, Senegal).

These agreements are negotiated on the basis of reciprocity and annual quotas. They enable young professionals aged between 18 and 35, who are either already working, or are just beginning their career, to visit the other country. They are encouraged to:

- Work in a company with a legal employment contract that guarantees them the same working conditions, remuneration and social protection as host country nationals in the same situation.

- Improve their language and professional skills and gain experience of salaried employment in another country.

- Enhance their knowledge of the other country's society and culture, to promote further understanding and dialogue between the two countries.

The temporary mobility of young workers can be organised and facilitated for periods ranging from a minimum of three months to a maximum of 18 months without labour market testing and in any sector (with the exception of restricted occupations). To enter France, young professionals receive a residence and temporary work permit valid for the duration of their employment. When this period is over, in theory, they cannot change status and have to return to their country of origin. Since 1989, the management of these agreements has been carried out by the OMI.

Assessment of bilateral agreements for young professionals

Agreements with satisfactory results tend to be those managed on both sides by a public or private operator who has a primary interest in their success. Private operators are usually appointed by government authorities, and receive financial compensation from future employers and internship managers, and young professionals (usually these persons pay much lower fees). Administrative arrangements in France are free of charge for young professionals, but employers are required to pay a modest sum to the OMI to cover the cost of the mandatory medical examination required to issue the residence permit. From the point of view of administrative procedures, the existence of a central operator with staff is critical. The operator hires personnel who can speak or read the language used for drafting the candidates' contracts and are capable of communicating with other central operators, *i.e.* their counterparts in sending countries. In the receiving country, the appropriate local authority plays a critical role, because it is responsible for giving an official opinion at the beginning of the process on the actual existence of a job, for issuing the work permit to young foreign professionals when they arrive and for approving the employers' ability to act as internship managers. This structure was adopted in France, even though it remains relatively cumbersome.

Complications can occur within these agreements, when employers submit a request for young foreign professionals to meet a need for highly-skilled labour, as was the case of the Polish welders sought after by companies working for shipyards. French authorities were forced to define their stance on this situation, which could easily have shifted the agreements on the exchange of all young professionals in a new direction which would have been inconsistent with the literal interpretation or spirit of the agreements.

Table 2 1. **Provisions of bilateral agreements with the Maghreb countries and Turkey**

Provisions of the agreements	Morocco	Tunisia	Turkey	Algeria
Equal treatment	X	X	X	
Non-discrimination	X	X	X	
Social security	X	X	X	
Transfer of savings	X	X	X	
Right to family reunion	X	X	X	X
Provision regarding recruitment	X	X	X	
Possibility of taking another job with working conditions according to French law	X	X	X	
Specification of a legal framework for work and residence				X
Clause regarding vocational training	X	X		
Provisions laying down an annual quota of workers				X

Source: Author for the OECD.

Table 2.2. **Inflows of Spanish and Portuguese seasonal workers, 1980-1992**

	Spanish	Portuguese
1980	93 751	10 666
1981	90 655	10 823
1982	89 539	10 497
1983	85 378	10 593
1984	76 843	11 199
1985	70 067	11 316
1986	64 681	12 453
1987	59 321	12 777
1988	51 978	14 020
1989	42 073	14 719
1990	33 960	16 592
1991	25 971	16 658
1992	Not recorded	Not recorded

Source: Office des migrations internationales.

Table 2.3. **Inflows of seasonal workers, by nature of job and nationality, 2000**

	Poland	Morocco	Tunisia	Former Yugoslavia	Other nationals	TOTAL
Agricultural activities						
Beet growing		16				16
Tree farming, plantations, nurseries	4	190	41	15	11	261
Forestry	11	127	13			151
Grape picking	1 996	4			7	2 007
Fruit and vegetable picking	943	457	473	4	2	1 879
Gardening and greenhouse cultivation		60		29	1	90
Varied agricultural work		2 885			3	2 888
Other	305	27	1	6	65	404
Subtotal	**3 259**	**3 766**	**528**	**54**	**89**	**7 696**
Industrial and commercial activities						
Construction		4				4
Industry		1			11	12
Hospitality and catering		125	8		5	138
Other	12	50	1		16	79
Subtotal	**12**	**180**	**9**		**32**	**233**
Total seasonal workers	**3 271**	**3 946**	**537**	**54**	**121**	**7 929**

Source: Office des migrations internationales.

Table 2.4. **Inflows of seasonal workers, by nature of job and nationality, 2001**

	Poland	Morocco	Tunisia	Former Yugoslavia	Other nationals	Total
Agricultural activities						
Beet growing		14		12	4	30
Tree farming, plantations, nurseries	71	209	105	1		386
Forestry	7	173	9		6	195
Grape picking	2 375					2 375
Fruit and vegetable picking	1 659	491	361	14	8	2 533
Gardening and greenhouse cultivation	26	39	13	13	1	92
Varied agricultural work		4 281			3	4 284
Other	482	21	1		8	512
Subtotal	**4 620**	**5 228**	**489**	**40**	**30**	**10 407**
Industrial and commercial activities						
Construction		4				4
Industry	13	1			100	114
Hospitality and catering		108	25		10	143
Other	1	45	3		77	126
Subtotal	**14**	**158**	**28**		**187**	**387**
Total seasonal workers	**4 634**	**5 386**	**517**	**40**	**217**	**10 794**

Source: Office des migrations internationales.

Table 2.5. **Persons admitted for family reunification by nationality, 2001**

	Families admitted		Families regularised		Total[1]	
	Number of cases	Number of persons	Number of cases	Number of persons	Number of cases	Number of persons
Algeria[2]	2 398	3 404	584	867	2 971	4 259
Morocco	3 627	6 626	298	400	3 916	7 015
Tunisia	911	1 758	72	107	982	1 863
Turkey	1 480	2 308	86	120	1 564	2 425
Total					**9 433**	**15 562**

1. In these two columns, the totals do not add up to the sum of the families admitted and regularised. The totals exclude those cases and persons whose situations are being re-examined for regularisation.

2. The OMI has no office in Algeria. Legal entry of Algerian family-related immigration is the responsibility of French consulates and a special department within the Ministry of Foreign Affairs, located in Nantes.

Source: Office des migrations internationales.

Table 2.6. **Existing agreements signed by France for young professionals**

Country	Date of signature
Former Yugoslavia*	29 July 1932
Switzerland	1 August 1946
Turkey*	2 December 1950
Haiti*	8 April 1952
Canada	4 October 1956
New Zealand	10 August 1983
United States OMI-AIPT	25 July 1988
Poland	29 September 1990
United States	4 June 1992
Argentina	26 September 1995
Hungary	2 May 2000
Morocco	24 May 2001
Senegal	20 June 2002

*These agreements are currently not in operation.

Source: Author for the OECD.

Table 2.7. **Mobility of young professionals under bilateral agreements signed with France, 2002**

Origin/Destination Country	Young professionals entering France	Young professional French nationals entering the country indicated
Switzerland	37	102
Poland	263	-
Hungary	15	-
Morocco	94	-
Senegal	7	-
United States	98	319
Canada	265	278
Argentina	7	-

Source: Office des migrations internationales.

Chapter 3

FROM LABOUR EMIGRATION TO LABOUR RECRUITMENT: THE CASE OF ITALY

by

Jonathan Chaloff

Fondazione Censis, Rome

Introduction

Italy was long a sending country of immigrants: between 1865 and 1940, more than 25 million Italians emigrated. After the Second World War, as the country was struggling to industrialise and to manage the transition of the economy, large numbers of Italians left to work abroad, both in Europe and further afield. It was not until the 1973 crisis that this emigration came to a halt. Towards the end of the 1980s, Italy began to receive foreign labour. This inflow increased during the 1990s – the balance of remittances became negative only in 1997 – and the population of foreign workers in Italy is now well over 1 million. These exit flows were a foreign policy priority during the period of mass emigration. The entry flows are now becoming a priority in Italian foreign policy, although most of the attention is devoted to the fight against irregular migration into the country. Some bilateral agreements specifically dealing with labour have been signed, and others are under discussion.

The key players in this process are: the government, the Ministries of Labour (Welfare), Foreign Affairs and the Interior; the regions; and the employers associations and federations (both local and national). Trade unions have played a very minor role in this process, as have other components of civil society. This chapter outlines the role that such agreements have played and are playing in managing labour flows in Italy.

Bilateral agreements for Italian workers going abroad

Immediately after the war, Italy was faced with a surplus of labour and dire economic conditions. Industry had been severely damaged during the war, and Italy had lost its colonies and had to accept returning refugees. As a consequence, the country sought to promote emigration to receiving countries. This was also the reason why Italy was a founding member of the Inter-Governmental Committee on Migration in Europe (ICME), the predecessor of the International Organization for Migration (IOM). South America was a major destination for Italians – first Argentina and Brazil, then Chile and Venezuela. European reconstruction led to a demand for Italian workers. Agreements were signed with Belgium, France and Switzerland. Between 1945 and 1961, 7.4 million

Italians went to work abroad. Some of these agreements are listed in Table 3.1. The most notorious was the 1946 agreement with Belgium, in which each Italian worker sent to the mines in the Walloon region was repaid with coal sent to Italian state enterprises. Each day of work by an Italian miner meant 200 kgs of coal for Italy. This gave an incentive to the Italian government to encourage migration and to institutionalise the mechanisms of recruitment, evaluation and transport of these workers. This process is well described by De Ledda in his autobiography *Padre Padrone*, in which he recounts the recruitment of illiterate and impoverished Sardinian shepherds for the Belgian mines.

A turning point in this process was the 1956 tragedy in Marcinelle, Belgium, when 262 miners died in an explosion; 136 of them were Italian, including many adolescents. This raised Italian public awareness of migration that had involved the poorest and least visible of Italian citizens. It also led to efforts by the Italian government to negotiate an improvement in the working conditions of Italian citizens abroad. This mobility of labour was one of the motivations in the development of the European Common Market. From the production of coal and steel, it was a short step to a market in workers who could extract and produce them. Even after the Common Market came into being, Italy continued to sign agreements for the management of its workers and their relationship with the countries in which they worked. Many of these agreements concerned social security and double taxation, but others involved recruitment for specific sectors of the economy in the receiving country. Finally, Italy was also involved in pressuring receiving countries to accept family reunification, since emigration was often limited to workers only, and not their families, thereby placing a burden on nascent social services in Italy.

Bilateral agreements for third country nationals

As can be noted in Table 3.1, between 1974 and 1997 no bilateral agreements were signed regarding foreign labour. Mass labour emigration from Italy was halted after the 1973 oil crisis. The rapid growth of the Italian economy in the 1980s led to profound changes in the labour market. The last ten years have seen a growing role for foreign-born workers in the Italian economy. The demographic decline of the Italian population has reduced the number of Italians entering the labour market. The movement of Italians from the south – where unemployment reached 25% – to the dynamic north has slackened off so much that it is no longer realistic to expect such a transfer of workers to meet the labour needs in the north. Finally, as elsewhere in industrialised countries, Italians are no longer willing to work in dangerous, unpleasant and low-paid jobs. The legal foreign labour force amounted to more than 800 000 in 2001. This number rises to 1.2 million, if family members of foreign workers, who also have the right to seek employment, are included. In 2001, 230 000 new workers arrived. In 2002, more than 700 000 people applied for the regularisation of their status as foreign workers. Therefore, it can be stated that there are at present at least 1.5 million foreign workers in Italy. More importantly, foreigners represent about 10% of new hires.

Nonetheless, it was not until 1997 that Italy signed a labour agreement with third countries – Albania and Tunisia – and the agreement was limited to seasonal work. Italian foreign policy regarding migration over the past five years has sought to sign bilateral agreements on readmission, rather than to support labour migration. This has been a constant concern, not only for the Ministry of the Interior, but for all ministries. The 2002 law, which made major changes to the 1998 framework immigration law, introduced an explicit foreign policy priority, by rewarding countries which "actively collaborate in the fight against undocumented migration" to Italy.[1] The mechanisms of this reward are described below.

The current recruitment system for foreign workers

Under the current Italian law (Framework Law 286/98, modified by Law 189/02), the employer requests an authorisation for individual foreign workers. In certain circumstances, such as for seasonal labour, employers associations can begin the process. The request can be nominative, for a specific worker known to the employer, or non-nominative, in which case the labour office uses registries held by Italian consulates abroad. Authorisation is given by the local office of the Ministry of Labour within the limits of the local quota and after the job offer has been listed nationally for a 20-day period. The authorisation is transmitted to the consulate abroad, which issues a Schengen work visa[2] for the appropriate period of the contract, but in any case for no more than two years. The employer must demonstrate the availability of adequate housing and post a bond to guarantee any repatriation costs in the event that the foreign worker loses the right to remain in Italy.

The quota system

In Italy, the discussion of the management of foreign labour flows essentially has become a discussion of the quota system. The 1998 framework law introduced a quota system for foreign labour, requiring the Prime Minister to publish an annual decree stating the maximum number of foreign workers whose entry would be authorised. This national quota can be divided according to at least four parameters:

- Territorial or regional, with the overall quota divided into sub-quotas for the 20 regions, which then allocate the quotas to 104 provinces.

- Type of labour, with the usual divisions being seasonal, contract (dependent) and independent work.

- Job category, with occasional sub-quotas given to certain categories (nurses, technology workers).

- Nationalities, with some sub-quotas reserved for citizens of specific nationalities.

This last parameter is the most closely related to signed bilateral agreements. Co-operation in the fight against irregular migration is a condition for preferential quotas for nationalities. Nonetheless, this preference is not formally stated in the bilateral agreements on readmission. Starting in 2002, seasonal work permits are issued only to citizens of European Union (EU) candidate countries (first and second round), to the citizens of those countries with which seasonal labour agreements have been signed (Albania and Tunisia), and to those individuals who had seasonal work permits the previous year (a "grandfather clause" allowing past workers to return).

The decision-making process to determine the size and distribution of quotas involves a number of different participants. The Ministry of Labour is at the centre of the discussions, and meets with employers associations, trade unions and social partners. At the same time, the local and regional labour offices of the Ministry provide their estimates

---

1.   Art. 1, Par. 2, Law 189/02.

2.   Italy has been in the Schengen system since 27 October 1997.

of the demand for foreign labour at a local level. Usually the local offices meet with the local representatives of the social partners, to develop estimates of labour requirements. This means that the social partners are able to influence the estimates at both a local and national level. Estimates of demand for foreign labour are then made, taking into account the local employment situation. For example, the south of Italy received no quotas in 2000 and 2001, despite a demand for agricultural workers. Once the total number of workers has been approved, the Ministry of Foreign Affairs has an opportunity to express its judgement regarding the preferences for specific nationalities. Finally, the Prime Minister issues a decree with the definitive number, categories and nationalities of foreign workers who may enter the country.

Readmission agreements

The priority in foreign policy has been to sign agreements on readmission, especially along the priority axes of North Africa and the Balkan States. Bilateral agreements on readmission have been signed with most neighbouring and nearby countries. Such agreements must be approved by the Italian parliament. The 1998 law states that "the Ministry of Foreign Affairs and the Ministry of the Interior must promote the appropriate measures of agreement with relevant countries to accelerate identification and issue of documents necessary to improve the effectiveness of the measures foreseen by this law". These readmission agreements follow more or less the same format. The person to be expelled is anyone who "does not meet or who no longer meets the conditions for entry and for stay in the territory of the contracting party". In most cases, Italy was able to sign agreements in which persons could be sent back to, and be admitted by, the countries of which they were presumed to be citizens. Presumption of citizenship is based on the presence of documents – even photocopies, self-declarations and reliable testimony. This process is qualified in certain cases. For example, Italy was unable to sign agreements for the readmission of presumed nationals with Morocco and Tunisia. Italy must therefore conduct a complex identification procedure before these persons can be readmitted into those countries. A total of 28 readmission agreements have been signed. Of these, 21 have been ratified and are currently in force. Some examples are listed in Table 3.2.

Second generation agreements

Any agreement on migration signed after a readmission agreement is considered to be a second generation agreement. The first type of second generation agreement is specifically related to labour migration. Up to now, these agreements have involved only seasonal work. The first country to sign such an agreement was Albania in 1997, and it was signed together with the readmission agreement. The only other country to have signed such an agreement with Italy is Tunisia, on 15 May 2000. Tunisia had already addressed the question of readmission in an exchange of notes on 6 August 1998. Another type of agreement which falls under the heading of second generation agreements is the launch of the Digital Registry of Foreign Workers (AILE). This registry, first tested with Albania in a joint project between the Italian Ministry of Foreign Affairs and the IOM, was meant to provide a list of foreign workers available for emigration to Italy under the anonymous request system. The AILE includes basic information on the training, skills and objectives of these foreign workers. The same principle underlies the registry of foreign workers open to Tunisians and Moroccans.

The Digital Registry of Foreign Workers was an ambitious project that did not have much success. Most employers, in fact, made nominative requests for foreign workers, rather than asking for an unknown worker from the registry pool. How these employers came to know and trust such foreigners, who had never been authorised to come to Italy, is a question frequently asked. The usual answer is that most workers came undocumented and worked unregistered for a while, before their employer was willing to undertake the complicated bureaucratic procedure necessary for legal entry. In other cases, friendship and kinship networks have been used to bring in workers. In any case, use of the AILE has been suspended. The Ministry of Labour has since launched a much more limited and effective database for seasonal workers (SILES).[3] This system registers eligible seasonal workers, either those with past experience or from authorised countries and allows employers to draw on this pool for rapid recruitment. The third kind of second generation agreement is for the training and recruitment of foreign labour. The Ministry of Foreign Affairs has prioritised this kind of activity in its development policy. Programmes are agreed upon in a bilateral statement, and the funding is then passed through Italian nongovernmental organisations (NGOs), training bodies and employers associations. This kind of co-operation has been slow to start. Italian regions have had more success in outlining their priorities and funding such projects (see below).

Preferential quotas

As stated above, those countries, which are actively involved in the fight against irregular migration to Italy, may be rewarded with preferential quotas within the quota system. This had been already an official policy position long before it was enshrined in the 2002 immigration law. In 1998, the Minister of the Interior stated: "It is Italy's intention to promote this sort of collaboration, by setting it as a prerequisite condition for the allocation of a preferential quota of legal entry work permits on a country basis." The preferential quotas for specific nationalities represent only a fraction of the overall quota and have never exceeded 25% (Table 3.3). Because the quotas are divided into regional and then provincial quotas, a labour office may have, for example, a single Somali or Moldovan to authorise under the preferential system. This makes authorisation an even more complex procedure. The list of countries which have received preferential quotas has expanded over the past few years. It is also worth noting that the quota for Morocco was reduced in 2001, due to dissatisfaction with the level of co-operation from the Moroccan authorities. The preferential quota assigned to Egypt for 2003 was due not to a specific readmission agreement, but more to the active collaboration by the Egyptian authorities in reducing migration flows through the Suez Canal, the usual transit route for Italy-bound Bangladeshis and Sri Lankans.

Another form of second generation agreement, codified in the 2002 law and of great interest to employers, is the possibility of supporting training programmes in the country of origin for workers who would then have priority for immigration to Italy. Such training courses have existed in the past. The Ministry of Labour signed an agreement with the Association of Italian Construction Companies (ANCE) in 2001 for the training of construction workers in Poland and Tunisia, who would then be able to enter Italy.[4] A similar agreement between the Ministry of Labour and the industrial association *Confindustria*, for training and immigration, involved Tunisia and the regions of Veneto, Emilia Romagna and Liguria. The Ministry of Foreign Affairs provides support for training courses in Albania, Tunisia and Morocco. These courses are conducted with funding from the Ministry and run by NGOs at a local level.

---

3. Registered employers can access the database *http://old.minwelfare.it/minlavoro/impiego/siles/*.

4. See Ministry of Labour Circulars 84, 91 and 98/2001.

Regional agreements

The Italian regions were created as administrative units in the 1970s, and since have acquired increasing independence and responsibility. Federalism or devolution in Italy is meant essentially as the transfer of powers to the regions. At present, regional public spending accounts for about 10% of GDP. Regions also pass framework laws covering migration and international co-operation. Most Italian regions emphasise in their regional laws the importance of training for the return migration of workers who have been employed temporarily in Italy.[5] Sometimes these laws address local demand for foreign labour in the context of international co-operation projects.

The Veneto region is at the forefront of this kind of initiative, for two reasons. First, Veneto is the home of numerous small and medium-sized enterprises, and is experiencing the most acute labour shortage in Italy. Second, local authorities are interested in regulating labour migration as part of their policy priorities. Vocational training is a key part of the Veneto regional strategy and about two-thirds of its immigrant funds are earmarked for training. The region has signed a protocol with local institutions and social partners to implement this project, which also includes a clause for "initiatives with the government authorities for immigration in source countries to evaluate the possibility of starting training activity [and] the subsequent organisation of such activity".[6] For the year 2002, Veneto budgeted EUR2.1 million for training programmes abroad. The training is meant both to "meet the needs of Veneto employers and local development in those countries". In addition, Veneto and the Ministry of Labour signed an agreement for a re-entry project involving training and socio-labour settlement for returning Argentinean Italian emigrants (EUR1.55 million in 2001). The funding is generally channelled through employers associations. The countries involved so far in the initiatives of various regions are Albania, Morocco, Senegal and Tunisia. Such activity requires agreements between the region and the country of origin. On an even more local level, provincial initiatives in Veneto facilitate immigration (e.g. a Chilean-Argentinean information desk in the Province of Padua and a Brazilian recruitment centre in the province of Vicenza).

Finally, another form of regionally-facilitated recruitment exists, in the absence of international agreements. The Trento-Alto-Adige autonomous province makes heavy use of foreign seasonal labour and has received the lion's share of the quotas for seasonal workers. The economy relies on tourism and requires large numbers of German-speaking personnel, who are recruited in Central Europe. The provinces have taken the unusual step of sending their own staff to work in Italian consulates in sending countries, to monitor and streamline the administrative procedures necessary for obtaining a seasonal work visa.

Other bilateral agreements on labour

Italy has signed an agreement with New Zealand on Working Holidays for young people; the agreement has been in force since 7 February 2001 and is currently under review. The scheme allows the issue of working holiday Schengen visas to New Zealanders aged 18 to 30 years, whose "primary intention is to holiday, with employment being an incidental rather than a primary reason for the visit". Up to

---

5.   See research by O. Frattolillo and A. Stocchiero (2001-2002), CeSPI.

6.   Single Regional Table for Coordination of Immigration, Veneto, Protocol Agreement 2000.

250 visas can be issued annually. This visa allows migrants to work for up to six months in Italy, but they cannot work for the same employer for more than three months. The visa-holder must first receive a residence permit and then register with the labour office, before seeking work. During the review of the agreement, the New Zealand government requested reciprocity in improved administrative procedures. A visa is now sufficient to work in New Zealand, so it was hoped that New Zealanders in Italy would be able to start work without the bureaucratic steps required (*i.e.* receiving a work permit and registering with the labour office). This was considered impossible to concede under current Italian labour and immigration law. Italy and Australia have negotiated an agreement containing similar terms to that with New Zealand. The suggested annual limit is 1 500 visas to be granted to Australian nationals. Canada has asked for a similar agreement, with an increase in the age limit to 35 years. Negotiations are under way.

Conclusion

The Italian labour market is fragmented seasonally, sectorally and regionally. Much of the growth and demand for employment comes from very small firms and enterprises; this means that large employers are unlikely to request groups of foreign workers, and employers must pressure government through their trade associations. Bilateral agreements in the near future are likely to fund vocational training for specific industries in source countries. Such agreements must respect the priority given to readmission agreements as a prerequisite for any preferences. Trade associations will play a key role in organising training courses and facilitating the admission of groups of trained foreign workers. Trade unions will continue to focus their efforts on workers who have already been admitted and whose settlement process is underway. Furthermore, the quota system, around which a strong political consensus has developed, will continue to be used by the Foreign Ministry as a means of rewarding those countries which have signed readmission agreements, irrespective of actual labour market preferences for single nationalities.

Table 3.1. **Selected bilateral agreements and diplomatic exchanges between Italy
and other countries on labour and migration, 1946-2000**

Date	Country	Agreement
23/06/1946	Belgium	Agreement to send 2000 workers weekly, in exchange for 200 kg. of coal for each working day by an Italian in the mines
14/01/1947	United Kingdom	Agreement and exchange of notes for recruitment of Italian workers for United Kingdom steel mills
26/01/1948	Argentina	Agreement on emigration
04/12/1948	Netherlands	Agreement on enlistment of Italian labour for Dutch mines
08/10/1949	Brazil	Agreement for increased collaboration, regulation of peace treaty questions and increase in immigration
01/12/1949	Chile	*Modus vivendi* for emigration
21/03/1951	France	Agreement on emigration; administrative agreement on emigration to France of Italian seasonal workers
15/06/1951	France	Three emigration agreements. 1) Medical selection of Italian candidates for emigration to France; 2) Agreement on financial transfers by emigrants; 3) Agreement on family benefit payments in Italy
25/06/1952	Argentina	Protocol on emigration of Italian farmers to Argentina
05/03/1954	Belgium	Protocol for the recruitment of Italian workers for the Belgian coal mines
04/06/1954	Netherlands	Agreement for the exchange of apprentices
16/01/1957	Luxembourg	Agreement for emigration of Italian workers
25/11/1957	Argentina	Commercial and financial agreement protocol on emigration and credit
11/12/1957	Belgium	Protocol for the regulation of the working conditions of Italian miners in Belgium and for the reactivation of emigration of Italian workers to Belgian mines
27/03/1958	France	Agreement on frontier workers
06/08/1960	Netherlands	Agreement on recruitment and employment of Italian workers
09/12/1960	Brazil	Agreement on emigration
10/08/1964	Switzerland	Agreement on emigration of Italian workers to Switzerland
26/09/1967	Australia	Treaty on emigration and settlement: Understanding on financially assisted emigration from Italy to Australia
20/09/1971	Canada	Exchange of notes on emigration
19/03/1973	Brazil	Administration agreement for application of articles of the 1960 agreement
30/01/1974	Brazil	Additional protocol for the 1960 agreement
18/11/1997	Albania	Agreement between Italy and Albania on seasonal workers
15/05/2000	Tunisia	Agreement between Italy and Tunisia on seasonal workers
07/01/2001	New Zealand	Agreement between Italy and New Zealand on working holidays

Source: Ministry of Foreign Affairs, Acli, other.

Table 3.2. **Readmission agreements signed by Italy, 1991-1999**

Country	Year
Poland	1991
Slovenia	1996
Albania, Austria, Croatia, Estonia, France, Georgia, Hungary, Latvia, Lithuania, FYROM, Romania, Former Yugoslavia	1997
Morocco, Tunisia	1998
Algeria, Bulgaria, Slovak Republic	1999

FYROM: Former Yugoslav Republic of Macedonia.

Source: Pastore F. (1998), "L'obbligo di riammissione in diritto internazionale: sviluppi recenti," *Rivista di diritto internazionale*, Vol. 81, No. 4; and Ministry of Foreign Affairs.

Table 3.3. **Preferential quotas for specific nationalities within the quota system, 2000-2003**

	Albania	Tunisia	Morocco	Egypt	Sri Lanka	Nigeria	Moldova	Somalia	Argentina*
2000	6 000	3 000	3 000	0	0	0	0	0	
2001	6 000	3 000	1 500	0	0	0	0	500	
2002	3 000	2 000	2 000	0	0	0	0	0	
2003	3 000	2 000	2 000	1 000	1 000	500	500	0	4 000

*Argentinean citizens of Italian descent (direct descendant, up to three generations removed).

Source: Ministry of Labour.

Chapter 4

ASSESSMENT AND EVALUATION OF BILATERAL LABOUR AGREEMENTS SIGNED BY ROMANIA

by
Dana Diminescu

Attachée de recherche, Maison des Sciences de l'Homme, Paris

Introduction

Ten years after the raising of the iron curtain, the barrier between the western world and the former "popular democracies" appeared to have been pushed back to the borders of Romania. The impression that this situation was at a standstill began to fade with the launch of negotiations on Romania's accession to the European Union (EU) in February 2000 and the right of Romanians to move freely within the Schengen area as of 1 January 2002. Successive governments in Bucharest have adopted numerous legislative and legal measures to bring the country into line with the requirements of the *acquis communautaire*. Particular attention has been paid to doing away with visas and protecting Romanian workers abroad. The act governing the status of foreigners in Romania, based on practices in EU member states, was adopted in April 2001, the same year as the act on border controls and border police operations, in June 2001. Regulations on the status and protection of Romanians working abroad, including a prescriptive framework for agencies recruiting and finding work for them, were adopted in July 2002. One of the provisions of this legislation created the Office for Labour Migration, *Oficiul pentru Migratia Fortei de Munca* (OMFM), effective from December 2001.

Several European countries have recently signed agreements with Romania, allowing Romanians to enter for seasonal work, in addition to existing agreements on the repatriation of irregular immigrants. This chapter looks first at the nature and content of those agreements, and then studies their implementation, distinguishing between the role of the Romanian authorities and recruitment intermediaries. The third section of the chapter draws initial conclusions and assesses the recent agreements.

Romania's bilateral agreements on labour recruitment and placement abroad

The main bilateral agreements signed by Romania are with Germany, Hungary, Luxembourg, Portugal, Spain and Switzerland. Additional arrangements concern the exchange or recruitment of Romanian workers and are the subject of agreements and protocols, for instance with Israel, or on a partnership basis with individual regions in the European Union.

Bilateral agreements recently signed by Romania

With Germany

- An agreement signed in 1992 by Romania and Germany sets an annual quota of 500 guest workers (*Gastarbeiter*) aged 18 to 35, to work in Germany for a period of 12 to 18 months. The duration of the agreement is three years, renewable annually. It specifies migrant recruitment criteria (notably German language and other skills), obligations on employers and details of the mediation process.

- Another agreement signed in September 1999 concerns Romanian workers employed for a fixed period in Germany. It covers two categories of seasonal workers: those employed for a three-month period in any branch of the economy and those working in leisure parks for nine months of the year. The agreement sets an annual quota of 17-18 000 seasonal workers and details their status in Germany, such as social welfare, tax concerns, accommodation requirements and obligations on employers and intermediaries (the OMFM recruitment and job placement and the German Central Office for Job Placement, the *Zentralstelle für Arbeitsvermittlung*, in Bonn).

With Switzerland

- The agreement between Romania and the Swiss Federal Council in November 1999 concerns the annual exchange of 150 trainees for a period of 12 months, with a possible six-month extension. The training may be in any of the sectors authorised for foreign workers. Trainees must be paid in line with Swiss pay standards and receive Swiss social welfare protection. If the quota is not filled in any given year, the remainder may be carried over to the following year.

With Hungary

- The agreement concluded between Romania and Hungary in May 2000 provides for a quota of 8 000 seasonal workers to be employed in the two partner countries for a period not exceeding six months a year.

- Another agreement signed between the two countries in May 2000 concerns the mutual exchange of a maximum of 700 trainees a year. Trainees may work for one year, with a possible extension of six months. They must be between 18 and 35 years old and may conduct their training in any sector of the economy.

With Spain

- Spain signed a multi-part agreement with Romania in May 2002 that deals with the movement of workers between the two countries. It also seeks to regulate flows more effectively and combat irregular immigration. It does not specify the number of Romanian workers concerned, but will do so at a later date, depending on the number of jobs available in Spain. These workers can be employed for a period of at least one year.

- The same agreement also applies to seasonal workers. They can stay in the country for a maximum of nine months per year, and their total number will also depend on the availability of job offers. Seasonal workers are required to sign a commitment to return to their country of origin once their contracts have expired.

- This agreement stipulates that trainees aged 18 to 35 may work in Spain for a period of 12 months, with a possible extension of six months. Their number is limited to 50 per year.

- The agreement gives details of the authorities and bodies acting as intermediaries (the Spanish Embassy in Bucharest and the OMFM), and of the terms of employment and social welfare for migrant workers. Both countries also agreed to provide support schemes to assist with voluntary returns and the integration of migrant workers in their country of origin.

With Luxembourg

- Romania signed an agreement with Luxembourg in August 2001, setting a fixed number of 35 trainees[1] per year for vocational and language training. The trainees must have completed their education, and be aged between 18 and 35 years old. Their training must not exceed 12 months (with a possible extension of six months). If trainees wish to remain in the country after the period covered by the agreement, they will no longer have trainee status and will be subject to statutory provisions on the employment of foreign workers in Luxembourg. Under the terms of the agreement, the onus is on the trainees to find an employer, but they are free to change employers during their training period.

With Portugal

- The agreement concluded between Romania and Portugal in July 2001 relates to temporary residence by Romanians in Portugal for the purpose of seeking employment. The agreement specifies the authorities responsible for managing these migrant workers in Portugal: the Ministry of Labour and Social Solidarity in Romania, the Institute of Labour and Vocational Training in Portugal and the International Organization for Migration (IOM). It also specifies the criteria that apply to such workers with regard to recruitment, admission and residence. It does not however specify worker quotas or age limits. The duration of stay will depend on their employment contract. The agreement was signed for a renewable period of five years.

Other arrangements for the exchange or recruitment of Romanian workers

An agreement was signed in July 1990 by Romania and Germany, concerning the transfer of Romanian staff employed by Romanian firms based in Romania, and under contract to German firms to carry out work on German soil. There is a circular on seasonal summer work in Germany by students aged 18 to 25 (a quota of 100 per year). There is a similar arrangement with the United Kingdom. There is also a protocol between Romania (the OMFM) and an Israeli employers association on job placement in Israel. As for relations with Italy, a partnership agreement has been signed for the employment of Romanian workers in catering, healthcare and the information and communications technology sector, between the OMFM and specific Italian regions, including Friuli-Venezia-Giulia (see Chapter 13 in this volume). Bilateral agreements are currently being negotiated with France, Italy and Ireland.

---

1.   The number of trainees may change, provided that notification is given to the intermediaries (Ministry of Labour and Social Solidarity of Romania, and Ministry of Labour of Luxembourg).

Implementation of agreements and the different intermediaries concerned

Most of the legislative measures adopted within the framework of the Ministry of Labour and Social Solidarity relate to guaranteed working conditions and protection for Romanians recruited to work abroad. Contacts between Romanian workers and receiving countries are also made through the intermediary of private agencies. These should, in principle, apply the statutory provisions referred to above. In most cases, they are in competition with the OMFM. Host country employers also have to comply with the legislation in their own countries on standards for the recruitment and placement of foreign labour.

Main intermediaries

The Ministry of Labour and Social Solidarity is responsible for signing bilateral agreements with other countries on the exchange of workers. The agreements then have to be ratified by the Romanian parliament. However, other ministries are also involved in the negotiations (including the Ministries of Justice, of the Interior and of Education and Research). Theoretically, this should lend greater coherence to government policy on the movement of labour. However, when these bilateral agreements are drawn up and signed, it appears that insufficient attention is paid to the following: the estimated number of migrants, in regular or irregular situations, already in the other country (party to the agreement); the employment rate and type of skills of the migrants; the job offers and skills required in the receiving country; and the labour supply and skills profile of Romanian workers applying to emigrate. This information, if available, would help assess the effectiveness of Romanian government policy in this area. While Romania operates a pre-selection process based on the applications and job offers received by the OMFM, the assumption is that the final selection is made by the receiving country. Local pre-selection offices currently have few resources, and the procedure is centralised at national level, at a high cost to applicants, who must travel to Bucharest.

In reality, a large share of the contacts between Romanian workers and host countries can be attributed to the private agencies that find jobs for Romanians abroad. Until December 2002, these agencies had to be accredited by the Ministry of Labour and Social Solidarity. The agencies work mostly with countries that do not have bilateral labour agreements with Romania. Under the Romanian legislation that came into force three years ago, however, these recruitment/placement agencies now have to register with local branches of the national employment and vocational training office (ANOFM). The private agencies are required to act as intermediaries in the migration process and sign firm contracts with foreign employers, guaranteeing at least the basic terms of employment for Romanian workers abroad, and ensure that emigrant workers have social welfare arrangements.

Protection of Romanians working abroad and competition with private recruitment agencies

Following the establishment of the OMFM in December 2001, the Romanian government specified that this new institution would be funded from the state budget and other financial sources. The OMFM, which reports to the Ministry of Labour and Social Solidarity, currently has 20 permanent staff and can call upon the services of more than 5 000 employees in the local branches of the employment and vocational training offices. The main responsibilities of the OMFM are: i) to enforce bilateral labour agreements between Romania and other countries, and ii) to recruit and find work for Romanians in countries with which Romania has no bilateral labour agreements. The main aim of the Romanian authorities, through the intermediary of the OMFM, is to protect Romanian workers and provide them with social welfare cover when working abroad. A further aim is to supervise the activities of private agencies, in order to reduce the number of cases of exploitation of Romanian workers. The media have been drawing attention to cases of fraud, in which Romanian workers paid employment agencies substantial commissions, without obtaining the services and jobs they had been promised. Others cases involved persons who managed to find jobs abroad, but were not paid by their employers.

The OMFM also competes with private firms which recruit and find jobs for Romanian workers. The cost of the transaction of finding a job abroad through the OMFM can be lower than private agency fees. Applicants can receive support from other state institutions that provide information on foreign labour demand. This may raise recruitment and job placement standards, enhance service provision and lower the costs of the services provided by intermediaries. Nevertheless, there is still a risk that the OMFM might find itself with a conflict of interest, given its dual role as regulator of, and competitor with, private agencies. Whether this situation might eventually oust private agencies from the market is currently the subject of debate in Romania, and is generating widespread discontent among the agencies. More than 50 private recruitment agencies have recently formed a management association for the recruitment and placement of workers abroad, with the aim of ensuring that their interests are defended and better represented *vis-à-vis* the Romanian authorities.

The act on the protection of Romanian citizens working abroad and its implementing decrees contains, in the second chapter, provisions relating to labour employment agencies (AOFMs). This means that any juridical person whose activity relates to the recruitment and placement of Romanian workers abroad (*i.e.* AOFMs) may provide services as intermediaries, only if the contracts with employers (foreign juridical or natural persons, or nationals) are for firm job offers.[2] This is a key provision, as there have been cases in which Romanian employment agencies have signed contracts with their foreign counterparts, thereby adding a further intermediary. The implementing decrees prohibit AOFMs from charging for inclusion in a database, or charging double fees for their services as intermediaries. A fee may be charged either by the Romanian agency or the foreign employer, but not by both. A Romanian citizen working in a country with which Romania has signed a bilateral agreement benefits from the rights granted under that agreement. The act also obliges AOFMs to submit employment contracts for verification and proposes model contracts for AOFMs to use with Romanian workers. The terms actually used in contracts however are not always those featured in the model proposed by the Ministry of Labour and Social Solidarity. This is because employers in the host country are obliged by their own authorities to assume certain responsibilities *vis-à-vis* their foreign workers. Such provisions also have implications for migrants. These institutional constraints will be described below, using the example of Romanians recruited to work in Israel.

2.   Job offers are considered to be firm if they specify: conditions of employment, type of job, duties, hourly wage, bonuses, allowances, working hours, rest time, overtime, date of wage payment, eligibility for additional family-related allowances, eligibility for compensation, employee's obligations, terms of accommodation, taxation and other contributions. The act also provides that Romanian nationals working abroad benefit from the services provided under the Romanian health insurance and unemployment insurance systems (or the state social insurance scheme), provided that they pay the necessary contributions to the appropriate Romanian institutions, by virtue of a declaration of monthly earnings abroad.

Provisional assessment of bilateral labour agreements

The chronology of the bilateral agreements listed above shows that there were virtually no agreements signed between 1992 and 1999. Most agreements are recent (2000 and 2001), yet Romania still has no agreements with Israel or Italy, two host countries popular with Romanian workers. In early 2002, the Israeli government temporarily suspended the issue of new work permits to Romanian nationals, to combat the illegal employment of Romanian workers. According to unofficial estimates, a large proportion of the 60-90 000 Romanians working in Israel are undocumented. Bilateral agreements usually set a quota for the number of work permits to be issued over a specific period. The agreement with Portugal is an exception, as it does not specify a quota. Agreements also specify migrant workers rights, and guarantee equal treatment with host country nationals.[3] These principles, however, do not exist in all bilateral agreements.[4] Moreover, there are no provisions to cover Romanian workers who entered the host country by their own means, legally or otherwise, instead of under an agreement.

The interviews conducted in Romania in preparation for the Montreux Seminar of June 2003 led to meetings with other institutional actors willing to play an innovative role using bilateral labour agreements. One example included three partners, the Italian region of Friuli-Venezia-Giulia, a French humanitarian foundation based in the Loire valley, the *Association Balkans Pays de la Loire*, and a Romanian healthcare workers union (UNISAT), which together perfected a special scheme for recruiting and placing healthcare workers abroad (Jean-Gabriel Barbin, Chapter 13). The scheme's advantage is to avoid the cumbersome bureaucracy involved in signing and implementing intergovernmental bilateral agreements, and instead to develop inter-regional agreements. This shift from the national to the regional arena provides an opportunity to open the European dimension of labour mobility. It also demonstrates how several regions throughout Europe can join forces and implement this kind of agreement.

Provisional assessment

The only source of data available is the annual assessment for 2002 conducted by the OMFM. The management association of private recruitment and placement agencies does not yet have centralised data on its members' activities. Other possible sources are the

---

3.   The Romanian perspective on the principles underpinning its bilateral agreements is clarified with this extract from Act No. 156 of 26 July 2000: "Agreements, understandings, treaties and conventions will be based upon: a) the principle of equal treatment, b) the application of more favourable clauses under the Romanian, foreign or international legislation to which Romania is a party. Agreements based on the above-mentioned principles shall specify at least: a) the basic wage, b) working hours and rest time, c) general terms of employment protection and occupational safety, d) insurance cover for work accidents and occupational diseases, as well as sickness occurring during working hours. Through the intermediary of the public authorities or the competent foreign institutions, Romanian citizens are guaranteed: a) the benefits due for the duration of the contract, b) the enforcement of labour protection measures provided for under the legislation of partner countries, and c) the resolution of any disputes, in compliance with the legislation applicable in each country".

4.   The agreement between Romania and Hungary on seasonal workers, for instance, merely stipulates that in exercising their rights and adhering to their specified obligations relating to their job, safety in the workplace and payment of contributions, seasonal workers will receive the same treatment as any other employees in the partner country. Equal treatment will include the legal protection of personal property, rights and interests, and access to judicial authorities. Furthermore, provisions relating to equal treatment will be harmonised with the provisions of the bilateral agreement on avoiding double taxation. Consequently, there is practically no explicit reference to a minimum wage, but only general remarks on the "protection of rights and interests". The agreement between Romania and Germany for guest workers contains a similar, very broad provision: pay and other terms of employment should comply with employment contracts and the provisions of labour and social insurance legislation in the receiving country.

consulates of countries issuing employment-related visas, but data are either unavailable or have not been sufficiently subdivided into visa categories to be very useful. Germany and Spain are probably the most committed partners in bilateral labour agreements with Romania. In 2002, the OMFM played a key role in the signing of 19 937 seasonal contracts with Germany (most of them for individually named workers). The leading sector for recruitment was agriculture, followed by catering, forestry and fairs/leisure parks. The quota for guest workers was set at a maximum of 500, the usual requirements being good vocational skills and a few years experience in healthcare or catering. To fill the quota, Germany introduced three successive selection procedures. The OMFM also recruited and selected 89 students for domestic work in Germany during the summer holidays.

Jobs for workers in Spain began with a pilot project in which two companies offered 961 seasonal farm labour contracts for three months (growing and harvesting strawberries). Recruitment was later extended to other types of seasonal work in the same industry (growing and harvesting vegetables and fruit). In 2002, the total number of seasonal contracts came to just under 2 000. The monthly wage for this work ranged from EUR460 to EUR700. For longer periods of work, the main sectors concerned are the construction and food processing industries, forestry, and data processing. More than 500 contracts of this type were signed in 2002. Other countries involved in the recruitment of Romanian workers include Hungary, Israel, Italy, Luxembourg and Switzerland. Romanian trainees obtained 133 contracts in Switzerland. Most migrants found their employers themselves, and 80% of applicants obtained their contracts in the healthcare sector through a Swiss company specialising in recruitment for this sector. One of the company's requirements was that applicants provide proof of previous employment in Germany. In fact, it is interesting to note that most applicants had already been *Gastarbeiter* in Germany.

Hungary and Luxembourg do not yet appear to have made use of the opportunities offered in their bilateral agreements with Romania. According to the information available, four people were selected to work in Luxembourg but have not yet managed to obtain work contracts. As for Hungary, in spite of a high quota (8 000 seasonal workers a year), the OMFM has managed to find work for only eight people so far. Hungary shares a border with Romania, so most Romanian applicants from the west of the country seem to prefer cross-border commuting and undeclared work, rather than benefiting from the terms of the bilateral agreement. In 2002, the OMFM recruited 700 people for contracts in Israel (particularly in the construction industry), and more than 350 people for the catering industry in Italy.

Evaluation of bilateral agreements concluded by Romania

Bilateral agreements on the repatriation of irregular Romanian immigrants, and on the recruitment and placement of Romanian workers abroad, are a major step forward in the formulation and implementation of migration policy. Legal and administrative steps have been taken to curb irregular migration and to promote the protection of Romanian workers abroad. Concerns about brain drain have also led to the adoption of measures to encourage highly skilled Romanian workers, particularly computer scientists, to return and settle in Romania. One incentive is tax exemption for the first five years of employment there.

A step towards European integration

The fact that Romanian nationals are employed in the European Economic Area (EEA) is seen as a step towards European integration. For Romanians, international mobility not only fosters movements of labour and capital, but also encourages innovation, and generates a change in attitudes and the work ethic. These factors should accelerate the modernisation of Romania and its transition to a market economy. In this respect, Romanian migrants can be said to be participating in the process of European integration.

A tool to combat unemployment and increase training opportunities for Romanian workers

Employment-related migration helps to alleviate the pressure of unemployment on the Romanian labour market and allows Romanian workers to acquire better vocational training. The country's official unemployment rate of 8% does not include the jobless who are not registered with the national employment office. The worsening unemployment situation has had adverse repercussions on the population, including the absence of a minimum wage, poor health, poverty and increasingly insecure housing. In the short term, labour emigration can ease these problems, particularly at a time when ongoing restructuring is the cause of a worsening in the job situation.

A significant source of capital and opportunities for local economic development

Labour flows give rise to financial flows in the opposite direction, that is, from the receiving country back to the sending country. The Romanian authorities have valued annual remittances by emigrants at USD2.5 billion, which represents 3% of national GDP in 2002. These transfers benefit migrants and their families financially, but also provide them with a degree of social mobility and better living standards. Apart from the material and financial benefits, this could eventually enable migrants to invest in forms of production that create jobs and generate wealth for their home region. Better living standards also help to broaden the tax base, in particular through indirect taxation. These extra resources for the local budget may go towards modernising the infrastructures (*e.g.* running water, sewage systems, better roads) and housing. This boost to local development is visible in northern Romania (the Oas area), as shown in studies of the village of Certeze.

A new work ethic

At the end of World War II, centralisation of the economy and ideological control at all levels of society hampered Romanian initiative and creativity. After 1990, people began to acquaint themselves with new economic practices, but there is still some reluctance to change. As Romanian emigrants become acquainted with market economies and democratic societies in Western countries, they will be able to facilitate the transition to a market economy with a new work ethic, eventually helping to disseminate another kind of know-how throughout Romania.

A factor in combating illegal immigration

Most Romanian bilateral labour agreements include provisions on the repatriation of undocumented Romanian migrants apprehended in the host countries party to these agreements. It is, by definition, impossible to set an exact figure on the number of

Romanians residing or working illegally in receiving countries but, given the number of people apprehended, it is very likely that irregular migration persists. The main challenge for Romania's new legislation and the government's efforts to co-operate with receiving countries, in particular those of the European Union, is to change attitudes and practices regarding irregular immigration. It is important for legal migration to become the norm, as people become freer to move and, in the longer term, settle throughout the EU. For the moment, bilateral labour agreements cover only a small share of Romanians employed abroad, but the trend to broaden the scope of these agreements and increase the number of countries involved, is a decisive step towards achieving the goal of combating irregular immigration. This goal is also relevant for Romanians employed in countries outside the OECD area. For example, Romania still has no bilateral labour agreement with Israel, although the number of Romanians working there, legally and illegally, is substantial.

Conclusions and recommendations

For the moment, Romania has signed a small number of inter-governmental agreements, to regulate the movement of Romanian workers abroad. The agreements impose a number of constraints (*e.g.* age limits, quotas, language requirements). By and large, reintegrating migrant workers back into Romania is not a priority in these agreements. Romanian authorities have begun to discuss possible measures to facilitate the return of migrants, but the agreements place more emphasis on the coercive aspects of returning upon completion of work contracts (*e.g.* the agreement with Spain), than on any form of support to help migrant workers re-enter Romanian society. The same applies to private agencies that find jobs for Romanian workers abroad.

It would be desirable to introduce a reporting system to monitor trends in employment-related emigration from Romania, and analyse the Romanian labour situation abroad. More generally for the moment there are no groups or research centres on migration to and from Romania which facilitate the practical implementation of this monitoring process.

To encourage Romanian migrants, especially the highly skilled, to give Romania the benefit of the skills and experience they have acquired abroad, it would be worthwhile to introduce a number of incentives to return, including:

- Temporary tax relief for those who return to the country and set up businesses, or participate in productive investments that create wealth and jobs.

- Recognition of the skills that migrants have acquired abroad.

- Training courses for returning migrants wishing to set up firms in Romania.

- Efforts to extend the work of Romanian consulates abroad to include business-oriented initiatives and to attract foreign investment, including investment by Romanians who have temporarily settled abroad.

Chapter 5

EMPLOYMENT OF FOREIGNERS IN AND FROM THE CZECH REPUBLIC

by
Michal Meduna

Ministry of Labour and Social Affairs, Czech Republic

Introduction

The Czech Republic has concluded many bilateral agreements on mutual employment (Annex 5.A.1). Several of these agreements were signed before 1989 and fall outside the scope of this chapter because, during communist times, there was no real movement of labour based on free market principles within the Eastern bloc. This chapter therefore concentrates on agreements concluded since 1989. The national legal framework for bilateral labour agreements is described, in order better to understand the basis on which they are concluded. With one exception,[1] all are classified as intergovernmental agreements under the Czech constitution. Bilateral agreements must comply with current legislation, they cannot grant any rights which go beyond it and cannot impose new obligations. This framework therefore directly influences their importance and regulatory power. The agreement with the Slovak Republic is described in more detail below, as are those with Germany. A brief description of other agreements is included. The future of Czech bilateral agreements is discussed in the section on accession to the European Union (EU) and an insider's view of the new Czech approach to bilateral labour agreements concludes the chapter.

Bilateral agreements on the employment of foreigners: the national legal framework

The conditions for the employment of foreigners in the Czech Republic are laid down in Act No. 1/1991 Coll. on employment. Under this act, foreigners or stateless persons may be employed in the Czech Republic, provided that they have been granted a work permit and a residence permit. A work permit also is required for a foreigner or stateless person who intends to work in the Czech Republic for a foreign employer who is posting him/her to work there, on the basis of a commercial or other agreement concluded with a Czech legal or natural person. Prior to the issue of a work permit, the labour office must have granted the employer a permit to recruit employees from abroad.

---

1.   Except for the agreement with the Slovak Republic, see below.

For this purpose, the labour office requires that the employer submit an application with a draft labour contract that must include: the type and the place of work; the date of commencement and the expected duration of employment; the gross salary; the address and the manner of payment of the accommodation. In addition, other documents must be produced, to verify the provision of accommodation for the expected term of employment, and to prove that financial resources are guaranteed for the repatriation of employees following the termination of their employment. The territorially competent labour office then issues the work permit, which is subject to payment of an administrative fee. The act provides that a work permit can be issued only on condition that there is no available Czech citizen to carry out the work and in particular, that nobody is registered as unemployed for the vacancy. Employers are required to register each vacancy with the labour office. This labour market test ensures that there is no direct competition between Czech and migrant workers.

An exception to the above provisions is made for citizens of the Slovak Republic, who are employed in the Czech Republic on the basis of Agreement No. 227/1993 Coll. between the Czech Republic and the Slovak Republic, on the mutual employment of citizens, and the Administrative Agreement between the Ministry of Labour and Social Affairs of the Czech Republic, and the Ministry of Labour and Social Affairs and Family of the Slovak Republic. A Czech employer registers a citizen of the Slovak Republic at the labour office in the place of its registered business location. A foreign employer who is posting a Slovak national to work in the Czech Republic registers that person at the labour office in the place where the work will be carried out. A foreigner receives a work permit for a fixed period of time not exceeding one year, but can apply for renewal an unlimited number of times. The permit is not transferable and contains information expressly stated in the decision of the labour office, namely the employer, the place of employment, the type of work to be performed and the term of the employment. A signed bilateral agreement published in the Collection of Law can provide that no work permits are needed for certain categories of foreign workers, or that work permits are issued regardless of the labour market situation.

Bilateral agreement on employment with the Slovak Republic

Between 1918 and 1989, Czechoslovakia was a state comprised of the Czech and Slovak areas, but changes after 1989 created two independent countries, effective on 1 January 1993. Relations between the two countries remained very close, not only between the governments, but also among enterprises and citizens. A special relationship developed between the Czech and Slovak Republics as independent countries, and during the process of preparation for the division, a complex set of agreements was concluded in 1992. One of these agreements was between the Czech Republic and the Slovak Republic on the mutual employment of citizens, signed in Prague on 29 October 1992. It was published under No. 273/1993 Coll., entered into force on 3 May 1993 and was implemented on a provisional basis from 1 January 1993. The agreement was approved by the parliaments of both countries, and thus can go beyond the respective national laws.

The agreement provides for the semi-free movement of workers,[2] and grants a wide range of rights to citizens of both countries. The rights to employment are supplemented with

---

2.   As referenced in Article 2 of the agreement:

a generous bilateral agreement on social security[3] which provides for sending unemployment benefits outside the country, and with an atypical non-visa agreement.[4] This entitles citizens of one contracting party to enter the territory of the other contracting party without a visa, at any point on the state border, for an unlimited period of time and for any reason. Slovak workers in the Czech Republic are not required to have either a work permit or a visa. Their employer is required to register them at the appropriate labour office. Slovak workers in the Czech labour market thus have an unprecedented status compared to all other foreigners. This very liberal regime, where no kind of permit is required from the Czech authorities, has considerably promoted the employment of Slovak workers. The distribution of these workers within the territory of the Czech Republic is uneven, however, because the vast majority are employed in border regions. The high level of unemployment in the Czech border regions neighbouring the Slovak Republic does not seem to be an important limiting factor because unemployment in Slovak border regions is two to three times higher.

The free access of Slovak workers to the Czech labour market does not endanger the status of unemployed Czechs, as is shown by an internal analysis conducted by the Ministry of Labour and Social Affairs. The study found that some regions accommodate large numbers of Polish workers, who are obliged to obtain work permits and thus cannot be in direct competition with Czech workers, who have priority over them. Minimal language barriers and a willingness to work under poor conditions make Slovak workers attractive to Czech employers (Table 5.1). Unfortunately, many Slovak nationals are working in the Czech Republic illegally, even though there are few administrative barriers to their access to the Czech labour market. The set of agreements, which are very generous and comprehensive, does not preclude abuse of the system. After working legally for the minimum amount of time to become entitled to Czech unemployment benefits, some Slovak workers apply for the benefits. They then return to the Slovak Republic, where they work legally while receiving Czech unemployment benefits. The extent of the problem has been limited by new administrative procedures in an agreement signed on 30 January 2001 which prolonged the minimum period of employment in the Czech Republic required for entitlement to unemployment benefits from 6 to 12 months, to avoid the eligibility of seasonal workers. The accession of both countries to the European Union, and the expected imposition of a transitional period by some member states on the free movement of Slovak workers, gives the Czech Republic the possibility of imposing a similar transitional period for Slovak workers, under the terms of the accession treaty. It is unlikely that the transitional period will be imposed when both the

---

a) Mutual employment of nationals of one Contracting Party by an employer with a site in the territory of the other Contracting Party is subject to the legislation of the country where the employer is situated, unless provided otherwise.

b) Mutual employment under this Agreement does not require the issue of a work permit. The employer is obliged to register citizens of the other Contracting Party at the local Labour Office covering the employer's site.

c) A work permit is also not required for employees who are posted to perform their job on the territory of the other State. The employer is obliged to register these employees at the local Labour Office covering the location where the work is done.

3. The Agreement between the Czech Republic and Slovak Republic on Social Security, signed in Prague on 29 November 1992, published as No. 228/1993 Coll., entered into force on 3 May 1993, but was implemented on a provisional basis from 1 January 1993.

4. The Agreement between the Czech Republic and Slovak Republic on the Cancellation of Visa Obligations, signed in Prague on 29 November 1992 and published as No. 149/1993 Coll., entered into force on the following 1 January.

Slovak and Czech Republics are EU member states, because both countries still enjoy the semi-free movement of workers.

Bilateral agreements with eastern countries

The Czech Republic concluded bilateral labour agreements with several eastern (or more accurately, non-western) countries – Bulgaria, Mongolia, Poland, the Russian Federation, Ukraine and Vietnam. These agreements are prepared from the same draft agreement (Annex 5.A.2). Their similarities enable a discussion in general terms, and to point out a few differences. The intergovernmental agreements require that workers are issued with work permits after labour market testing in the receiving country, so that the country's nationals retain priority over foreign workers. The duration of the work permit is up to one year, with the possibility of a maximum one-year extension. Applicants seek employment in the receiving state themselves, and the responsible authorities may only give certain defined assistance, which is free of charge. A reasonable charge is made for the issue of work permits. Employment is governed by the law of the country in which the employer is established. Wages may not be lower than those of a national of the receiving country performing equivalent work for the same employer, or producing comparable results. Compensation for work injury or an occupational illness occurring during or in direct connection with the work is governed by the legislation of the country where the work is performed. Workers employed under these agreements may transfer their income to the country where they are permanently resident in freely exchangeable currency. Their entry into the country where they will work temporarily, and their stay and exit, are governed by the appropriate legislation of the receiving country.

The agreement with the Russian Federation permits an extension of the work permit for up to 18 months only (24 months is common). This restriction should be removed in future negotiations. Agreements with Poland and Vietnam do not limit the number of possible extensions of the duration of work permits. The agreement with the Ukraine was concluded for five years only and terminated on 4 February 2002. This agreement did not limit the number of possible extensions of work permits. Some interesting findings can be drawn from the figures in Table 5.2. First, a high proportion of the foreign workforce is self-employed. The reason for this may be that work permits can be issued only when all the conditions are fulfilled. For trade licences, there is no test as to whether the self-employment can be carried out by a Czech national. There is also no right to have a work permit issued for self-employment. Many foreigners, especially from Ukraine, enter the Czech labour market as self-employed, simply to avoid the strict regulation of the labour market by Czech legislation. The new Act on Employment should prevent of this form of avoidance. The Vietnamese self-employed are to a large extent really self-employed, for example, by running small shops. Another interesting finding is that the end of the agreement with Ukraine has not affected the number of Ukrainian workers entering or being employed in the Czech Republic.

This review confirms that the power of regulation of Czech bilateral agreements with these countries is low and their function is more in setting out administrative procedures for employment. The low level of regulatory power is illustrated by the addition of only one extra-regulatory element to the agreements – yearly quotas. These quotas are set as ceilings not to be exceeded, even though Czech employers are interested in having many foreign workers available. The only time a quota was exceeded was in 1997 with Ukraine and it was quickly adjusted to allow more Ukrainian workers into the Czech Republic (Table 5.3). Generally speaking, bilateral labour agreements with eastern countries have not fulfilled the original aim of regulating the inflow of foreign workers and their contribution to their employment is more in setting administrative procedures for processing employment applications. All this occurs within the limits set by current Czech legislation, as such agreements cannot go beyond it.

Bilateral agreements with western European countries

The Czech Republic currently has three bilateral labour agreements with only one Western European country, Germany. All these agreements were signed by the former government of the Czech and Slovak Federal Republic, but after 1 January 1993, the Czech Republic continued all agreements that were valid and binding. The agreement between the former government of the Czech and Slovak Federal Republic and the government of Germany on Mutual Employment of Czechoslovak and German Nationals with a View to the Enhancement of their Vocational and Language Proficiency was signed and entered into force on 23 April 1991. The agreement covers nationals aged between 18 and 40 who have finished vocational training, and who wish to enhance their vocational and language proficiency. Migrants need a work permit, which is limited to one year with the possibility of an 18-month extension. A work permit is issued regardless of the labour market situation. The authorities of both contracting parties can help with mediating employment as they exchange applications for work with the other contracting party. Such mediation is free of charge. Should a person's employment be terminated before the expiry of the agreed term, the relevant authorities will endeavour to find other suitable employment. The yearly quota is 1 400, and any unused vacancies are not transferred to the following year.

The agreed quota (1 400 persons per year) has not been fully used in recent years. As of 1 April 2003, 118 working permits were issued (Table 5.4). The majority of the 639 work permits issued in 2002 were in the fields of catering (cook, waiter/waitress), nursing and construction. Catering and nursing were also the most attractive professions, as 80 to 90% of applicants received a work permit when applying, without having an employment contract. The annual quota is not totally used, as the number of applications for work in Germany is always lower than the quota, and work permits are actually issued to between 60 to 70% of all applicants. Germany requires a certain level of German language proficiency before issuing the work permit, and German experts interview Czech applicants to assess their proficiency several times a year. The agreement aims to give Czech workers the possibility to improve their German language skills, enhance their vocational skills, and learn about the culture and people of a neighbouring country.

Nevertheless, some flaws have arisen in the implementation of the 1991 Agreement. The German authorities do not allow a Czech worker to work under this agreement more than once, and workers sometimes need to acquire long professional practice before submitting an application. None of this is provided for in the agreement. The agreement between the former government of the Czech and Slovak Federal Republic and Germany on the secondment of Czechoslovak workers from companies with registered business locations in the Czech and Slovak Federal Republic, to work under service contracts, was signed and entered into force on 23 April 1991. The agreement is one-way only, and covers Czech workers who have completed vocational training and are seconded to work under a service contract for a limited period of time. The worker needs a work permit, the duration of which is limited to two years, with the possibility of extension up to 30 months (in exceptional cases 36 months). Key personnel can be issued a work permit for up to four years (the maximum is four workers per company). A work permit is issued regardless of the labour market situation. The Czech Ministry of Industry and Trade distributes the quota of 4 000 workers per year among Czech companies. This is supervised by the German authorities. After finishing the earlier contract, each worker can be issued a new work permit for another service contract for up to two years, on condition that there is a certain period of time between the two contracts. The agreed quota has not been fully used in recent years, as only about 2 000 work permits are issued annually. Virtually all Czech applicants receive a work permit.

The implementation of this agreement also differs from its text, as the German authorities do not allow the provision of services in the region of the former German Democratic Republic and the entire area of Berlin (the so-called list of forbidden districts). This list is updated each month and an exemption is possible only on the basis of a written exception by the locally competent authority. The third agreement with Germany is a concord between the Ministry of Labour and Social Affairs of the Czech Republic and the Federal Labour Office, on how to facilitate employment in Germany for Czechoslovak applicants for a maximum period of three months a year. It was signed in Nürnberg on 11 March 1991 (Table 5.5). This agreement is one-way only, and sets out administrative procedures for helping Czech applicants who have either already found work, or who are only willing to work without already having found a job in Germany. This agreement covers temporary work only, for example, in agriculture, forestry, viniculture, entertainment, hospitality, bars and construction. The majority of work permits issued were in agriculture, forestry, entertainment and the hotel trade. On a separate note, the German Green Card System for information technology specialists as of the end of February 2003, was used by 313 Czech experts (Table 5.6).

An agreement with Austria[5] was signed in Vienna on 24 August 2001. This agreement has not entered into force, as the internal process of approval by the Austrian parliament is not yet completed. The agreement is limited to cross-border workers who live in the border region with Austria and commute on a daily basis. Work permits are required, issued for up to one year and, exceptionally, can allow a commuter to work in the whole of Austria beyond the border regions. Work permits are issued only after testing whether the vacancy can be filled by domestic labour sources. Annual quotas are negotiated between the two countries. Austria maintains its regime of an overall quota for foreign workers and the Czech quota will be included in this, securing part of it for Czech workers only. In March 2003, there were 3 992 Czech workers in Austria[6] and they represented only 1.86% of the foreign workforce (Table 5.7). The Czech Republic also concluded a small number of agreements on the exchange of trainees. These agreements have low quotas and their actual use did not have an impact on either the Czech labour market or on the employment of Czech nationals abroad.

Accession to the European Union and the consequences

The accession of the Czech Republic to the European Union on 1 May 2004 changes the conditions for Czech nationals wanting to access the labour markets of the other 24 EU member states. Participation in the free movement of persons as defined by the *acquis communautaire* is the biggest asset for Czech nationals, and the Czech administration will strive to make the best use of it. Free movement of labour is the least flexible instrument of the single market, and is also the most restricted one, adding more

---

5.   The Agreement between the Czech Republic and Austria on the Employment of Citizens in Border Regions.

6.   AMS on-line statistics, *www.ams.or.at/amsallg/index.htm.*

obstacles to already fairly heavy restrictions. The actual implementation of the free movement of Czech workers in the European Union as part of the Accession Treaty is relevant to the topic of this chapter. Current EU member states will be allowed to introduce a transitional period for the free movement of Czech workers following accession. During this period, these states will continue to apply national measures, or measures contained in existing bilateral agreements on mutual employment.

Bilateral agreements are thus a very important instrument, capable of implementing measures to work towards the complete freedom of mobility of labour. The current EU member states national measures are quite restrictive, and require that Czech nationals obtain work permits on the same terms as third country nationals. Thus, bilateral agreements will be the only measure available to liberalise further the access of workers from the candidate countries to the labour markets of current EU member states. The set of three bilateral agreements, signed at the beginning of the 1990s, that the Czech Republic has in force with one EU member state, Germany, are not the most appropriate tools to regulate the free movement of labour between two EU member states, even during the transitional period. A new kind of bilateral agreement is needed to reflect better the reality of the situation.

The European Agreement for the Czech Republic obliged current EU member states to try to improve the access of Czech workers to their labour markets. Since then, no bilateral labour agreement has entered into force, with the exception of one agreement on the exchange of trainees with Luxembourg effective 1 May 2001, with a yearly quota of 30 trainees. All current EU member states were asked to enter the negotiation process on bilateral agreements; all except Austria declined to do this. The lengthy negotiation process with Austria is not yet completed, because two signed agreements are still under consideration by the Austrian parliament, after two years. A bilateral agreement can only be concluded when both countries are in agreement. This might be a possible obstacle in the way of the Czech Republic realising its hopes for improving the position of its workers in the labour markets of other EU member states.

New approaches

The Czech Republic has been an immigration country for the past ten years. There are more foreigners working and residing in the Czech Republic than there are Czech nationals working abroad. The attraction of the Czech Republic for foreign workers (including the self-employed) is so high that there are more foreigners residing there than in Poland, the Slovak Republic and Hungary combined. The legal framework for the residence of aliens, including visa policy, the possibility of earning a high income, the standard of living, or perhaps the attitude of Czech society towards migrant workers, makes the Czech Republic attractive to foreign workers. The number of economically active foreigners can also be interpreted from a different perspective. The Czech Republic is interested in having a foreign workforce. Despite the tripling of the official unemployment rate since 1996, which passed 10% at the beginning of 2003,[7] the share of foreigners in the Czech labour market has not been significantly affected. Furthermore, their share is likely to grow as the Czech population is growing older due to rising life expectancy,[8] and falling because of an unprecedented low total birth rate.[9]

---

7.   In January and February 2003, the unemployment rate reached 10.2 %.

8.   Life expectancy for males is 72.14 years and for females 78.45 years, according to the *Czech Statistical Yearbook*, 2002.

These factors, together with a closer integration into European structures, are slowly creating a need for a brand new migration policy better suited to meet current and future challenges. The former policy of short-term working visas was successful in meeting the needs of the Czech labour market in the short term, but it failed both to give the foreign workforce the necessary guarantee of a lengthy residence to encourage them to integrate into Czech society and, *vice versa*, to give Czech society the certainty that integrating foreign workers is a worthwhile investment. Integrated foreign workers are more likely to have their human capital used fully for their own benefit and that of the society. Since 1999, the new government's approach toward the integration of all groups of foreigners residing for more than a year in the Czech Republic is producing results. It has created a more foreigner-friendly environment and improved the acceptance of foreigners by the majority of people in the society. Since 2000, the Ministry of Labour and Social Affairs of the Czech Republic has been preparing a pilot project[10] which will test the management of the new migration approach. Better management of migration flows of workers ensures that the state administration will be able to actively select those foreign workers deemed beneficial to the Czech Republic.

These improved controls create the possibility of providing a much more flexible legal system, and thus create further incentives for highly qualified foreign experts to settle in the Czech Republic. It is evident that better conditions can be offered to groups of foreign workers who are carefully chosen to better suit the long-term needs of the Czech labour market and the whole of society. Bilateral agreements on the employment of foreigners are sure to play a decisive role in the implementation of this new approach. These agreements should better meet the needs of the Czech Republic and at the same time allow the country to benefit from all the possibilities of the enhanced legal status of the chosen group. To illustrate the approach, the simplified "equation in time" can be used (Box 5.1):

Box 5.1. **Equation in time**

Management of migration flows

= Enhanced control of migration
= Better fulfilment of the Czech Republic labour market needs
= Improved legal framework for groups of better managed workers
= Improved situation of foreign workers

Such bilateral agreements facilitate the management of migration flows and allow the creation of a legal framework for labour market access of migrant workers. The Ministry of Labour and Social Affairs and the Ministry of the Interior have agreed to enter into informal talks on a new type of bilateral labour agreement. This new approach should take into account the following aspects of the presence of foreigners in the Czech Republic:

---

9.   Total fertility rate was 1.136 in 2001 according to the *Czech Statistical Yearbook*, 2002.

10.   The Pilot Project on the Active Selection of Qualified Foreign Workers, Government Resolution No. 720 of 10 July 2002 and Resolution No. 975 of 26 September 2001.

- A higher level of consideration to be given to the security aspects connected with labour migration.

- New channels to be opened for legal migration and decreasing numbers of illegal migrants.

- The position of migrant workers covered by the agreement to be improved, compared to other migrant workers.

- A higher level of workers security to be developed in all areas (*e.g.* employment, social security, occupational health and safety, guaranteed transfer of income to home country).

- Employment to be linked with a guaranteed income and help to return to the home country, by means of foreign aid projects (as remittances are the world's second largest money transfer).

The result should be that foreign workers are both legally employed and legally resident, giving a higher level of security for them and the Czech Republic. This new approach will be to some extent unilateral, as it will be aimed towards eastern European countries. Membership of the European Union will, to a large extent, open up the labour markets of the countries in which Czech migrants are mostly interested in working.

Annex 5.A.1
Bilateral Labour Agreements Concluded by the Czech Republic

Country	Type of agreement	Signed	Entry into force	Published	Administrative procedures	Annual quota
Germany	Service contracts	11.3.1991	11.3.1991	Not published	Not agreed	4 000
Germany	Employment	23.4.1991	23.4.1991	Not published	Not agreed	1 400
Germany	Seasonal employment	11.3.1991	11.3.1991	Not published	Not agreed	No quota agreed
Poland	Employment	16. 6.1992	16.6.1992	Not published	Not agreed	No quota agreed
Slovak Republic	Employment	29.10.1992	1.1.1993	227/1993 Coll.	30.1.2001	No quota agreed
Vietnam	Employment	4.6.1994	9.8.1994	239/1994 Coll.	1.3. 2002	200 (for year 2002)
Switzerland	Exchange of trainees	19.5.1997	6.6.1997	188/1997 Coll.	8.8.2000	100
Russia	Employment	25.6.1998	21.9.1998	284/1998 Coll.	Not signed yet	No quota agreed
Hungary	Exchange of trainees	9.9.1999	11.4.2000	91/2000 Coll.	Not signed yet	300
Bulgaria	Employment	6.12.1999	5.5.2000	90/2000 Coll.	Not signed yet	No quota agreed
Mongolia	Employment	8.12.1999	13.12.2000	114/2001 Coll.	Not signed yet	No quota agreed
Lithuania	Exchange of trainees	31.3.2000	29.9.2000	6/2001 Coll.	Not signed yet	200
Luxemburg	Exchange of trainees	11.11.1999	1.5.2001	42/2001 Coll.	Not signed yet	30
Austria	Employment	24.8.2001	-	-	-	-
Austria	Exchange of trainees	24.8.2001	-	-	-	-

Source: Boušková, P. (2002), Ministry of Labour and Social Affairs, Employment Administration Service, Prague.

Annex 5.A.2
Draft Bilateral Agreement between the Czech Republic and Selected Partnering Eastern Countries

The draft Agreement between the Government of the Czech Republic and the Government of XYZ on the mutual employment of citizens of the Czech Republic and the citizens of XYZ.

The Government of the Czech Republic and the Government of XYZ (hereinafter "the signatories") proceeding according to the principles of good mutual relations and led by the desire to expand economic co-operation taking into account the needs of both states' labour markets, have agreed on the following:

Clause 1

1. This Agreement applies to citizens of the Czech Republic with permanent residence in the Czech Republic and citizens of XYZ with permanent residence in XYZ (hereinafter "the citizens") who, in accordance with the laws of the two states, temporarily carry on work in the state of the other signatory (hereinafter "the receiving state").

2. Citizens may be employed in all occupations the performance of which is not restricted for foreigners under the law of the receiving state. In the case of professions requiring a special permit such permit must be obtained.

Clause 2

1. The authorities of the signatories responsible for implementing this agreement (hereinafter "the responsible authorities") are: in the Czech Republic, the Ministry of Labour and Social Affairs of the Czech Republic; in XYZ ...

2. Differences in the interpretation or use of the provisions of this Agreement will be resolved by direct talks or consultations between the responsible authorities.

Clause 3

In accordance with this Agreement, citizens may carry on work in the receiving state for such time as the duration of their work permit:

a) based on a work agreement with an employer of such state (these citizens are reffered to below as "Employees").

- for a period of up to one year with the possibility of at most a one-year extension,

- for a period of up to six months in a calendar year for seasonal work and work carried on by students during holidays;

b) as part of their employment by an employer that sent them to work in the other state under a contract made with a legal entity or natural person of the receiving state (hereinafter "the contract"):

- for a period of up to one year with the possibility of an extension by the amount of time necessary to complete the work in accordance with the contract.

Clause 4

1. Applicants seeking employment with an employer in the receiving state seek the employment themselves. The responsible authorities may only give assistance in the search for a job by means of suitable measures.

2. The mediation of employment under this agreement and the formalities associated with issuing a work permit through the relevant government offices are performed free of charge.

3. Citizens must not carry on in the receiving state any other gainful activity, nor may they be taken into other employment than that for which they were granted a work permit. The government office authorized to issue work permits may in justified cases approve a change in employment.

4. Before leaving the state of permanent residence or, if both parties to the work agreement so agree, after arriving in the receiving state, the employee shall obtain one copy of the work agreement. In the latter case, the employee must be notified in advance of the general employment conditions and of the work, in particular of the minimum sum to be paid in wages.

Clause 5

1. Employees must be medically fit for the work and must have suitable medical confirmation thereof.

2. Employees who are employed for a period of up to one year with the possibility of a one-year extension must have the necessary qualification, confirmed by the relevant documents.

3. In accordance with its state law, each signatory shall recognize the education and qualification documents necessary for performing the employees' work, issued in the state of permanent residence and translated into the official language of the receiving state and officially authenticated.

Clause 6

1. The employment of citizens takes place in accordance with the law of the state in which the legal entity or natural person that is their employer has its registered address or place of residence respectively.

2. The employee's wage must not be lower than the wage of an employee who is a citizen of the receiving state performing the equivalent work for the same employer and displaying comparable results.

3. The means of compensating for damages caused to an employee by a work injury, occupational illness or other injury to health incurred during the performance of the work or in direct connection with the work is governed by the law of the receiving state.

Clause 7

1. The issuing and extending of work permits takes place in accordance with the law of the receiving state.

2. For a work permit and residence permit for work purposes to be issued, besides the documents laid down by the receiving state's law, there must be a written agreement between the parties to the work agreement or the parties to the contract on the means of paying for the expense of the citizen's travel to the place of his permanent residence after finishing work in the receiving state.

3. If the employment ends prematurely and the employee is dismissed in connection with the end of the economic activity of the employer in the receiving state or with the performance of actions designed to reduce the number of employees or permanent jobs, the employee is provided with the compensation prescribed in the receiving state's labour legislation.

4. In the event of the employment being ended under the terms of paragraph 3 of this clause, the employee's employment in the receiving state may be prolonged for the time envisaged by the first work agreement on the basis of a new work agreement with another employer on the condition that at least two months remain until such time.

Clause 8

1. The employment of employees may take place solely through the responsible authorities or organisations or the government offices charged by them with the implementation of this Agreement.

2. After the agreement is signed, the responsible authorities and organisations or government offices charged by them shall without undue delay approve a mechanism for the practical implementation of the Agreement and the form to be taken by co-operation.

Clause 9

Citizens employed under this Agreement may transfer their employment income to their state of permanent residence in fully exchangeable currency.

Clause 10

The entry of citizens to the receiving state on the grounds of temporary employment, their stay and exit shall take place in accordance with the law of the receiving state.

Clause 11

The import and export of citizens' personal belongings and other items takes place in accordance with the law of the receiving state.

Clause 12

In accordance with the state of the labour market of the Czech Republic and that of XYZ the responsible authorities shall by 30 November of the current calendar year set out in working protocols the numbers of citizens that can be employed in the receiving state during the following calendar year.

Clause 13

1. This Agreement becomes valid on the day of delivery of the last communiqué in which the signatories confirm that the internal conditions necessary for it to become valid have been satisfied.

2. This Agreement will be preliminarily implemented from the day on which it is signed.

3. This Agreement runs for a period of five years and will automatically be extended by two years unless one of the signatories notifies the other of its intention to terminate the agreement and does so in writing and six months before its expiry at the latest.

4. In the event of the Agreement's expiry the work permits issued to citizens according to this Agreement remain valid for the period stated in them.

This Agreement was made in …… on …… in two original counterparts, each in both Czech and XYZ, with both wordings being equally valid.

For the Government of the Czech Republic   For the Government of XYZ

Table 5.1. **Stocks of Czech workers in the Slovak labour market and *vice versa*, 1993-2002**

Year	Czech workers in the Slovak Republic	Slovak workers in the Czech Republic
1993	1 439	23 367
1994	1 198	39 209
1995	1 179	59 323
1996	1 499	72 244
1997	1 718	69 723
1998	2 119	61 320
1999	2 229	53 154
2000	2 227	63 567
2001	2 013	63 555
2002	2 023	56 558

Source: Horáková, M. (2003), "Mezinárodní pracovní migrace v R", *Bulletin č. 10*, VÚPSV, Prague.

Table 5.2. **Numbers of workers from countries with a bilateral agreement, 1998-2002**

	1998			1999			2000		
	WP	TL	Total	WP	TL	Total	WP	TL	Total
Ukraine	19 255	9 942	29 197	16 646	19 521	36 167	15 753	21 402	37 155
Russia	1 129	816	1 945	1 151	1 550	2 701	1 016	1 842	2 858
Poland	9 941	874	10 815	6 880	1 033	7 913	7 679	1 033	8 712
Bulgaria	2 721	734	3 455	1 657	1 104	2 761	1 523	1 174	2 697
Mongolia	942	76	1 018	623	174	797	660	231	891
Vietnam	50	15 454	15 504	62	18 938	19 000	75	19 307	19 382

	2001			2002		
	WP	TL	Total	WP	TL	Total
Ukraine	17 473	21 590	39 063	19 958	19 047	39 005
Russia	887	1 890	2 777	930	1 667	2 597
Poland	6 661	1 051	7 712	7 338	1 081	8 419
Bulgaria	1 863	1 123	2 986	1 985	1 004	2 989
Mongolia	976	228	1 204	1 185	190	1 375
Vietnam	63	20 403	20 466	150	20 081	20 231

TL: trade licences; WP: working permits.

Source: Horáková, M. (2003), "Mezinárodní pracovní migrace v R", *Bulletin č. 10*, VÚPSV, Prague.

Table 5.3. **Yearly quotas with Vietnam and Ukraine, 1994-2002**

	1994	1995	1996	1997	1998	1999	2000	2001	2002
Vietnam	3 000	1 500	800	500	500	150	150	150	200
Ukraine	-	-	36 000	60 000	30 000	30 000	30 000	30 000	-

Source: Boušková, P. (2003), Ministry of Labour and Social Affairs, Employment Administration Service, Prague.

Table 5.4. **Agreement with Germany: enhancement of vocational and language proficiency 1998-2002**

Number of applications and actual work permits issued to Czech workers

	1998	1999	2000	2001	2002
Applications	569	749	994	1160	925
Work permits	320	446	649	783	639
%	56.2	59.5	65.3	67.5	69.1

Source: Dvo áková, L. (2003), Ministry of Labour and Social Affairs, Employment Administration Service, Prague.

Table 5.5. **Number of work permits issued to Czech workers, 1998-2003, Germany**

	1998	1999	2000	2001	2002	2003*
Total	2 078	2 157	3 126	3 036	2 958	893

* Includes permits issued up to 1 April 2003.

Source: Dvo áková, L. (2003), Ministry of Labour and Social Affairs, Employment Administration Service, Prague.

Table 5.6. **Numbers of German workers in the Czech Republic, 1998-2002**

	1998			1999			2000			2001			2002		
	WP	**TL**	**Total**	**WP**	**TL**	**Total**	**WP**	**TL**	**Total**	**WP**	**TL**	**Total**	**WP**	**TL**	**Total**
Total	1 545	868	2 413	1 466	941	2 407	1 452	837	2 289	1 218	940	2 158	1 306	949	2 255

TL: trade licences; WP: working permits.

Source: Horáková, M. (2003), "Mezinárodní pracovní migrace v ČR", *Bulletin č. 10*, VÚPSV, Prague.

Table 5.7. **Numbers of Austrian workers in the Czech Republic, 1998-2002**

	1998			1999			2000			2001			2002		
	WP	**TL**	**Total**	**WP**	**TL**	**Total**	**WP**	**TL**	**Total**	**WP**	**TL**	**Total**	**WP**	**TL**	**Total**
Total	455	238	693	421	272	693	384	206	590	396	248	644	432	250	682

TL: trade licences; WP: working permits.

Source: Horáková, M. (2003), "Mezinárodní pracovní migrace v ČR", *Bulletin č. 10*, VÚPSV, Prague.

PART II

ALTERNATIVES IN FOREIGN LABOUR RECRUITMENT

Chapter 6

LABOUR MIGRATION TO THE UNITED STATES:

Programmes for the Admission of Permanent and Temporary Workers

by

Jacquelyn Bednarz

Office of International Policy
Directorate for Border and Transportation Security
US Department of Homeland Security

and

Roger G. Kramer

Former Director, Division of Immigration Policy and Research
Bureau of International Labor Affairs
US Department of Labor

Introduction

This chapter provides a broad overview of the many ways persons may enter the United States, either to pursue business interests or to work in the US labour force. Immigration law, which governs all admissions to the United States, is generally considered to be the second most complex set of US laws, after tax law. Fundamental to deciphering this maze of legislation and regulations is the realisation that there are two rather distinct and separate admissions systems: one governing permanent admissions and the other covering persons admitted for a temporary purpose. US immigration law defines immigrants as persons who are lawfully admitted to the United States for permanent residence. After a period of residence (generally 5 years), immigrants are eligible to apply for US citizenship. In contrast, US law designates persons who are lawfully admitted temporarily as non-immigrants. These non-immigrants have an entirely different set of admissions criteria and are discussed in the second half of this chapter.

The United States is proud to be a nation of immigrants and proud that its admissions systems for admitting both permanent and temporary migrants are open to all countries. In recent history, there are only a few cases of temporary worker programmes which have been directed to one or two specific countries: the Q-2 visa for the Irish peace process cultural and training programme and the TN visa facilitating the entry of Canadian and Mexican professionals entering under the North American Free Trade Agreement (NAFTA). The vast majority of US admissions programmes are open to citizens of all countries of the world and all countries are treated equally.

Permanent labour immigration to the United States

How does a person qualify for admission to the United States as a permanent immigrant? The grounds for admission of immigrants and specific numerical limitations, if any, are set by the US Immigration and Nationality Act (INA). These criteria have changed over time. Given the often strong feelings (both pro and con) concerning immigration in the United States, as well as the number and diversity of different groups involved in the issue, the system for admitting legal immigrants is modified only infrequently. The last major modification to the legal immigration admissions system occurred with the passage of the Immigration Act of 1990. Prior to that, the last major change occurred in 1965. While there are numerous ways to qualify for immigration to the United States, classes of admission can be generally categorised into four major groups: family reunification; employment-based; refugees and asylees; and diversity. Many people have the mistaken perception that labour immigration is the principal avenue to permanent settlement in the United States. This is not the case. Immigration to the United States is strongly rooted in the humanitarian principles of family reunification and refugee resettlement which accounted for nearly three-fourths (73.6%) of all immigration in fiscal year 2001. Even those admissions systems for filling employment needs, and for increasing the diversity of countries in immigration flows, allow for the admission of the immigrant's immediate family (*i.e.* spouse and unmarried minor children). It is, however, the case that all immigrants to the United States are authorised to enter the US labour market.

Table 6.1 shows the number of immigrants admitted each year for 1999-2001, by class of entry. While the absolute numbers of employment-based permanent immigrants are fairly large, ranging from some 57 000 to 179 000 immigrants, these accounted for only 8.8% to 16.8% of all immigration to the United States. For each of the past 10 years (1992-2001), employment-based immigration has fallen within these ranges, both in absolute and relative terms. It should be noted, however, that changes in immigration levels in recent years do not necessarily represent corresponding changes in demand to immigrate to the United States. Rather, changes in the level of immigration are often an artefact of new legislative initiatives, increasing documentation requirements and backlogs in the processing of applications.

The employment-based preference categories for permanent immigration

A minimum of 140 000 employment-based immigrant visas are available each year. These are divided among five preference categories based on percentages mandated by immigration law. The employment-based preferences are oriented toward the admission of skilled workers. Even in years when the numerical limit is raised above 140 000, the number of immigrant visas granted on the basis of unskilled labour remains at 10 000 world wide. At this time, visas for all of the employment-based preferences are current, that is numbers are available for all qualified applicants. By law, the 140 000 employment-based immigrant visas are distributed as follows:

Preference 1: Priority workers

40 000 visas:[1]

- Extraordinary ability (proven by sustained national or international acclaim) in the sciences, arts, education, business and athletics. No US employer is required.

- Outstanding (internationally recognised and having at least three years of experience) professors and researchers seeking to enter in senior positions. A US employer must petition for the worker.

- Executives and managers of multinationals (requires one year of prior service with the firm during the preceding three years). A US employer must petition for the worker.

Preference 2: Members of the professions with advanced degrees and aliens of exceptional ability in the sciences, arts or business

40 000 visas.[1]

A US employer is required. However, the Secretary of Homeland Security can waive this requirement if it is in the national interest. Requires a labour certification.[2]

Preference 3: Skilled workers, professionals and other workers

40 000 visas.[1]

Labour certification is required.[2]

- Skilled workers with at least two years vocational training or experience.

- Professionals with a Bachelor's degree.

- Other workers (unskilled workers). This subcategory is limited to no more than 10 000 visas per year.

Preference 4: Special immigrants

10 000 visas.

This category includes ministers of religion and persons working for religious organisations, foreign medical graduates, alien employees of the US government abroad, alien retired employees of international organisations, etc.

---

1. The number of visas available for each of the first three employment-based preferences may be increased through redistribution if usage in other employment-based preference categories is low throughout the year. Employment-based first preference receives the extra visas not being utilised by preferences 4 and 5. Second preference receives visas unused by first preference. Third preference receives visas unused by first and second preference.

2. A labour certification is granted by the US Department of Labor upon a finding that there are not sufficient US workers who are able, willing, qualified and available for the employment offered to the alien, and that the wages and working conditions of similarly employed US workers will not be adversely affected. The labor certification process is initiated by the employer, and requires recruitment of US workers at prevailing wages and working conditions at the location where the employment will take place. Labour certifications are required for certain employment-based immigrants, as well as H-2A and H-2B non-immigrants.

   In contrast, the labour condition application (LCA) requirement for H-1B specialty workers is less demanding (and, some would say, less protective of US workers). The Labor Department is not involved in any recruitment efforts – in fact, the LCA only requires recruitment of US workers when an employer is H-1B dependent or has been a wilful violator.

Preference 5: Employment creation (investor) visas

10 000 visas.

For investors of at least USD1 million. However, a minimum of 3 000 visas are reserved for investors of USD500 000 in rural or high unemployment areas. Investment must create employment for at least 10 US workers. Investors are granted only conditional lawful permanent resident (LPR) status for two years; there are extensive anti-fraud provisions in the bill.

Prior to 1992, employment-based immigration accounted for an even lower percentage of all immigration to the United States. In fact, one of the major changes brought about by the 1990 Immigration Act (IMMACT 90) was increased numbers for employment-based immigration. In the decade prior to fiscal year 1992, the year that IMMACT 90 was implemented, less than 7% of all immigrants to the United States entered as employment-based immigrants. Under IMMACT 90, the numbers available for annual employment-based immigration increased from 54 000 to a minimum of 140 000. Despite this expansion in the numbers, employment-based principals (*i.e.* not their accompanying families) have accounted for 3.7% to 7.8% of annual immigration during the fiscal years 1992-2001 (see Table 6.2 for detailed breakdowns for 1996-2001). The reason this percentage has remained low despite increasing numbers for employment-based immigration since 1992 is that other types of immigration have also increased during this period.

Temporary labour migration to the United States

Aliens lawfully admitted to the United States for a specific purpose are defined in US immigration law as non-immigrants. The criteria for the admission of non-immigrants are very different from those for immigrants. Nearly 33 million non-immigrants were admitted temporarily in fiscal year 2001 (Table 6.3). While some 29 million of these are visitors for business or pleasure, non-immigrants are playing an increasing role in the US labour market. A word of caution about the statistics, however – the non-immigrant admissions data include multiple entries by the same person over time. Consequently, they should not be interpreted as the number of individual non-immigrants entering the United States. Currently, there are over 20 broad classes of non-immigrant visas, most of which have no numerical limitations. A complete listing is given in Box 6.1. Many of these allow the holder to participate in the US economy, including:

- E-1   Treaty trader
- E-2   Treaty investor
- H-1A   Temporary workers – Registered nurses (programme ended in 1995)
- H-1B   Temporary workers – Specialty occupations and fashion models
- H-1C   Registered nurses in health professional shortage area
- H-2A   Temporary agricultural workers
- H-2B   Temporary worker performing other services
- L-1   Intracompany transferee

- O   Aliens of extraordinary ability in the arts, sciences, education, business or athletics

- P   Athletes and entertainers

- Q   International cultural exchange visitor

- R   Aliens employed by nonprofit religious organisations

- TN   Canadian and Mexican professionals entering under North America Free Trade Agreement (NAFTA)

- TC   Canadian professionals entering under the US-Canada Free Trade Agreement (suspended by NAFTA on 1 January 1994)

and some

- J-1   Cultural exchange visitors such as au pairs, researchers, scholars, trainees, and certain F-1 students.

Other non-immigrant visas allow foreigners to pursue foreign-based business and communication interests in the United States: B-1 (visitors for business) and I-1 (representatives of the foreign media), while still others allow employment, but only in connection with diplomacy (the A visa) or international organisations (the G and NATO classes). The H-3 trainee visa differs from training visas of other countries in that it is highly regulated and requires that training occurs in a structured programme, and not on-the-job. Displacement of US workers is prohibited and the employer must explain why practical training in the United States is necessary. The number of non-immigrants entering in a year underestimates their impact on the US labour force, since many of these visas permit stays longer than one year. The H-1B visa, for example, permits work in the United States for as long as six years. In fact, the American Competitiveness in the 21st Century Act, signed into law in October 2000, effectively increased the length of stay beyond six years for workers who have labour certification or permanent immigrant applications pending for longer than one year. Now, stay under the H-1B visa has no definitive duration, since workers can continue to reside and work in the United States until a final decision on their case is reached.

All temporary worker programmes in the United States are demand-driven, that is, petitions on behalf of foreign workers must be submitted by their US employers, rather than from the workers themselves. As will be apparent in the next section, most of these programmes incorporate various types of worker protection, based on the premise that the least educated, least skilled workers require the highest level of protection. Thus, employers petitioning to hire low-skilled workers through the H-2A and H-2B programmes must first show evidence that they have been unable to hire US workers for those jobs. In some instances, they must also provide support to foreign workers, such as free housing and transportation. In contrast, employers wishing to hire foreign professionals through the H-1 programmes are simply asked to attest that they have met certain labour conditions. In the case of professionals admitted under NAFTA and intra-company transferees, the foreign worker's education, skill and/or wage levels alone are sometimes considered sufficient to prevent adverse domestic impacts. Employers of persons of extraordinary ability, athletes or entertainers, are required to consult with peer groups and/or relevant labour organisations before sponsoring foreign workers. Finally, admissions in certain visa categories are also subject to numeric limits, which act as a form of protection for US workers.

Box 6.1. **Non-immigrant classes of admission**

A-1	Ambassador, public minister, career diplomat or consular officer, and immediate family
A-2	Other foreign government official or employee, and immediate family
A-3	Attendant, servant, or personal employee of A-1 or A-2, and immediate family
B-1	Temporary visitor for business
B-2	Temporary visitor for pleasure
B-1/B-2	Temporary visitor for business and pleasure
C-1	Alien in transit
C-2	Alien in transit to United Nations Headquarters district under Section 11 (3), (4) or (5) of the Headquarters Agreement
C-3	Foreign government official, immediate family, attendant, servant or personal employee, in transit
D	Crewmember (sea or air)
E-1	Treaty trader, spouse and children
E-2	Treaty investor, spouse and children
F-1	Student (academic)
F-2	Spouse or child of student
G-1	Principal resident representative of recognised foreign member government to international organisation, staff, and immediate family
G-2	Other representative of recognised foreign member government to international organisation, and immediate family
G-3	Representative of non-recognised or non-member foreign government to international organisation, and immediate family
G-4	International organisation officer or employee, and immediate family
G-5	Attendant, servant or personal employee of G-1 through G-4, and immediate family
H-1A	Temporary worker – Registered nurse under 1989 law *(Note*: no new admissions)
H-1B	Other temporary workers in specialty occupations
H-1C	Temporary worker – Registered nurse in health professional shortage areas
H-2A	Temporary worker performing agricultural services unavailable in the United States
H-2B	Temporary worker performing other services unavailable in the United States
H-3	Trainee
H-4	Spouse or child of alien classified H-1, H-2A/B, or H-3
I	Representative of foreign information media, spouse and children
J-1	Exchange visitor
J-2	Spouse or child of exchange visitor
K-1	Fiancé(e) of US citizen
K-2	Child of fiancé(e) of US citizen
K-3	Spouse of US citizen awaiting issue of an immigrant visa
K-4	Child of US citizen awaiting issue of an immigrant visa
L-1	Intracompany transferee (executive, managerial, and specialised personnel continuing employment with international firm or corporation)
L-2	Spouse of child of intracompany transferee
M-1	Vocational student or other nonacademic student
M-2	Spouse or child of alien classified M-1
N-8	Parent of an alien classified SK-3 special immigrant
N-9	Child of N-8 or of an SK-1, SK-2 or SK-4 special immigrant
NATO-1	Principal permanent representative of member state to NATO
NATO-2	Other persons affiliated with NATO, including other representatives of member states of NATO, spouses and children of NATO officials,
To NATO-7	NATO experts, clerical personnel, and servants
O-1	Aliens of extraordinary ability in the arts, sciences, education, business or athletics
O-2	Accompanying aliens with critical skills that form an integral part of an O-1 alien's performance
O-3	Spouses and children of O-1 or O-2
P-1	Athletes and entertainers of international stature
P-2	Athletes and entertainers entering under a reciprocal exchange agreement
P-3	Artists and entertainers offering a culturally unique programme
P-4	Spouses and children of P-1, P-2 or P-3

Q-1	International cultural exchange visitor
Q-2	Irish nationals entering under Irish Peace Process Cultural and Training Programs
R-1	Aliens employed for nonprofit religious organisations
R-2	Spouses and children of R-1
S-1	Aliens supplying critical information on a criminal enterprise
S-2	Aliens supplying critical information relating to terrorism
TN	Canadian and Mexican aliens entering as professionals under North America Free Trade Agreement
TD	Spouses and children of TN aliens
TC	Canadian aliens entering as professionals under the US-Canada Free Trade Agreement (suspended by NAFTA on 1 January 1994)
TB	Spouses and children of TC aliens
T-1	Alien victim of human trafficking who is assisting investigation or prosecution and who is likely to suffer extreme hardship or harm upon departure
T-2	Spouse or child of T-1. Also parents, if T-1 is under age 21
U-1	Victim of criminal activity who suffered physical or mental abuse and who possesses information on the criminal activity (rape, torture, domestic abuse, etc.) and is likely to help investigation/prosecution
U-2	Spouse or child of U-1. Also parents, if U-1 is under age 21
V-1	Spouse of a lawful permanent resident who has an approved petition filed prior to 21 December 2000 and who has been waiting three or more years for an immigrant visa
V-2	Child of a lawful permanent resident who has an approved petition filed prior to 21 December 2000, and who has been waiting three or more years for an immigrant visa
V-3	Child of a V-1 or V-2

Selected non-immigrant classes of admission for temporary business and labour migration

B-1 Business visitors

Although prohibited from working in the US labour force, B-1 business visitors may be admitted to engage in those commercial transactions not involving gainful employment and remuneration from a US source, such as consultations with clients, contract negotiations and litigation. Other activities permitted by the B-1 visa would include facilitating import and export of goods, undertaking marketing and sales activities, fulfilling obligations under a sales contract and participating in professional meetings and conventions. The B-1 visa is bound in the NAFTA and is included in the trade agreements that have recently been negotiated with Chile and Singapore. These trade agreements have yet to be submitted to the US Congress for approval.

E-1 Treaty traders and E-2 treaty investors

The E-1 and E-2 visas are available to nationals of countries which have a Friendship, Commerce and Navigation (FCN) Treaty, a Bilateral Investment Treaty (BIT) or other arrangements, such as NAFTA, with the United States. This visa is also bound in the NAFTA and is included in the negotiated trade agreements with Chile and Singapore. Treaty traders are persons carrying on substantial trade in goods or services between their own country and the United States. Treaty investors establish, develop, administer or provide advice or key technical services to the operation of an investment to which they or their enterprise have committed (or is in the process of committing) a substantial amount of capital. Only persons in supervisory or executive roles or those having essential skills relevant to the business of the enterprise are eligible for these temporary entry categories. Legislation passed in 2002 grants work authorisation to the spouses of E-1 and E-2 non-immigrants.

H-1B Workers in specialty occupations and distinguished fashion models

Although the H-1B visa covers a wide range of jobs requiring a baccalaureate degree, it is often referred to as the "high-tech visa" because more than half the visas are granted for computer-related occupations. The majority of H-1B beneficiaries come from India (nearly half in 2001) and from China (a distant second, accounting for 8%). As mentioned earlier, the maximum length of stay now exceeds six years for those workers having labour certification or permanent immigrant applications pending for longer than one year. These workers can continue to reside and work in the United States until a final decision on their case is reached. Although most non-immigrant categories do not have numeric limits, the H-1B visa is an exception. When the visa was first implemented in 1992, the ceiling had been set at 65 000. However, growing employer demands for H-1B workers led to legislation raising the ceiling to 115 000 for 1999 and 2000. In October 2000, the H-1B programme was expanded for the second time to 195 000 annually for three years, beginning with 2001. Moreover, the law no longer applies the numeric cap to H-1B workers employed at colleges and universities, their affiliated non-profit organisations, and non-profit and governmental research institutions. Undoubtedly, the numeric limitation will be debated heavily in the US Congress this year, as the cap is scheduled to revert to 65 000 in October 2003.

Employers desiring to bring in H-1B workers must file a labour condition application (LCA) with the US Department of Labor, in which they attest to four conditions: *1)* The H-1B worker will receive the appropriate wage, *2)* The employment of H-1B workers will not adversely affect the working conditions of similarly employed workers, *3)* There is no strike or lockout, and *4)* The bargaining representative has been notified, or a notice of intent to employ H-1B workers has been posted. Unlike the permanent programme's labour certification requirement, it is not a requirement for most H-1B labour condition applications that employers first recruit US workers. The two requirements – to recruit US workers before hiring foreign professionals and to not displace US workers with H-1B professionals – apply only to a small subset of employers, specifically those who are H-1B dependent employers (*i.e.* whose workforce includes at least 15% H-1B foreign workers) and employers who have been found to have wilfully violated their H-1B obligations within the last five years. These recruitment and no lay-off requirements are scheduled to expire on 1 October 2003, unless the Congress takes action to retain them. Two other worker protections – that is, authorisation for the Department of Labor to investigate complaints from credible sources who are not themselves aggrieved persons or organisations, and a USD1 000 fee per H-1B worker who has been assessed to train comparable US workers – will also be removed, unless there is congressional action to do otherwise.

H-1C Registered nurses in health professional shortage areas

Created by the Nursing Relief for Disadvantaged Areas Act of 1999 as a short-term solution to nursing shortages in health professional shortage areas (HPSA), this relatively small programme provides for a maximum of 500 visas to be issued annually for the four years of the programme's existence. The H-1C visa allows for a period of admission of three years with no extensions. Although the programme is small by design and only 29 H-1C admissions were recorded in 2001, it is interesting to note that there were some nurses already in the United States who converted to H-1C status during the year.

H-2A Temporary agricultural workers

The H-2A temporary worker programme permits agricultural employers who anticipate a shortage of US workers to bring non-immigrant workers to the United States for up to one year to perform agricultural labour or services of a temporary or seasonal nature. Like the permanent labour certification programme, the H-2A programme requires a labour certification by the US Department of Labor that sufficient US workers are not able, willing, qualified and available at the time and place of employment to perform particular agricultural work, and that the importation of foreign workers will not adversely affect the wages and working conditions of similarly employed US workers. There are no limits on the number of H-2A workers who can be admitted each year. The H-2A programme has numerous conditions covering wages, provision of free housing, of meals or cooking facilities, transportation, etc. Although the H-2A programme is open to all countries, the requirement that the employer pay transportation between the place of recruitment and of work results in workers from nearby countries being more attractive to employers. Of the nearly 28 000 H-2A admissions in 2001, 79% were from Mexico and 13% from Jamaica.

H-2B Temporary workers performing other services

The H-2B programme permits workers to come temporarily to the United States to perform work not covered by the other H visas. The employer must show the need for work to be performed on a temporary rather than a permanent basis. The process for obtaining an H-2B labour certification is very similar to that required for permanent labour certification, but it is not as extensive or time-consuming. The labour certification may be issued for a period of up to one year, renewable for a maximum of three years. The H-2B programme is numerically limited by law at 66 000 per year. As with the H-2A programme, Mexico and Jamaica are the major senders of H-2B non-immigrants. Although the programme is not specifically limited to low-skilled labour, these occupations tend to dominate the programme. In 2002, the principal occupations receiving certifications were, in descending order, landscape labourers, forest workers, housekeeping cleaners, stable attendants, tree planters, non-farm animal caretakers, construction workers, dining-room attendants and kitchen helpers.

H-3 Trainees

As mentioned earlier, the H-3 visa is highly regulated, to ensure that US workers are not displaced. These regulations mandate that: 1) The training not be available in the trainee's own country, 2) The trainee not be placed in a position in the normal operation of the business and where US workers are regularly employed, 3) The trainee will not engage in productive employment unless it is incidental and necessary to the training, and 4) The training will benefit the trainee in pursing a career outside the United States. In fact, one of the many restrictions on training programmes is that they cannot be designed to recruit and train persons for the ultimate staffing of operations within the United States. As a result of the narrow scope of this visa and the fact that there are so many other visas that permit work, the number of H-3 trainees entering the United States has been at a fairly low level of approximately 3 000 annually.

L-1 Intracompany transferees

The L-1 visa allows foreign workers to continue working for the same employer or its affiliate or subsidiary within the United States. The worker must have been continuously employed abroad for one of the past three years. This prior work requirement is reduced to six months under the blanket petition procedures, covering those companies using the L visa frequently (*i.e.* more than 10 approvals in the last 12 months). The L visa is restricted to managers, executives and workers with specialised knowledge. The maximum length of stay permitted under this visa is five years for workers with specialised knowledge and seven years for executives and managers. Legislation passed in 2002 grants work authorisation to the spouses of L-1 non-immigrants.

There are no limits on the number of L-1s who may be admitted to the United States, and virtually every country of the world is represented in the incoming flows of L-1 intracompany transferees. This visa is also bound in the NAFTA and is included in the recently negotiated trade agreements with Chile and Singapore. The visa is considered indispensable for the smooth operation of multinational corporations, which often require the movement of key personnel between sites and affiliated companies in various countries. However, technical personnel admitted under this category are not subject to a prevailing wage requirement and there have been anecdotal reports in recent years of multinational companies trying to take advantage of this by bringing in low-wage contract workers as intra-company transferees.

O-1 Aliens of extraordinary ability in the arts, sciences, education, business or athletics

Both the O-1 visa and the O-2 visa (which covers accompanying workers with critical skills that form an integral part of the O-1 performance) permit stays in the United States that provide for the scheduled event or events, initially up to three years. However, extensions of the event are permissible in increments of one year. In the motion picture or television business, consultations are required with the union and the management group. For all other O-1 and O-2 visas, a written advisory opinion is required from a peer group (a person or persons with expertise in that area).

P-1, P-2 and P-3 Athletes and entertainers

These three non-immigrant visas cover a variety of athletes and entertainers, notably athletes at an internationally recognised level of performance and entertainers who are part of an internationally recognised group, a reciprocal exchange programme or a culturally unique programme. A written advisory opinion from an appropriate labour organisation is required. The visa for entertainers covers the length of time necessary to complete the event, not to exceed one year. P-1 athletes may be admitted for 10 years, that is for an initial five years with an extension for an additional five years.

Q-1 International cultural exchange visitors

The Q-1 visa is designed for participants in international cultural exchange programmes which provide practical training, employment, and the sharing of history, culture and traditions. The Q-1 visitor must receive comparable wages and working conditions as the similarly employed US workers. Maximum duration of stay is 15 months. The Q-1 worker visa differs from all other non-immigrant visas in that the law does not provide for accompanying spouses and children. Because of the narrow focus of this visa, usage is fairly low, with approximately 2 000 admissions annually.

Q-2 Irish Peace Process Cultural and Training Program

The Irish Peace Process Cultural and Training Program Act of 1998 established "a program to allow young people from disadvantaged areas of designated counties suffering from sectarian violence and high structural unemployment to enter the United States for the purpose of developing job skills and conflict resolution abilities in a diverse, co-operative, peaceful and prosperous environment, so that those young people can return to their homes better able to contribute toward economic regeneration and the Irish peace process". This Q-2 visa programme allows for the admission of 4 000 aliens[3] in each of three consecutive years. The Q-2 visa itself would be valid for three years. To participate in the programme, Irish nationals must be aged 35 years or younger with a residence in Northern Ireland, or the counties of Louth, Monaghan, Cavan, Leitrim, Sligo and Donegal in the Republic of Ireland.

R-1 Religious workers

The R-1 visa covers both *1)* Persons who are coming to carry out the vocation of religious minister, and *2)* Persons coming to work for a religious organisation or for an organisation affiliated with the religious organisation. Maximum duration of stay is five years, after which they must reside outside the United States for one year to be eligible again.

TN Canadian and Mexican professionals entering under the North American Free Trade Agreement

The North American Free Trade Agreement between the United States, Canada and Mexico came into effect on 1 January 1994, superseding the US-Canada Free Trade Agreement. Four groups of business persons are permitted temporary entry to the United States under Chapter 16 of the NAFTA, three of which (business visitors, treaty traders and investors, and intracompany transferees) have already been discussed. The NAFTA facilitates entry under these three, with little change to the current criteria for entry under US immigration law. The fourth category, NAFTA professionals, is unique to this trilateral trade agreement. A similar concept to the NAFTA professional has been included in the recently negotiated trade agreements with both Chile and Singapore, although these agreements have yet to be submitted to the US Congress for approval. Unlike the NAFTA, which covers specific professions, these proposed free trade areas (FTA) use a general definition for professionals based on educational achievement, which will be more flexible and able to accommodate the changing workforce over time.

Certain professionals are covered under the NAFTA (a complete listing is shown in Box 6.2), provided they meet minimum educational requirements, or possess alternative credentials and seek to enter the United States to engage in business activities at a professional level. With regard to the movement of professionals between United States and Canada, the liberal provisions and absence of numeric limitations which existed in the US-Canada Free Trade Agreement have continued under NAFTA. The United States and Mexico have agreed to a temporary annual numerical limit of 5 500 Mexican professionals entering the United States.[4] This number is in addition to those admitted

---

3. Spouses and minor children are counted in the 4 000 annual limitation. The numbers used in the Q-2 visa programme are deducted from the 66 000 H-2B visas available each year.

4. The ceiling will be removed by 1 January 2004 (ten years after NAFTA went into effect), unless the two countries decide to remove it earlier.

under a similar category in US law, specifically H-1B non-immigrants. Statistics on the flow of Canadian and Mexican non-immigrant professionals to the United States under the NAFTA, since its implementation on 1 January 1994, are shown in Table 6.4.

Box 6.2. **Professions covered under Chapter 16 of NAFTA**

GENERAL:

Accountant
Architect
Computer Systems Analyst
Disaster Relief Insurance Claims Adjuster
Economist
Engineer
Forester
Graphic Designer
Hotel Manager
Industrial Designer
Interior Designer
Land Surveyor
Landscape Architect
Lawyer (including Notary in the Province of Quebec)
Librarian
Management Consultant
Mathematician (including Statistician)
Range Manager/Range Conservationalist
Research Assistant (working in a post-secondary educational institution)
Scientific Technician/Technologist
Social Worker
Sylviculturist (including Forestry Specialist)
Technical Publications Writer
Urban Planner (including Geographer)
Vocational Counsellor

MEDICAL/DENTIST/ALLIED:

Dietician
Medical Laboratory Technologist (Canada)/
Medical Technologist (United States, Mexico)
Nutritionist
Occupational Therapist
Pharmacist
Physician (teaching or research only)
Physiotherapist/Physical Therapist
Psychologist
Recreational Therapist
Registered Nurse
Veterinarian

SCIENTIST:

Agriculturist (including Agronomist)
Animal Breeder
Animal Scientist
Apiculturist
Astronomer
Biochemist
Biologist
Chemist
Dairy Scientist

Entomologist
Epidemiologist
Geneticist
Geologist
Geochemist
Geophysicist (including oceanographer in Mexico and United States)
Horticulturist
Meteorologist
Pharmacologist
Physicist (including Oceanographer in Canada)
Plant Breeder
Poultry Scientist
Soil Scientist
Zoologist

TEACHER:

College
Seminary
University

The provisions for entry of Mexican professionals into the United States under NAFTA differ somewhat from those for Canadians, because US immigration law changed after the US-Canada Free Trade Agreement entered into force. Thus, Mexican admissions are patterned after the H-1B specialty worker visa. As with the H-1B, Mexican NAFTA professionals are now subject to an annual numeric limit. Also, the US employer must file the labour condition application, attesting that the prevailing wage will be paid for the occupation, and the location of intended employment. The employer is also required to petition the Department of Homeland Security (DHS) for permission to bring in the Mexican citizen as a NAFTA professional. All three of these requirements will be lifted on 1 January 2004, the tenth anniversary of entering into force of NAFTA.

Entry of Canadian NAFTA professionals to work in the United States

A Canadian citizen seeking temporary entry to the United States as a NAFTA professional must have pre-arranged employment in the United States in one of the aforementioned professional occupations. At the port of entry, the professional must present Department of Homeland Security officials with:

- Proof of citizenship (a passport or birth certificate and a picture ID, *e.g.* driver's license).

- A written offer of professional employment in the United States, signed by the potential employer. This letter must include detailed information about the entrant's job duties, expected length of stay and salary arrangements. The employer is not obliged, however, to pay the Canadian professional the prevailing wage for the occupation and locality of employment.

- Supporting documentation regarding the entrant's professional status (*i.e.* educational qualifications or appropriate credentials). NAFTA does not negate the need for workers to satisfy applicable state and local licensure requirements.

Entry of Mexican NAFTA professionals to work in the United States

A US employer wishing to hire a Mexican citizen as a NAFTA professional must first file a labour condition application with the US Department of Labor, attesting that he/she will pay the professional at least the prevailing wage for the occupation and locality of intended employment. The employer must also petition DHS for permission to bring in the Mexican citizen as a NAFTA professional, based on the following supplemental documentation:

- Certification from the Department of Labor that the employer has filed an LCA.

- Evidence that the worker's educational qualifications or credentials meet the predetermined minimum requirements.

- The employer's statement of the professional activity in which the applicant will be engaged, and a full description of the job duties.

- Evidence that all applicable licensure requirements in the state or locality of intended employment are satisfied.

- Proof of Mexican citizenship.

The Mexican professional must possess a valid Mexican passport and must obtain a non-immigrant (*i.e.* temporary migrant) visa from the US embassy or consulate. These two documents and a copy of the prospective employer's statement submitted in support of the petition must be presented at the port of entry.

Conclusion

As shown in this chapter, the vast majority of US temporary admissions programmes are open to citizens of all countries. With the sunset of the Q-2 visa for the Irish Peace Process Cultural and Training Program, NAFTA's TN visa, directed specifically to Canadian and Mexican professionals, is the only exception to worldwide programmes. The United States recently negotiated free trade agreements with both Singapore and Chile which contain provisions to facilitate the entry of professionals between these two countries and the United States. However, as of May 2003, neither agreement had been submitted to the US Congress for approval.

Table 6.1. **Permanent immigration, by entry class, fiscal years 1999-2001**

	1999		2000		2001	
	Total	%	Total	%	Total	%
1) Immediate relatives of US citizens	258 584	40.0	347 870	40.9	443 035	41.6
2) Family preferences	216 883	33.5	235 280	27.7	232 143	21.8
3) Employment preferences	56 817	8.8	107 024	12.6	179 195	16.8
4) IRCA legalisation	8	-	421	-	263	-
5) Refugees and asylees	42 852	6.6	65 941	7.8	108 506	10.2
6) Diversity	47 571	7.4	50 945	6.0	42 015	3.9
7) NACARA entrants	11 267	1.7	23 641	2.8	18 926	1.8
8) Others	12 586	1.9	18 685	2.2	40 235	3.8
TOTAL	**646 568**	**100.0**	**849 807**	**100.0**	**1 064 318**	**100.0**

NACARA: 1997 Nicaraguan Adjustment and Central American Relief Act

Note:
Percentages may not add up to 100, due to rounding-up of figures

With the exception of immediate relatives of US citizens, immigrants in a class of admission include principal beneficiaries, *i.e.* those aliens who directly qualify for the class of admission under US immigration laws, and derivative beneficiaries, *i.e.* the spouses and unmarried children of principal immigrants.

Brief descriptions of the entry classes:

1) Numerically unrestricted immigrants comprising spouses, unmarried minor children, and orphans adopted by US citizens, as well as parents of adult US citizens.

2) Numerically restricted family-sponsored immigrants comprise the following four preference classes: i) Unmarried adult sons and daughters of US citizens, ii) Spouses and unmarried sons and daughters of US permanent resident aliens, iii) Married sons and daughters of US citizens, and iv) Brothers and sisters of adult US citizens.

3) The employment-based preferences are described in detail in the text of this chapter.

4) Under the 1986 Immigration Reform and Control Act, certain persons who had been in the United States illegally were granted legal permanent residence.

5) The distinction between refugees and asylees is the location of the alien at the time of application: asylees are already in the United States or at a port of entry, whereas refugees apply while still outside the United States.

6) A programme of 55 000 visas annually began in fiscal year 1995 aimed at increasing the diversity of countries sending immigrants to the United States. (As of 1999, 50 000 visas will be allocated annually – this decrease is a result of the NACARA legislation.) Eligible countries are determined on the basis of previous levels of immigrant admissions from the specific country and region of the world.

7) Under the 1997 Nicaraguan Adjustment and Central American Relief Act, immigrant status was provided to nationals of Nicaragua and Cuba who had been in the United States for at least two years.

8) Includes groups such as persons receiving cancellation of removal (including under NACARA section 203), Soviet and Indochinese parolees, and persons receiving immigrant status under the Haitian Refugee Immigration Fairness Act of 1998 (HRIFA).

Source: US Department of Justice, 1999-2001 Statistical Yearbook(s) of the Immigration and Naturalization Service.

Table 6.2. **Employment-based permanent immigration, by preference, fiscal years 1996-2001**

Employment-based preference	1996	1997	1998	1999	2000	2001
Total, employment 1st preference	**27 501**	**21 810**	**21 408**	**14 898**	**27 706**	**41 801**
Aliens with extraordinary ability	2 060	1 717	1 691	1 250	2 002	3 376
Outstanding professors/researchers	2 633	2 097	1 835	983	2 667	3 903
Multinational executives /managers	6 354	5 325	5 183	3 608	6 783	9 783
Spouses and children of 1st pref.	16 454	12 671	12 699	9 057	16 254	24 739
Total, employment 2nd preference	**18 462**	**17 059**	**14 384**	**8 581**	**20 304**	**42 620**
Members of the professions holding advanced degrees or persons of exceptional ability	8 870	8 393	6 933	3 946	9 815	20 623
Spouses and children of 2nd pref.	9 592	8 666	7 451	4 635	10 489	21 997
Total, employment 3rd preference	**62 756**	**42 596**	**34 317**	**27 966**	**49 736**	**86 058**
Skilled workers	16 001	10 564	8 515	7 285	13 651	19 320
Baccalaureate holders	5 507	3 972	3 927	2 490	8 771	20 115
Spouses and children of the above	28 998	19 216	15 579	13 171	22 723	41 909
Chinese Student Protection Act	401	142	41	19	22	19
Principals	373	132	32	16	13	16
Spouses and children	28	10	9	3	9	3
Other workers (unskilled workers)	6 010	4 036	2 701	2 141	1 951	2 089
Spouse and child of unskilled workers	5 839	4 666	3 554	2 860	2 618	2 606
Total, employment 4th preference	**7 844**	**7 781**	**6 584**	**5 086**	**9 052**	**8 523**
Special immigrants	3 494	3 652	2 695	2 324	4 403	3 858
Spouse and child of 4th preference	4 350	4 129	3 889	2 762	4 649	4 665
Total, employment 5th preference	**936**	**1 361**	**824**	**286**	**226**	**193**
Employment creation, not target area	143	129	83	38	47	34
Spouses and children	301	211	156	73	83	74
Employment creation, targeted area	152	315	176	61	32	33
Spouses and children	340	706	409	114	64	52
Excluding Chinese Student Protection Act:						
Total, employment preference, principals	**51 224**	**40 200**	**33 739**	**24 126**	**50 122**	**83 134**
Percentage of all immigration	5.6	5.0	5.1	3.7	5.9	7.8
Total, employment preference, dependants	**65 874**	**50 265**	**43 737**	**32 672**	**56 880**	**96 042**
Percentage of all immigration	7.2	6.3	6.6	5.1	6.7	9.0
Total, employment preferences	**117 098**	**90 465**	**77 476**	**56 798**	**107 002**	**179 176**
Percentage of all immigration	12.8	11.3	11.7	8.8	12.6	16.8
Including Chinese Student Protection Act:						
Grand total, employment preferences	**117 499**	**90 607**	**77 517**	**56 817**	**107 024**	**179 195**

Note: Percentages may not add to totals due to rounding-up of figures. Also, the number of admissions in a given year may exceed the numerical ceiling on visas issued, as immigrant visas may be used up to six months after issue.

Source: US Department of Justice, Statistical Yearbook(s) of the Immigration and Naturalization Service.

Table 6.3. **Non-immigrants admitted, by class of admission: fiscal years 1994, 1999-2001**

Non-immigrant class	1994	1999	2000	2001
Foreign government officials, spouses and children (A)	105 299	133 005	138 230	131 313
Temporary visitors for business (B-1)	3 164 099	4 592 540	\ 30 511 125	29 419 601
Temporary visitor for pleasure (B-2)	17 154 834	24 104 371		
Transit aliens (C)	330 936	385 768	437 671	456 174
Students (F-1)	386 157	557 688	648 793	688 970
Vocational students (M-1)	7 844	9 458	10 288	9 625
Spouses and children of students (F-2 and M-2)	33 720	36 641	40 872	43 326
Int'l representatives, spouses and children (G)	74 722	91 829	97 555	94 109
Temporary workers				
• Registered nurses (H-1A)	6 106	534	565	627
• Registered nurses in disadvantaged areas (H-1C)	*	*	*	29
• Specialty occupations: professionals (H-1B)	105 899	302 326	355 605	384 191
• Temporary agricultural workers (H-2A)	13 185	32 372	33 292	27 695
• Temporary non-agricultural workers (H-2B)	15 687	35 815	51 462	72 387
• Industrial trainees (H-3)	3 075	3 462	3 208	3 245
• Professional workers: US-Canada FTA (TC)	5 031	*	*	*
• Professional workers: NAFTA (TN)	19 806	68 354	91 279	95 479
• Workers with extraordinary ability (O-1)	5 029	15 946	21 746	25 685
• Workers accompanying O-1 non-immigrants (O-2)	1 455	3 248	3 627	3 834
• Athletes and entertainers (P-1, P-2, P-3)	28 055	48 471	56 377	55 791
• International cultural exchange (Q-1)	1 546	2 466	2 447	2 089
• Irish Peace Process Cultural and Training (Q-2)	*	19	279	299
• Non-profit religious organisation workers (R-1)	5 951	12 687	15 342	17 122
• Intracompany transferees (L-1)	98 189	234 443	294 658	328 480
• Treaty traders and investors and families (E)	141 030	151 353	168 214	178 534
Families of temp. workers (H-4,O-3,P-4,Q-3,R-2)	43 207	109 681	128 993	146 427
Families of CFTA and NAFTA professionals (TB and TD)	6 033	19 087	22 181	21 509
Spouses, children of intracompany transferees (L-2)	56 048	111 891	132 105	144 911
Foreign media representatives and dependants (I)	27 691	31 917	33 918	34 488
Exchange visitors (J-1)	216 610	275 519	304 225	339 848
Spouses and children of exchange visitors (J-2)	42 561	43 841	47 518	49 587
Fiancés(ées) of US citizens (K-1)	8 124	15 940	20 558	23 634
Children of fiancés(ées) (K-2)	764	2 268	3 113	3 487
Parent/child of intl. org. special immig. (N-8, N-9)	*	75	47	69
Legal Immig. Family Equity (LIFE) Act (K3, K4 V1-V3)	*	*	*	7 557
Victims of Trafficking and Violence (T1-T4, U1-U4)	*	*	*	96
NATO officials, spouses and children (N-1-N-7)	9 135	12 992	14 133	13 805
Unknown	878	47	656	58
TOTAL	**22 118 706**	**31 446 054**	**33 690 082**	**32 824 088**

* Not applicable

Note: These numbers include multiple entries by the same person over time. Consequently, they should not be interpreted as the number of individual non-immigrants entering in a particular fiscal year.

Source: US Department of Justice, 1994, 1999-2001 *Statistical Yearbooks of the Immigration and Naturalization Service.*

Table 6.4. **Inflows of Canadian and Mexican non-immigrant professionals to the United States under the NAFTA, 1994-2002 (calendar years)**

	1994	1995	1996	1997	1998	1999	2000	2001	1st half of 2002
Canadian professionals	25 104	25 598	28 237	48 430	60 742	60 755	89 864	70 229	35 933
Their spouses/children	6 707	7 436	7 868	14 687	17 202	15 504	20 799	14 725	6 130
Mexican professionals	16	63	229	436	785	1 242	2 354	1 806	1 035
Their spouses/children	11	13	57	172	313	431	728	555	292

Note: Admission statistics for 1996-1998 have been revised. NAFTA professionals do not have to surrender their INS Form I-94 (Arrival/Departure Record) if they leave the United States for 30 days or less, or if they travel within Mexico, Canada and the United States. Nonetheless, the above numbers may reflect multiple entries by those people who travel outside of these criteria. Consequently, these numbers should not be interpreted as the precise number of individual professionals entering under the NAFTA each year.

Chapter 7

PRINCIPAL LABOUR MIGRATION SCHEMES IN THE UNITED KINGDOM

by
Anaïs Loizillon
Consultant to the OECD

Introduction

Steady economic growth during the 1990s was accompanied by an internal government revision of labour migration policies in the United Kingdom. Taking into consideration the increased importance of labour migration in the latter portion of the 1990s, as well as the globalisation of the labour market, the UK government responded with a comprehensive review of its migration system. The publication by the Home Office in 2002, *Secure Borders, Safe Haven: Integration with Diversity in Modern Britain* outlines a vision for a co-ordinated labour migration system which responds to its labour market needs. The managed approach is underscored by the cultural, economic and social benefits brought by migrant workers to the United Kingdom.

The particular status of the United Kingdom with New and Old Commonwealth countries is unique among the former colonial powers of Western Europe. It can certainly help to explain why, contrary to other OECD countries, migration schemes in the United Kingdom are not managed through bilateral agreements. The old Commonwealth countries, Australia, Canada, New Zealand and South Africa, provided a steady trickle of emigrants to the United Kingdom; yet, the migration balance remained a net emigration to these countries from the United Kingdom. Beginning in the 1950s, the incorporation of the New Commonwealth countries significantly increased inflows. Legislation in the 1970s which required work permits for citizens from the Commonwealth reduced these flows. Immigration from India and Pakistan peaked respectively in the 1960s and the 1970s (Hatton and Price, 1999, p. 6). Retaining these post-colonial links was critical to UK foreign policy and provided Commonwealth citizens with a special status among other migrant populations. This chapter examines the principal labour migration programmes operating in the United Kingdom, chosen for their unique characteristics and targeted migration population. As an aggregate of labour migration, the schemes attract a wide variety of immigrants from low-skilled to highly-skilled migrants for short or medium-term settlement in the United Kingdom. The characteristics of the UK labour market relative to these schemes are addressed in the last section of the chapter.

Description of the principal schemes

Seasonal Agricultural Workers Scheme

The Seasonal Agricultural Workers Scheme (SAWS) dates from the immediate post-war years, when organisations were set up to bring thousands of young people from Europe to help restore land and gather harvests. The programme evolved into the current SAWS when it was consolidated in the 1960s by the Home Office. Considered a youth mobility scheme, it has grown into an essential source of temporary seasonal labour for UK farmers and growers. SAWS permits non-European Economic Area (EEA) nationals enrolled in full-time university studies, aged between 18 and 25, to work in agriculture and horticulture in the United Kingdom.[1] There is no limit to the number of times young people can participate in the programme, as long as they return to their home country for a minimum of three months. The SAWS programme is managed by seven operators who enlist connections with universities abroad, review applications and place students within farms. Two of the seven operators are charities and work with approximately 90% of all SAWS participants. The remainder are independent farms that hire SAWS participants for their own needs. Operators are responsible for issuing work cards that specify the farm to which students have been assigned. Operators also attest to ensuring that farmers provide acceptable subsidised housing and appropriate work conditions for SAWS participants, according to the Code of Practice (Box 7.1).

The Home Office establishes quotas in response to demands from operators who report annually the demand from farms. In 2003, the annual quota was first increased to 20 200 participants and later supplemented by an additional 4 800. Table 7.1 shows the increase in the quota system governing SAWS since 1996. At each interval, the request for increases in SAWS participants has stemmed from operators responding to farmers' needs. According to the Home Office and a major operator, the take-up rate of the quota is approximately 100% each year. SAWS participants can earn a net average of GBP200 per week in a variety of agricultural and horticultural work including but not limited to sowing, planting, harvesting, sorting and packing. Meat production and animal husbandry are prohibited to participants. SAWS participants fall under the legal category of agricultural workers and benefit from the unionised sector. According to the UK Agricultural Wages Board (AWB), the first 12 weeks of employment by an inexperienced worker are paid at the harvest rate (GBP4.30 per hour) which is slightly higher than the national minimum wage (GBP4.20 per hour). After a 12-week period of work, agricultural workers receive the standard wage (GBP4.91 per hour) according to AWB regulations.

Most SAWS participants originated from Central and Eastern European countries (CEECs), because operators have established strong and reliable connections with universities favourable to SAWS. Therefore, they have not resulted from formal bilateral agreements signed between the United Kingdom and sending countries (Table 7.2). For example, Poland requires that all agricultural university students work abroad as part of their diploma requirement for about the same duration as SAWS. Not astonishingly, Polish universities have been regular feeding mechanisms for SAWS for many years. In 2002, the majority of students reporting for work under SAWS came from four countries: Poland (26.42%), Ukraine (20.96%), Bulgaria (11.99%) and Lithuania (11.72%). New

---

1.   The period during which seasonal agricultural workers were allowed to come to the United Kingdom used to be restricted to between May and November, but in 2003 the scheme was extended to a full year.

sending countries have recently appeared in the SAWS programme. Ghana and India registered participants for the first time respectively in 2002 and 2003. Seventy Chinese students also benefited from the programme in 2003. One charity operator reported that new countries are interested in participating in SAWS, due to its strong work experience and reputation in developing countries. Moreover agricultural sectors in the sending countries can benefit from new technologies and methodologies students have learned in the United Kingdom when they return to their home countries, which are run with less modern agricultural production means.

Evidence suggests that SAWS participants are very eager to gain paid work experience in the United Kingdom and that their primary motivation in joining SAWS is "to earn money in an area of work which is relevant to their studies" (Home Office, 2003c). Nonetheless, SAWS stipulates a cultural component to the programme, which ensures that farmers provide students with access to recreational and linguistic activities. The balance between the two components of the programme (work and cultural experience) is a personal choice made by the student. Most often, though, SAWS participants work as many hours as possible to reap the benefits of overtime pay (GBP6.45 for harvest rate or GBP7.37 for standard pay). SAWS was placed under consultation after the publication of the Home Office's analysis of labour migration and asylum policies in the United Kingdom, commonly known as the White Paper. The review process, which ended in August 2002, consulted many interested parties, including 23 employers or employer unions, seven scheme operators, two trade unions, ten foreign universities and several government departments. The purpose of the review was three-fold:

- To examine whether a continuing need for SAWS existed, especially given the imminent EU accession of several sending countries.

- To determine how SAWS and improved recruitment of seasonal workers could meet labour shortages in the agriculture sector.

- To reflect on whether the scheme could be extended to other sectors with shortages in short-term casual (temporary) labour.

The consultation exercise provided a critical forum for the discussion of temporary unskilled labour in the United Kingdom, as until 2003 SAWS was the only existing migration scheme specifically targeting low-skilled workers. There is a high demand for short-term casual labour in the UK labour market and it is especially important in seasonal activities such as agriculture. Growers and farmers face increasing difficulty in recruiting the resident workforce to meet their needs, due to the difficult work conditions of agriculture and competitive employment alternatives in the service sector. Moreover, the farming industry – hurt by the mad cow and foot-and-mouth disease outbreaks – has been shedding regular labour, to cut costs over the past years (Cabinet Office, 2002, p. 38). The lack of workers to pick daffodils in the Cornwall region of the United Kingdom exemplifies the acute labour shortage: in 2002, more than one-third of the GBP3 million crop went unharvested (Johnston, 2003). The availability of on-demand temporary labour has been poor throughout the United Kingdom.

Box 7.1. **Code of practice for the SAWS programme**

The SAWS Code of Practice for operators and participants was initiated by SAWS operators in the late 1990s, due to concern that the programme was unregulated. It outlines the rules and regulations of the programme, including the responsibilities of each contracting party (the operator, the farmer and the student). Operators are responsible for verifying that farmers adhere to work and pay conditions established by the national Agricultural Wages Board and other governing legislation. The code of practice establishes the criteria for student acceptance and the type of work in which they can be engaged.

The Home Office report on the consultation exercise found that the code of practice did not provide sufficient standards to ensure "clarity and consistency" across the scheme (Home Office, 2002, § 5.5.3). Although the Code of Practice is employed by all operators, it is subject to much interpretation and considered more of a guideline than an enforceable document. For example, the amount of information provided to students concerning their rights as migrant agricultural workers and regulations of the scheme varies among operators. Each operator imputes fees to students, which may differ significantly, to cover the organisation's costs for processing the application, providing health insurance and following up on other services for students. These fees are not regulated by the Home Office and are chosen individually by the operators, who are either charitable organisations or private farmers.

As of January 2004, the existing code of practice between the Home Office and the operators will be replaced by a contract which will form the basis of performance monitoring and evaluation of the operators. This contract is expected to implement new target goals for operators and farmers. While the tendering offer notes that operators will have to supply management information to the Home Office, there is no indication of how the contract will be monitored. One charity organisation raised the concern that the intermediary operators, as opposed to those operators hiring for their own needs, will be able to provide an external (perhaps unbiased) review of acceptable practice: that is, external validity of monitoring programmes will be critical to the implementation of the contract. The Home Office is reviewing the option of its direct involvement in monitoring.

Seasonal labour provided through SAWS does not represent a large proportion of the total labour migration channels in the United Kingdom, but is a critical factor in the agriculture sector. In 2000, for example, SAWS participants accounted for slightly more than 5% of total labour immigration admissions (190 830) in the United Kingdom (Home Office, 2001, p. 41). Yet, the vitality of SAWS to the agriculture sector is decisive. Throughout the late 1990s, seasonal labour composed more than 10% of the UK agricultural workforce. Removing managers and farm owners, seasonal workers accounted for more than one-third of the workforce on UK farms during this same period (Table 7.3). Comparing SAWS admissions data with seasonal agricultural labour market data, SAWS participants were estimated to represent 28.5% of all agricultural seasonal workers in 2002. Another factor that compounds political interest in SAWS is that low-wage sectors are magnets for undocumented workers because of the high availability of work. Many such workers are hired by farmers through the intermediary of unscrupulous gangmasters (more than 2 000 estimated to exist in the United Kingdom) who knowingly exploit seasonal agricultural workers. These workers are denied wage protection under the AWB, as well as entitlements to national insurance, sick leave and other regularised social benefits. Controlling, managing and broadening SAWS are critical factors in the fight against illegal seasonal work (Home Office, 2001, p. 44).

During the consultation period, organisations (including employer and employee unions, nongovernmental organisations) raised several issues. Generally, the programme was well received and respondents believed that it should be continued, especially in light of the EU accession of Central and Eastern European countries, which might reduce the participation of some of the larger sending countries. Those respondents representing employers supported an increase in the quota, a year-round scheme and the removal of the upper age limit. The use of operators in administering the scheme was considered a key strength in recruiting and allocating workers to meet demand in farms. The cultural component and the management of operators were favoured because they provide external validity to the scheme.

Certain employers and their unions were concerned that the expansion of the scheme would delay the creation of an alternative, wide-scale programme to permit short-term casual labour to enter the United Kingdom. The National Farmers' Union (NFU), which represents farmers across England and Wales, suggested creating an additional scheme which would allow all workers (*i.e.* not only students) to enter the United Kingdom temporarily to meet seasonal labour shortages. Expanding the programme to align with farmers' current needs could bring "the entire scheme into disrepute", as it is not equipped to handle a much larger population. The actual figure of current labour shortages is difficult to establish due to the lack of data on seasonal workers. In addition, some seasonal labour is composed of undocumented migrants and there is no reliable evidence on what proportion of seasonal workers they represent. The government's Curry Commission (named after its chairman Sir Donald Curry) recommended that annual quotas for SAWS be raised to 50 000 (Cabinet Office, 2002, p. 38). This figure remains unsubstantiated however and is considered in some circles to be too high. The NFU suggested that 50 000 would be an accurate figure of the need for seasonal workers only if all illegal workers were displaced. In fact, the existing quota is not related to an explicit and detailed analysis of labour market needs but is set according to i) the self-declared needs of the employers, ii) the ability of the operators to manage a larger quota, and iii) an informal evaluation of labour market needs by the Home Office after consultation with the social partners.

A report on the review, including policy recommendations and changes in the scheme, was presented in October 2002, with the changes to come into effect in January 2004. Numerous modifications of the criteria were made directly in response to the growing request for short-term labour in the agriculture sector. SAWS will be able to operate year-round, thereby extending the programme by five months. The upper age limit of 25 years for participants was removed, so that mature university students could apply and increase the number of potential workers. Several new areas of agriculture were added to the programme at the request of farmers and their union representatives. The 2003 quota was increased by 4 800 participants from a pre-consultation level of 20 200 to 25 500. Despite positive comments on the current organisational management of SAWS, the Home Office decided to restructure SAWS so that operators now must apply through a tendering exercise to run the scheme.

Working Holidaymakers Scheme

The Working Holidaymaker Scheme (WHM) targets Commonwealth citizens between the ages of 17 and 27 who wish to enter the United Kingdom to take an extended holiday. The Home Office clearly defines the WHM scheme objective as a youth mobility scheme and not a work permit allowance. While the extended holiday for a maximum of two years is the basis of entry into the United Kingdom, WHM scheme participants are allowed to work under certain conditions. Information provided on the scheme states that employment must be incidental to the holiday, that is, working holidaymakers can work in full-time employment (more than 25 hours a week) for 50% or less of the working holiday period or, alternatively, in part-time employment for more than 50% of their stay (Home Office, 2003d, § 2.5). Restrictions in the type of employment include "engaging in business or providing services as a professional sportsman or entertainer or pursuing a career". In other words, employment must be either temporary in nature or in relatively junior positions. Working holidaymakers can engage in the WHM scheme only once in their lifetime.

The WHM scheme is operated through a UK mission overseas (usually consulates) which accepts WHM scheme applications. Among several immigration forms, the application also requires a statement of evidence of funds to cover the return journey, and at least two months of accommodation and living expenses. Dependants or spouses are not allowed to join the holidaymaker unless they can qualify independently for the WHM scheme. In 2000, approximately 38 500 working holidaymakers were granted entry into the United Kingdom, with a 16% decrease compared to 1999 (45 800). In 2000, the majority of working holidaymakers were aged 23 (5 230) and half of that year's admissions were between the ages of 22 and 25. The scheme was placed under review by the Home Office with a consultation exercise which ended in August 2002. Similar to the SAWS programme, the consultation exercise was initiated by the government's White Paper analysis on labour immigration. The stated objectives are numerous and wide-ranging and included: i) to increase the cultural benefits of the scheme, ii) to ensure the scheme is as inclusive as possible, iii) to contribute to sustainable economic growth, and iv) to achieve a balance with other economic routes of entry into the United Kingdom (Home Office, 2003d, § 4.1). Yet, it is unclear to what extent this scheme can be modified to meet the primary concerns that led to the consultation document. The government's main concern is that the majority of applicants are from traditional Commonwealth countries (Australia, Canada, New Zealand and South Africa), so that the WHM scheme is not inclusive of the Commonwealth as a whole (Table 7.4). The existing criteria for the application process, including the income requirement and the work restrictions, appear to preclude applications from less affluent applicants. Given that the newer Commonwealth countries are mostly developing countries with low-income populations and ethnic minorities, the current application process may be considered discriminatory.

The Home Office is also considering how to minimise abuse of the scheme and to remove unnecessary employment restrictions. Most abuses fall into the category of admitted working holidaymakers who overstay their two-year limit, and continue to live and work in the United Kingdom, but it is difficult to estimate the extent of the phenomenon. For those individuals with at least a university degree or equivalent qualification, it appears to be quite easy to shift from the working holidaymaker scheme to a work permit, despite the fact that the scheme mandates that participants leave the United Kingdom at the end of their two-year stay.[2] Anecdotal evidence suggests that an increasing number of working holidaymakers stay legally in the United Kingdom to work in more high-skilled posts in the financial and information technology sectors. While such employment falls within the confines of the scheme, it is clear that the working holidaymakers can be beneficial to the UK labour market, especially in shortage occupations. In particular, this migrant category "can help alleviate recruitment difficulties, contribute to economic growth and reduce the demand for illegal working, *so it might not be in the United Kingdom's economic interests to fully enforce the current employment restrictions* (emphasis added)" (Home Office, 2003d, § 3.2).

---

2. Logistically, working holidaymakers have to leave the United Kingdom to process the work permit application, but this does not appear to be a big constraint as they do not have to return to their origin country. In practice, most people leave the country for a few days, and make their application for a work permit at the border when they come back to the United Kingdom.

The fact that working holidaymakers are not followed up in any way by the government after their entry into the United Kingdom renders any attempt to understand and monitor working holidaymaker labour market activities nearly impossible. For example, WHM scheme employment restrictions (*e.g.* number of hours, type of employment) are practically impossible to control; it is even more difficult to impose sanctions for violating those conditions. Even though working holidaymakers pay national insurance, this information is not collected per type of visa. The migration policy is torn between extending employment opportunities to working holidaymakers and wanting "to retain the requirement that working holidaymakers take a holiday period during their time in the United Kingdom in order to maintain the distinctive cultural aspects of the scheme" (Home Office, 2003b). Furthermore, working holidaymakers are frequently isolated in the labour market, and do not receive appropriate information on employment rights. While application rules clearly state that this employment is incidental to the holiday, the scheme is often categorised as labour migration (in various documents, including the White Paper). In fact, in 2000, WHM scheme admissions were the second largest category of labour inflows (the first was work permits), with more than 20% of total labour migration (Home Office, 2001, p. 41). It is a unique programme within that migration channel, as the WHM scheme has a restricted application base (only Commonwealth countries) but no quotas. Expanding the programme by either opening employment possibilities (or even extending to new countries, see below) has the consequence of opening a migration channel of unlimited proportions, that is, of providing a more explicit connection between the labour market and the WHM scheme.

Future policy developments for the WHM scheme considered in the consultation included an expansion of the programme to countries outside the Commonwealth, with a particular focus on the EU candidate countries. This development might be unnecessary for the ten candidate countries: the UK government has allowed unrestricted access to the labour market for those citizens immediately upon entry into the European Union (May 2004) (Guba and Turner, 2002, p. 5). Nonetheless, an expanded WHM scheme would be expected to apply quotas "to not erode its benefits to Commonwealth users" (Home Office, 2003d, § 7.2). Several organisations submitted public comments to the consultation process.[3] Representatives of employers from sectors facing labour shortages (*e.g.* hospitality, medical professions, information technology) associate the benefit of expanding the present scheme beyond Commonwealth countries with filling gaps in the UK labour market. They hope to see the WHM scheme provide labour market flexibility by expanding the age criterion to 30 years of age, removing restrictions for choice of employment, increasing work hours to fulltime employment for two years and allowing more than one scheme entry. The Trades Union Congress (which represents many employers in the hospitality sector) is particularly concerned with protecting working holidaymakers from unscrupulous employers: it expects a monitoring mechanism to be put in place. The workers union remained concerned that abuses exist in the current system with, for example, foreign employers using the WHM scheme to avoid hiring local staff when working on UK projects.

From the perspective of the working holidaymakers, comments centred on the age restriction which limits the pursuit of professional training in the United Kingdom

---

3.   The following description of commentaries stems from those provided by the Immigration Advisory Service (a legal advocacy group), the Southern Cross Group (a non-profit international advocacy agency), the Trades Union Congress (general employers union), the Recruitment and Employment Confederation (trade association for recruitment and staffing industry) and BECTU (trade union for workers in the audiovisual and live entertainment sectors), all of which consulted their members. Accessed 12 March 2003.

(forbidden under the current scheme) and the entrance of highly skilled workers. In addition, they favoured allowing working holidaymakers to switch into work permit employment at the end of their stay, as long as the current work permit conditions were also met in these cases (*e.g.* labour market testing). In June 2003, the Home Office presented results of the WHM scheme review, enacting several changes effective immediately for current working holidaymakers, and from 25 August 2003 for new applicants. The most significant changes centred on the removal of most employment restrictions. Working holidaymakers now can be employed in any sector, on a full-time basis for the duration of their stay (still a maximum of two years). After one year of employment in the United Kingdom, they are permitted to switch into work permit employment. The scheme also was expanded to include older participants, with the maximum age limit now set at 30 years. The goals of the WHM scheme review, however, as noted earlier, were not completely fulfilled. Expanding the employment opportunities will not ensure an increase in applicants from poorer Commonwealth countries, as income restrictions are still in place. In addition, the scheme continued to exclude non-Commonwealth country applicants. The cultural benefits of the scheme were not addressed in the results of the review. A similar programme was set up with Japan in 2001 in a bilateral agreement (Box 7.2).

Box 7.2. **United Kingdom/Japan exchange programme**

In February 2001, the Home Office launched the only bilateral scheme existing in the UK immigration system (Home Office, 2003b, Chapter 17, Section 10).[4] Based on the Working Holidaymaker Scheme, the United Kingdom/Japan Youth Exchange Scheme allows Japanese nationals aged 18 to 25 to spend up to one year in the United Kingdom on an extended holiday to experience UK "culture, people, society and way of life". On a discretionary basis, applicants up to age 30 might be considered if they are able to demonstrate that "a genuine and compelling impediment" prevented them from applying at an earlier age. Such circumstances include being engaged in full-time studies or caring for a sick relative. The current quota, which is subject to review, has been set at 400 participants. Applicants must submit their file to the United Kingdom embassy in Tokyo. Selected candidates are invited for an interview, where they must show that they have sufficient funds to purchase a return ticket and be able to maintain themselves for at least two months upon arrival. As in the WHM scheme (before recent changes), applicants must prove that they do not intend to settle in the United Kingdom. Scheme participants cannot be accompanied by children or their spouse, unless the latter is accepted by the United Kingdom embassy through an independent application.

This bilateral scheme has few differences compared to the WHM scheme. The United Kingdom-Japan Youth Exchange Scheme instructions state that participants should have the intention of working in the United Kingdom as part of their holiday. The type and number of hours of employment are limited with similar conditions to the pre-review WHM scheme. Japanese scheme participants are allowed to engage in junior professional activities (*i.e.* supply teaching, agency nursing) where specific labour shortages exist.

Work Permit Scheme

The Work Permit Scheme was designed to facilitate the recruitment of foreign nationals (specifically non-EEA) for posts that cannot be filled with the resident labour supply.[5] This scheme is the main labour migration channel for entry into the

---

4.   The scheme also allows UK nationals to live in Japan for up to one year under similar conditions.

5.   The resident labour supply includes EEA countries.

United Kingdom, and targets skilled and highly-skilled workers. Work permits are granted for up to five years[6] and remain specific to the employer. Applicants must have a minimum level of qualification, which has recently been lowered.[7] Reflecting the needs of the UK labour market, the downgrading of required qualifications has enabled all UK university degree holders to apply for a work permit. That is, foreign students can remain in the United Kingdom upon graduation if they have a supporting employer, instead of returning to their home country, as in the past. The Home Office's Work Permits (UK) administers the permit system and has a turnaround of 24 hours for completed applications. The number of work permits issued is not limited by quotas and Table 7.5 shows that admissions have steadily increased since 1994. In 2000, the number of entrants to the United Kingdom with such permits (67 100) accounted for 35.1% of all labour migration entries. This labour migration channel allows the entrance of dependants, although they are not given the right to work in the United Kingdom without a separate work permit application.

The Work Permit Scheme increasingly has become a sector-based labour migration channel. Two industries which have been the focus of significant labour shortages account for nearly half of all work permits issued in 2000: health and medical services (23%) and computer services (20%) (Home Office, 2001, pp. 39-41). Most recently, the Work Permit system has benefited from the creation of a Shortage Occupation List that allows the expedition of permit applications for sectors facing hiring difficulties. Work Permits (UK) consults with representatives from sectors sensitive to current labour shortages through frequent Sector Panels. Representatives from trade unions, employer organisations, major companies, government agencies and other stakeholders, participate in frequent meetings to discuss the status of labour shortages in the specified sector. Sector Panels currently exist for the following sectors: finance; engineering; healthcare; hotel and catering; and teaching.[8] Work Permits (UK) reviews the conclusions from these meetings with relevant government agencies and makes an internal decision whether an adjustment to the shortage occupation list is warranted. As of August 2003, the shortage occupation list consisted of the following occupation areas: engineering sector (railway, structural, transportation); healthcare sector (doctors, nurses); actuaries; licensed aircraft engineers; teachers; and veterinary surgeons.

The critical measuring point of the Work Permit system relies on labour market testing, a mechanism designed to test the availability of the resident labour supply. UK employers apply for work permits on behalf of the overseas applicant and must demonstrate that the recruitment process fulfils a labour market test. The test consists of advertising with the national job centres, showing the post remains unfilled for four weeks and providing evidence that interviewed applicants, if any, were unqualified. The completed application must include this evidence, as well as the skill level of the overseas national. Under the shortage occupation list, however, the labour market test is waived and applications are processed with high priority. Moreover, current permit holders may request an extension of a work permit, or a new work permit for another employer,

---

6. Most applicants obtain a permit for two to three years.

7. The minimum qualification level for a work permit used to be a degree plus two years of professional experience, or five years of professional experience. As of October 2000, it is now set to a degree without professional experience or three years of professional experience.

8. Until recently, the information technology communications and electronics sectors as well as electronic and opto-electronic engineers were also included on this shortage occupation list; they were removed due to an apparent end of hiring difficulties in these sectors.

regardless of the sector and without a labour market test, provided the skills and experience required are similar.

In 2000, the Work Permit system was streamlined to increase the processing efficiency of permits issued by the Home Office. Employers can complete applications on-line with supporting documents sent by fax, reducing the amount of original paperwork engaged in the process. The application turnover standard held by the Home Office is commendable: 90% of complete applications should be decided within one day of receipt (Home Office, 2001, p. 12).

Box 7.3. Special agreements between countries and the Department of Health

In the United Kingdom, 31% of all doctors and 13% of all nurses are foreign-born; in the London area, these figures attain respectively 23% and 47%. Over the last ten years, the immigration of medical personnel has contributed to 50% of the increase in personnel of the National Health Service (NHS) that is, 8 000 out of 16 000 posts created (Glover *et al.*, 2001). There is a wide consensus among the social partners on the great need for healthcare workers in the United Kingdom, and most particularly for nurses (78% of public sector employers declare having recruitment difficulties). The Department of Health intends to recruit at least 35 000 extra nurses before 2008, while it will be necessary to replace 50 000 retirement departures during that period.

All types of healthcare professionals are included in the shortage occupation list (*http://www.workpermits.gov.uk/default.asp?pageid=2594*), which allows for a simplified international recruitment procedure. The Department of Health officially acknowledges the necessity for immigration: "We are expanding the workforce and have increased the number of training places, but international recruitment helps stabilise the nursing workforce and reduces the shortfall in the short to medium-term".

In order to cope with these difficulties, the United Kingdom has concluded agreements with several countries to recruit nurses or doctors. In November 2000, the then Health Secretary, Alan Milburn, agreed with his Spanish counterpart to recruit 5 000 Spanish nurses for the NHS. About 375 of them were recruited in the period 2001-02. Austrian, German and Italian doctors are also targeted to come to work in the United Kingdom, and recruitment agreements have been signed with India and the Philippines for nurses (*http://www.doh.gov.uk/international-recruitment/*).

The recruitment of nurses who are citizens of third countries especially has increased in recent years, passing from 3 621 in 1998-99 to 13 721 in 2001-02. Taking into account the fact that a majority and an increasing volume of health worker migrants come from developing countries, the UK authorities have decided to enact a code of good practice in the matter of international recruitment for the NHS employers (*Guidance on International Recruitment*, DoH, 1999; *Code of Practice for NHS Employers Involved in International Recruitment of Healthcare Professionals*, DoH, 2001). These documents stipulate the conditions in which recruitment should occur, as well as the receipt and employment of healthcare professionals from member countries of the European Union, and third countries. The code defines the linguistic competences required and the role of private recruitment agencies. It also identifies a list of countries (more than 150 in total) in which the Department of Health engages not to organise recruitment drives. The code stipulates that NHS employers must not target developing countries, unless the government of the country concerned officially accords its permission to the Department of Health through a Memorandum of Understanding, to encourage exchanges of medical personnel and expertise between the two countries.

During 2002, the Home Office proposed the development of a new scheme known as the Sector Based Short-Term Work Scheme for low-skilled workers. As proposed, this scheme would enable non-EEA workers between 18 and 30 years of age to enter the United Kingdom for up to 12 months to supplement labour in a sector with significant labour shortages. While the scheme is based on the successful operation of SAWS, it also shares characteristics of the Work Permits Scheme. The number of permits approved would be limited by quotas distributed among the sectors, with proposed subdivisions within sectoral components. The scheme and quota allocations would be monitored by employer and industry representatives in conjunction with the Home Office. Similar to the aforementioned sector panels, internal inter-governmental meetings would discuss proposed changes before their implementation.

As of May 2003, the Home Office introduced the re-named Sector Based Scheme (SBS) for the hospitality and food processing. While there was limited public information during the scheme's development, the Home Office suggested that they developed the scheme in response to requests for additional supply of labour by industry leaders. Yet, sources indicate that the food processing industry is not facing a labour shortage and initially had requested their removal for the future operation of the short-term scheme. Unions are concerned with the independent development of the scheme, which does not appear to respond to specific industry requests. Nonetheless, the expansion of labour migration schemes to incorporate low-skilled migrants is innovative among most OECD member countries. Box 7.3 describes the special agreements between countries and the Department of Health.

United Kingdom policy

The findings of the Home Office's report *Migration: An Economic and Social Analysis* showed the positive impacts of migrant workers in the United Kingdom. However, the report highlighted the heterogeneous origin of migrants, their uneven experiences in the UK labour market and the mixed social and economic benefits provided to the United Kingdom. The report states that: "migrants create new businesses and jobs and fill labour market gaps, improving productivity and reducing inflationary pressures. Continued skill shortages in some areas and sectors suggest that legal migration is, at present, insufficient to meet demand across a range of skill levels" (Glover *et al.*, 2001, p. viii). In concluding remarks, the report highlights the problems with migration policies that remain unco-ordinated with the work of other government authorities. It supposes that "migration is neither a substitute nor an alternative for other labour market policies, notably those on skills, education and training; rather, migration policies should complement other policies and contribute to a well-functioning labour market" (Glover *et al.*, 2001, p. ix).

Labour market driven policy

The White Paper, written in response to the growing demand for a revised migration system, emphasised the need for a UK migration policy driven by the labour market. In particular, the paper responded to a growing need for a coherent migration policy recognising the complexity in labour migration patterns because of globalisation. Since the publication of the White Paper, the UK government has centred its efforts on an economic growth environment. Politically, the United Kingdom was under much pressure to provide a fresh labour supply in industries that faced shortages. Yet, the government was also dealing with an increasing number of asylum seekers entering the United Kingdom illegally in search for economic opportunities and political protection. The complexity of migration patterns in the United Kingdom – recognising both inflows and outflows of UK and non-UK migrants – is often obscured in the face of political realities. An overall increase of inflows during the late 1990s of working-age non-UK citizens was characterised by large proportions of managerial and professional workers. While the UK labour market is characterised by a higher proportion of unemployed foreign-born than UK-born, the more skilled occupation groups contain higher proportions of foreign-born workers (Dobson *et al.*, 2001).

The labour migration schemes presented in this chapter provide a glimpse of the diversity and flexibility of the current UK labour migration system. The underlying argument for increasing the foreign labour force lies in an expanding economy and the inability of the resident labour force adequately to supply the market. The revised labour market driven policy has created a two-pronged approach to enabling a more diverse group of foreign workers to enter the UK labour market. The first concentrates on increasing the diversity of migrant groups, while the second centres on the qualifications of migrants. The diversity of migrant groups is based on their country of origin, their immigration purpose and characteristics specific to their employability in the UK labour market. Work Permits (UK) has facilitated the application process so that previous groups of migrants can remain in the United Kingdom after their initial entry. These exceptions are geared to widen the resident labour supply with foreign workers. For example, foreign students in the United Kingdom are now allowed to seek a work permit immediately upon graduation from a UK educational institution. Previous policies required that foreign students return to their home country to apply for a work permit. In the revised policy, graduate students, student nurses and post-graduate doctors benefit from their status as potential high-skilled workers.

The UK government further demonstrated its interest in an enlarged foreign workforce through its unexpected announcement related to the immigration of foreigners from EU accession country candidates. The United Kingdom had the option to retain border controls for workers from these ten countries for up to seven years, even though they could be admitted to live in the United Kingdom upon accession in May 2004. In December 2002, the Home Secretary, David Blunkett, announced that the United Kingdom would allow these migrants to enter the United Kingdom for work purposes. The government defended the policy as a practical method for controlling migration flows in a system already burdened with irregular flows. Insider government reports stated that the policy towards EU accession countries would benefit the UK labour market by providing a supply of regular migrants at both the top and bottom end of the skill levels (Guha and Turner, 2002).

The second prong of labour market-driven migration seeks to encourage a greater diversity of skill levels among entering labour migrants. National shortages across all skill levels – recognised by employer and employee organisations alike – have facilitated the expansion surrounding the aforementioned schemes. SAWS clearly targets low-skilled agricultural workers who fill the casual, seasonal needs of the UK agriculture sector. The expansion of the scheme reflects its validity among farmers, and the economic benefits provided by migrant SAWS students. Even though the review of the scheme opened the debate on the general need for low-skilled workers, it is primarily the agriculture sector which has suffered from an acute shortage. The new SBS should provide a glimpse of how low-skilled migrant workers take up opportunities of labour shortages in other sectors in the United Kingdom. Recent changes in the WHM scheme support anecdotal evidence that an increasing number of working holidaymakers are employed in skilled and high-skilled occupations in the finance and information technology sectors, for example. The shortage occupation list (as well as the high-skilled migrant programme not discussed here) enables high-skilled migrants to benefit from an accelerated process to enter the United Kingdom for employment.

Flexibility and control

However, from the public perspective, economic labour migration is closely linked to the need for a reduction in irregular migration flows. The two channels are managed independently by the UK government within the Home Office, and the sensitivity of the resident labour market to foreign workers has created political problems in the past. Thus, expansion of worker inflows through the aforementioned two-pronged system requires a controlling mechanism in times of economic difficulties. That is, the labour market driven migration policies outlined above need to be equally responsive to future economic recessions through flexible and rapid responses. Managed migration can occur at any point in the migration process through a variety of internal processes directed by the Home Office. The schemes presented in this chapter can be limited in their scope through explicit or implicit controlling mechanisms. SAWS and SBS can be limited through quotas which are reviewed annually by the Home Office, in response to the needs of the relevant sectors. Since the establishment of the scheme, though, SAWS quotas have been raised (and never lowered), and there is no evidence that the casual seasonal labour supply will increase within the resident labour force. Nonetheless, the increasing and reducing of the quota can provide a constrained response to changes in the labour supply.

At the other end of the spectrum, the work permit system, especially through the accelerated track of the shortage occupation list, has several tightening points integrated into its procedures. The shrinking labour market for information technology workers, and the subsequent removal of this category from the shortage occupation list, demonstrate an increased sensitivity to changing economic conditions. External panels composed of private sector representatives provide reasonable forums for soliciting information in real time. At any point, though, the Home Office can restrict the number of foreign worker entries by delaying or complicating the application process. For example, the 24-hour turnaround for work permit applications can be prolonged on a case-by-case basis, by requiring more information to satisfy the market test. Work Permits (UK) can choose to implement these additional restrictions in a more rapid fashion than quotas would allow. The WHM scheme is a more difficult scheme to manage, as it is currently operated without any quotas. Similar to the Work Permit Scheme, the application process could be controlled internally by requiring additional information to fulfil the entrance criteria. This is unlikely, though, as historical co-operation among Commonwealth countries underscores the political importance of this scheme. Moreover, the recent review process has suggested an expansion to overcome potential discrimination factors in the application process. Limiting the scheme in response to future economic recessions might question the government's intent to improve diversity in migration flows.

Partnerships

A singular characteristic of the UK migration system is the checks and balances system of the Home Office. Through partnerships and consultation with nongovernmental sources, the Home Office actively recruits information from employer and employee representatives, industry organisations, charities and other interested parties, to inform changes in the schemes highlighted in this chapter. The incorporation of the interested parties helps formulate a migration policy that is reactive to changes in the economy or in the labour force. Not only can programmes be adjusted quickly (*i.e.* increase quotas, reduce application delays), but also new schemes, such as the new SBS, can be developed in response to specific needs.

Partnerships among the public and private sectors are interesting, specifically because a consensus appears to be created around labour-related migration issues in the United Kingdom. Of course, implementation and monitoring activities create some discord among these groups. The general opinion, though, is that the schemes operate more or less effectively to match labour market needs. By engaging the private sector and NGOs in revising migration policy, the Home Office has succeeded in providing a base for public support. These schemes are not controversial and criteria changes appear to lead to greater efficiency. Labour migration in the United Kingdom has greatly benefited from the checks and balances notion, as it has successfully avoided being linked to the public debate on the overburdened asylum system.

BIBLIOGRAPHY

Agricultural Wages Board for England and Northern Ireland (2003), "Board Confirms its Proposals for a New Agricultural Wages Order from 1 October 2002", 30 August 2002, available at *www.defra.gov.uk/news/awb/awb302.htm*, accessed 20 March 2003.

Cabinet Office (2002), *Farming and Food: A Sustainable Future*, Policy Commission on the Future of Farming and Food, January.

Crawley, H. (2003), *Managing Migration: Current Entry Routes Into the UK Labour Market*. Institute for Public Policy Research, available at *www.ippr.org.uk/research/files/team19/project22/Athens1.doc*, accessed 25 February 2003.

Department of Health (1999), *Guidance on International Recruitment*.

Department of Health (2001), *Code of Practice for NHS Employers Involved in International Recruitment of Healthcare Professionals*.

Dobson, J. *et al.* (2001), "International Migration and the United Kingdom: Recent Patterns and Trends", Final Report to the Home Office, December 2001.

Ethical Trading Initiative (2003), "Seasonal and Foreign Labour in the British Food Industry", available at *www.eti.org.uk/pub/publications/2002/05-ukagric-sem/index.shtml*, accessed 19 March 2003.

Glover, S. *et al.* (2001), *Migration: An Economic and Social Aanalysis,* Home Office Research Development and Statistics Directorate Occasional Paper No. 67, Home Office, London.

Guha, K. and D. Turner (2002), "Workers from New EU States Let In Early for Practical Reason", *The Financial Times*, 14 December 2002.

Hatton, T.J. and S.W. Price (1999), "Migration, Migrants and Policy in the United Kingdom", Institute for the Study of Labour (IZA) Discussion Paper No. 81, December.

Home Office (2001), *Secure Borders, Safe Haven: Integration with Diversity in Modern Britain: Working in the United Kingdom*, Home Office, London.

Home Office (2002), "Report on the Review of the Seasonal Agricultural Workers' Scheme 2002", October, available at *www.workpermits.gov.uk/file.asp?fileid=611*, accessed 17 January 2003.

Home Office (2003a), *Guidance – Working Holidaymakers (INF 15),* available at *www.ukvisas.gov.uk*, accessed 25 February 2003.

Home Office (2003b), *Immigration Directorates' Instructions,* Chapter 17, Section 10, "Japan: Youth Exchange Scheme", available at *www.ind.homeoffice.gov.uk/default.asp?pageid=1352*, accessed 27 February 2003.

Home Office (2003c), "Review of the Seasonal Agricultural Workers' Scheme 2002", available at *www.workpermits.gov.uk/file.asp?fileid=481*, accessed 18 March 2003.

Home Office (2003d), "Working Holidaymaker Scheme: Consultation Document", available at *www.workpermits.gov.uk/default.asp?pageid=2830*, accessed 17 January 2003.

Johnston, P. (2003), "Extra Foreign Farm Workers", *The Telegraph*, 28 November 2002, *www.telegraph.co.uk/news/main.jhtml?xml=/news/2002/11/28/nbudi28.xml*, accessed 25 February 2003.

National Farmers' Union (NFU) (2002), "NFU Response to Home Office Review of the Seasonal Agricultural Workers' Scheme", August.

Table 7.1. **SAWS quotas**

Year	Annual quota	Annual increase
Up to 1996*	5 500	
1997-2000*	10 000	82%
2001	15 200	52%
2002	18 700	23%
2003	25 000	34%

Note: * Figures are *per annum*

Source: Home Office.

Table 7.2. **Nationalities of SAWS participants, 2002**

Nationality	Number of cards issued	Number reporting for work	Reporting (% total)
Poland	4 867	4 826	26.42
Ukraine	4 003	3 829	20.96
Bulgaria	2 252	2 190	11.99
Lithuania	2 161	2 140	11.72
Russia	1 089	1 046	5.73
Latvia	1 029	1 012	5.54
Slovak Republic	942	931	5.10
Belarus	774	746	4.08
Czech Republic	594	576	3.15
Romania	425	383	2.10
Estonia	362	345	1.89
FYROM	158	107	0.59
Hungary	95	95	0.52
Turkey	40	38	0.21
Ghana	7	2	0.01
Others	574	505	2.76
Total	**18 798**	**18 266**	**100.00**

FYROM: Former Yugoslav Republic of Macedonia.

Source: Home Office.

Table 7.3. **Seasonal agricultural workers on UK farms, 1996-2002**

(thousands)

	1996	1997	1998	1999	2000	2001	2002
Total labour force on UK agricultural holdings	616.3	611.1	608.2	586.0	556.9	549.9	550.5
Other workers (non-managerial, non-owners)	237.9	235.1	233.0	215.7	193.3	184.2	180.6
Seasonal, casual or occasional workers (total)	81.5	80.9	78.4	72.0	64.4	63.2	64.2
Male	55.6	55.4	53.9	51.0	45.9	44.6	46.2
Female	25.8	25.6	24.5	21.0	18.5	18.6	18.0
% of total agricultural labour force	13.22	13.24	12.89	12.29	11.56	11.49	11.66
% of other workers	34.26	34.41	33.65	33.38	33.32	34.31	35.55

Note: Fundamental changes in data collection in 1998 makes comparison with previous years impossible.

Source: Department for Environment, Food and Rural Affairs, 2002.

Table 7.4. **Working holidaymaker admissions to the United Kingdom, 1999-2000**

	1990	1991	1992	1993	1994	1995	1996	1997	1998	1999	2000
All nationalities (non-EEA)	23 200	23 700	24 100	21 600	31 600	36 000	33 000	33 300	40 800	45 800	38 500
Australia	13 400	14 200	15 400	13 700	18 500	17 400	15 000	15 200	17 000	18 800	17 000
Bahamas	0	0	†	†	†	0	†	0	0	†	†
Bangladesh	†	†	†	†	†	10	10	†	†	10	10
Barbados	0	10	†	10	10	10	†	10	†	†	10
Belize	0	0	0	0	0	0	0	0	0	†	0
Bermuda	0	0	0	†	10	†	†	†	†	0	†
Botswana	†	†	0	†	0	†	†	†	†	10	10
Brunei	0	†	0	0	0	0	0	0	†	0	0
Cameroon	0	0	0	0	0	†	0	0	†	†	0
Canada	1 940	1 740	1 740	1 460	1 810	1 880	1 910	2 560	3 510	3 730	3 770
Cyprus	†	†	†	†	10	10	20	†	10	20	†
Dominican Rep.	0	0	0	0	0	†	0	0	†	0	0
Fiji	†	†	†	0	0	†	†	†	†	10	10
Gambia	†	0	†	0	10	40	10	0	0	0	†
Ghana	0	†	†	†	20	40	30	20	40	120	220
Grenada	0	†	†	†	†	†	†	0	†	†	†
Guyana	0	0	†	†	†	10	†	†	†	10	10
Hong Kong, China	10	0	†	†	10	20	10	†	†	†	10
India	†	10	20	10	20	40	40	40	50	50	60
Jamaica	50	30	70	120	150	170	100	70	130	190	100
Kenya	†	†	†	†	10	40	20	10	20	10	10
Lesotho	0	0	†	0	†	0	0	0	0	0	0
Malawi	0	0	†	†	0	†	†	†	10	10	40
Malaysia	30	40	30	20	30	70	40	20	100	120	120
Malta	0	0	†	10	†	10	10	10	30	20	20
Mauritius	†	10	10	10	20	50	10	10	10	20	20
Mozambique	0	0	0	0	0	0	0	0	0	0	†
Namibia	0	0	0	20	20	60	80	60	140	230	180
New Zealand	7 440	7 260	6 500	6 000	8 060	7 650	6 300	6 820	7 650	8 080	6 350
Nigeria	†	†	10	20	30	50	20	10	30	40	40
Pakistan	†	†	†	10	20	60	20	20	20	40	70
Papua New Guinea	0	0	0	0	†	†	†	†	0	†	0
Samoa	†	0	0	0	0	†	0	†	†	†	†
Seychelles	0	0	0	0	†	0	†	0	†	†	†
Sierra Leone	†	†	0	†	†	10	†	0	0	†	0
Singapore	10	20	10	†	10	20	20	20	30	50	30
South Africa	0	†	†	†	2 330	7 610	8 960	7 780	11 300	13 200	9 570
Sri Lanka	†	†	†	†	10	20	10	10	10	20	20
St. Helena	0	0	0	20	30	20	10	10	10	20	20
St. Lucia	0	0	0	0	0	0	0	0	0	0	†
St. Vincent and	0	0	0	0	0	0	0	0	0	0	†
Swaziland	0	†	0	†	†	†	†	†	10	10	†
Tanzania	0	†	0	†	†	10	†	†	†	†	†
Tonga	†	†	0	†	0	†	0	0	†	†	†
Trinidad and Tobago	0	10	10	†	20	60	60	110	220	330	300
Uganda	†	†	0	†	†	†	0	†	0	†	†
Zambia	†	†	10	40	50	80	60	50	20	40	40
Zimbabwe	200	190	170	140	220	270	200	220	260	260	210
Other Commonwealth	10	20	20	0	0	0	0	0	0	0	0
Other nationalities	60	80	50	50	160	190	110	120	150	300	230

† indicates five or fewer admissions *Note*: Provisional data rounded to three significant figures unless number is less than 1 000, in which case it is rounded to the nearest 10. *Source*: Home Office.

Table 7.5. **Non-EEA work permit holders and dependants given leave to enter, 1991-2001**

Number of persons

	All nationalities				Europe			
Year	Total	Employment for 12 months or more	Employment for 12 months or less	Dependants of work permit holders	Total	Employment for 12 months or more	Employment for 12 months or less	Dependants of work permit holders
1991	46 920	11 060	21 740	14 120	8 760	1 630	5 230	1 800
1992	51 140	9 940	26 320	14 890	9 190	1 390	5 860	1 940
1993	48 000	9 350	24 520	14 130	9 730	1 440	6 440	1 850
1994	47 500	10 200	23 000	14 300	6 450	830	4 600	1 030
1995	52 100	11 700	26 100	14 300	7 630	1 000	5 570	1 060
1996	58 200	11 400	29 400	17 400	6 870	970	4 730	1 160
1997	62 975	16 270	27 385	19 320	7 260	1 400	4 550	1 310
1998	68 385	20 160	28 020	20 205	8 330	1 875	4 920	1 535
1999	76 180	25 090	28 445	22 645	9 330	2 195	5 385	1 750
2000	92 045	36 290	30 785	24 970	9 880	2 815	5 190	1 875
2001	108 825	50 280	30 785	27 760	10 040	3 725	4 665	1 650

Note: Year corresponds to year of admission. Work permits total includes only new permits, that is first permissions and standard work permits.

Source: Institute for Public Policy Research.

Chapter 8

LABOUR RECRUITMENT FOR SKILL SHORTAGES IN THE UNITED KINGDOM

by
Nicolas Rollason

Partner, Kingsley Napley Solicitors, London

Introduction

Since 1998, the government of the United Kingdom has been actively reviewing its policies towards labour migration, principally to deal with shortages of skills and labour in the labour market. In 1998, the Department of Trade and Industry (DTI) published its Competitiveness White Paper (formally known as *Our Competitive Future: Building the Knowledge Driven Economy*). One of the conclusions of the report was to examine "whether there is scope to lower barriers to immigration that prevent entrepreneurs and skilled professionals from coming or remaining in the UK". This theme was developed in the pre-budget report of November 1999, which made clear the government's thinking on immigration and skills shortages, as well as innovation and investment. Under the chapter title "Meeting the Productivity Challenge," the government recognised that the United Kingdom needed:

> "to attract the most skilled and most enterprising people from abroad to add to the skills pool of resident workers. This will increase the quality of the UK's human capital and will allow greater economic activity and more employment opportunities for all in the longer term. Skilled foreign workers will help the UK address skill gaps, both where there are transient shortages in particular areas, for example amongst IT workers, or where skills shortages persist. The Government is therefore making it easier for skilled foreign workers in key areas to come and work in the UK, where they have the skills and attitudes to help generate an enterprise economy" (H.M. Treasury, 1999).

A number of significant policy initiatives were announced, including adding relevant categories of information technology (IT) workers to the list of work permit shortage occupations, undertaking a fundamental policy review of work permit arrangements to better reflect the global labour market, and investigating ways to make it easier for foreign entrepreneurs and small investors to come and start businesses in the United Kingdom. These were followed through in the budget in March 2000, which in looking at the problem of skills shortages concluded "access to skilled people from overseas is also part of the answer. Equally important is to enhance the UK's image as an attractive location for talented overseas students and entrepreneurs" (H.M. Treasury, 2000).

This budget also set out the government's thinking on the work permit system. "The UK has always benefited from a market-driven work permits system, so that employers can recruit skilled people from abroad without any artificial limits or quotas on the number of work permits that can be issued. This rationale will remain the same" (H.M. Treasury, 2000). It is precisely this rationale which has driven the recent changes to labour migration in the United Kingdom. The government has introduced a number of significant changes to existing migration schemes, introduced new migration routes and reviewed other long-standing schemes under the generic heading "Managed Migration". These policy changes have been underpinned by an unprecedented level of research into the effects and benefits of labour migration (for example, Glover *et al.*, 2001; Gott and Johnston, 2002; Kempton, 2002). This chapter will review the major changes to labour migration which have resulted from this policy.

Main trends

The main trends in labour migration can be summarised as follows:

- A move towards a more informed policy based on research, statistics and consultation.

- A reduction in obstacles to issuing work permits.

- A shift in the sources of highly skilled migrants from the Old Commonwealth to the New Commonwealth, mirroring the global skills pool.

- A move towards more flexible immigration categories, covering both labour and self-employed migration.

- The extension and creation of temporary guest worker schemes for young people combined with quotas, temporal restrictions and no access to settlement.

The United Kingdom and bilateral agreements

It should be noted at the outset that the United Kingdom has not concluded any significant bilateral agreements on labour migration in the past 40 years. Labour migration has been regulated by the UK Immigration Rules, generic schemes such as the work permit scheme and administrative concessions outside the Immigration Rules (notably on domestic workers). There have also been a small number of schemes agreed on a bilateral informal basis, involving very small numbers. They are tied to cultural exchanges and recruitment initiatives in various sectors, which again appear to be in the form of memoranda of understanding or exchange of letters. The use of quotas has been extremely limited, and only applied in two existing schemes and one newly announced scheme. Contrary to the statements made by the Chancellor of the Exchequer (H.M. Treasury) on the use of quotas, the increase of existing quotas and the new quota-based scheme (see below) indicate that the United Kingdom is shifting towards assessing labour market demands and setting annual quotas at the lower end of the labour market. It should also be noted that the only significant bilateral agreements signed by the United Kingdom in the field of migration are the UK Treaties on Illegal Migration with Bulgaria and Romania.

The Work Permit Scheme

In March 2000, the Department for Education and Employment (DfEE) announced the results of its review of the work permit arrangements and confirmed that these would continue to be labour market driven (DfEE, 2000). A specific commitment was given to identify shortages in information technology communications and electronics (ITCE), with skills shortages being established more quickly and effectively through a rolling programme of sector analysis and consultation. The most significant change was to the skills criteria which determine who may qualify for a work permit. Previously, these had required a prospective employee to have a university degree plus two years experience, or for those without degrees at least five years senior experience (usually at board level). As of 1 October 2000, the skills criteria of the scheme were changed so that the prospective employee would only now need to meet the following criteria:

- A UK equivalent degree level qualification; or

- A Higher National Diploma (HND) level qualification relevant to the post on offer; or

- A HND level qualification which is not relevant to the post on offer, plus one year's relevant work experience.

or the following skills:

- Three years experience of using specialist skills acquired through doing the type of job for which the permit is sought for at least three years. This type of job should be at national vocational qualification (NVQ) level 3 or above and would include head or second chefs, specialist chefs with skills in preparing ethnic cuisine, and those with occupational skills and language or cultural skills not readily available in the European Economic Area (EEA).

The change in the criteria marks a significant departure from the previous scheme, now enabling overseas graduates to apply for work permits upon graduation (subject to the usual resident labour testing through advertising). This change was driven partially to achieve the government's aims of attracting the best students to the United Kingdom, who might wish to remain to work after graduation. The previous requirement for graduate students, which required that they show an intention to leave the United Kingdom when coming for studies, was removed from the Immigration rules in April 2003. The training aspect of the Training and Work Experience Scheme (TWES) was incorporated into the main part of that scheme, enabling those completing their professional training to remain as work permit holders beyond their period of training. This had previously not been possible, as those completing training were excluded from obtaining a work permit for two years. The work experience and training aspect of the scheme has been retained for supernumerary posts, prohibiting those who have completed their work experience/training (typically 12 to 24 months) from remaining in the United Kingdom as work permit holders, until they have been abroad for 12 or 24 months (depending on the length of their work experience).

Importantly, labour market testing through advertising is now no longer needed in two cases: i) when the employer applies for an extension of an overseas national's approved employment where the job remains the same, or ii) when the individual changes employment in the United Kingdom, provided the job requires similar skills and experience. Supplementary employment with another employer in the United Kingdom is also allowed without the need for a work permit, provided the work is in the same field as the work permit employment. Work permits can now be issued for five years (increased from four years). It appears that the opening up of the Work Permit Scheme fuelled the existing upwards trend in the number of work permit applications since 1995. In 1999, 58 245 work permits were granted (an 11.7% increase from 1998). In 2000, the number of work permit applications approved increased dramatically to 85 638. After rising again in 2000 to over 100 000 for the first time, the provisional figures for 2002 stand at around 155 000 permits approved, 108 000 of which were first permissions (Work Permits, UK).[1]

Acute shortage of skills: the use of the Shortage Occupation List

The Shortage Occupation List was introduced in 1991, when a two-tier work permit system was created. Tier 1 covers intra-company transfers, board level posts, posts connected to inward investment and shortage occupation posts, and allows employers to dispense with labour market testing, while Tier 2 covers all other posts. The shortage occupation list includes occupations recognised to be in acute short supply, for which labour market testing is not required when applying for work permits. The criticism of the list was that it did not reflect the rapid changes in the labour market and the demands of employers for new skills, particularly in technology-driven sectors. The current government's commitment to improving sectoral labour market analysis resulted in the establishment of a number of sector-based panels to review shortages on an ongoing basis. Sector panels are now held regularly with representatives from industry bodies, key employers and other government departments, to assess industry issues such as training, recruitment, skills and pay. There are currently six sector panels covering ITCE, health, engineering, hotel and catering, teaching and finance. As will be demonstrated below, the use of the shortage occupation list in the IT and health sectors has had significant impacts not only on the numbers of permits issued, but also on the distribution of the geographical origin of work permit holders.

The information technology sector

In March 2000, following the recommendation of the ITCE Skills Strategy Group, the shortage occupation list was dramatically altered to reflect ITCE skills shortages. For the first time, specified ITCE occupations, agreed between the DfEE and sector organisations, as well as specific skills seen as being in short supply, were set out in the list. These included IT managers, analyst programmers, business analysts, database specialists, network specialists and software engineers. Employers wishing to hire foreign workers within those categories needed to demonstrate that the post on offer met the description of these shortage posts and that the employee met the basic skills criteria of the scheme.

While information technology work permits increased significantly in the period 2000 to 2002, the labour market situation with regard to skills shortages was also changing, following a significant downturn in the sector. The ITCE Sector Panel's main source of information, the e-skills quarterly report on labour market trends within the sector, indicated in August 2002 that a resident pool of skills was available for UK employers. Coupled with an increase in the number of reported fraudulent IT permit applications and "body shopping" practices by UK employers, all shortage occupations in the IT sector were removed from the list as from 2 September 2002. Work Permits (UK) also

---

1.   For a full analysis of work permit approvals up to 2000, see Dobson *et al.* (2001).

undertook a major review of all IT work permits and requested additional information from existing and new work permit applicant companies. This now means that all IT posts must be advertised, unless an employer can demonstrate that the skills (or combination of skills) cannot be located in the EEA labour market. The impact of the changes to the shortage occupation list in the end of 2002 can be seen in the increase in the refusal rate of work permits for Indian nationals to 15% in the last quarter of 2002, as against an overall refusal rate of 7% in 2001. Most recently, complaints by British unions and concerns about large companies abusing the work permit system and undercutting local pay rates have led the National Audit Office to carry out a review of Work Permits (UK) operations (*The Times*, 12 May 2003).

The recognition of shortages in the IT sector had led not only to a significant increase in the issue of permits in this sector, but to a substantial change in the distribution of work permits between countries of origin. Historically, the majority of work permits had been issued to US and Japanese nationals. For the first time, in 2001 the number of permits granted to Indian nationals (29 171) significantly exceeded those issued to US nationals (23 306). In 2002, 20.5% of all work permits were issued to Indian nationals, the majority of which were in IT related occupations. It is clear that the United Kingdom was able to react to a significant shortage in IT skills through expanding the shortage occupation list and effectively targeting specific nationalities with relevant skills. The creation of the sector panels and the removal of all IT posts from the shortage occupation list in September 2002 also demonstrate the ability of the new system to respond to changes in the labour market, as well as sensitivity towards allegations of abuse felt by the Home Office.

Health

Work permits issued in the health and medical services sectors accounted for 22.5% of all work permits issued in 2000, with nurses accounting for 18.4% of all work permits granted. The increases in the number of health permits has been driven not only by the inclusion of all nursing posts in the shortage occupation list, but also as a result of a number of specific initiatives aimed at facilitating the recruitment of overseas nurses and doctors. One of the most significant areas of international recruitment by the United Kingdom has been in the area of nursing, where shortages have remained acute. Shortages continue despite a 92% increase in applications for nursing and midwifery courses for the 1999 academic year compared to 1998, and despite government schemes to increase staff retention and pay within the National Health Service (NHS) nursing, and to speed up the registration of overseas nurses. All nursing posts are currently listed on the Work Permits (UK) shortage occupation list.

The Department of Health issued a *Guidance on International Nursing Recruitment* in November 1999. The guidance stated clearly that recruitment practices should not target developing countries and that "international recruitment should never be carried out against the interests of those countries and we are clear about how NHS organisations should decide from where they should and should not be recruiting". The guidance followed a major review of nursing strategy published in July 1999, which aimed to deal with shortages (Department of Health, 1999b). At that time, ten nursing specialties were acknowledged as being in short supply. In terms of overseas recruitment, NHS trusts (include NHS hospitals, regional/national speciality centres, university-based centres) will usually contract private recruitment agencies for assistance and selection of appropriate nursing or midwifery staff from abroad. All agencies must abide by the NHS Code of Practice (Department of Health, 2001) and the Department for Health publishes a list of agencies recognised as operating in line with the code of practice. The code of practice recommends, *inter alia*, that developing countries should not be targeted for the recruitment of care professionals. The Department of Health together with the Department of International Development produced a definitive list of relevant countries from which they should not recruit, based on the list by the OECD/Development Assistance Committee List of Aid Recipients. The code prohibits the NHS from advertising in these countries unless there is intergovernmental co-operation in this area to allow recruitment, usually by way of memorandum of understanding. The code does not exclude recruitment of nurses when they make personal applications for posts in the United Kingdom.

The Department of Health has established a number of nursing recruitment initiatives with the Spanish Ministry of Health, which aim to provide Spanish nurses with the opportunity to go to the United Kingdom for work purposes. Agreements have also been signed with the Philippines and India, and provide for individual nurses to apply to come to work in the United Kingdom. It is understood that these agreements are informal arrangements and not bilateral treaties. Between April 2002 and March 2003, 43% of all new UK professional registrations for overseas nurses were from the Philippines (5 594), with the number of nurses registered from India almost doubling to 1 833. The next most significant provider of nurses was South Africa (1 480), despite the exclusion of recruitment from South Africa through the code of conduct. In addition, Nigeria and Zimbabwe, also on the excluded list, provided 524 and 493 registrations respectively. Total recruitment from Africa increased by 41% during this period (Nursing and Midwifery Council, 12 May 2003). There have naturally been ongoing concerns about the poaching of nurses from countries, and it is clear that the code of conduct and the recruitment agreements have had little impact in reducing the migration of nurses from developing countries (Laurance, 2003; Nursing and Midwifery Council, 2003).

Perhaps the most significant impact of shortages in nursing has been on the geographical distribution of work permits. The Philippines was the third largest source of work permit holders in 2000, with the number of permits issued to Philippine nationals tripling as against the previous year. Of 6 772 permits issued to Philippine nationals, 6 214 were for nurses. The numbers of permits granted to nationals has continued to increase, with 10 432 permits approved in 2001 and 11 318 permits issued in 2002 (Work Permits, UK). At the same time, there has been a dramatic increase in the numbers of work permits granted to South Africans from 4 437 (approximately 40% of which were for health associate professionals) in 2000, to 11 956 in 2001 and 11 357 in 2002 (Work Permits, UK). Recruitment of doctors has also been driven by severe shortages. The shortage occupation list published in October 2002 contains no less than 52 specialities for consultant posts, together with all salaried general practitioners and 11 other posts, including social workers, physiotherapists, speech therapists, pharmacists and occupational therapists.

A number of Department of Health initiatives have taken place, including the Global Scheme which aims to attract doctors at consultant level into the NHS. The global campaign was launched on 31 August 2001 with significant advertising in the medical press in North America, Europe and Australia, and through seminars arranged in specific countries. The Department of Health contracted TMP Worldwide, a private recruitment agency, to deal with responses to the campaign. Under the scheme, the department compiles a database of doctors on the specialist register, which is then matched to vacancies registered by NHS Trusts. The department funds support arranging informal visits to NHS trusts as well as interviews, police checks and applications for work permits. In addition the NHS operates a Managed Placement Scheme where doctors are invited to live and work in the United Kingdom for a trial period of six months as consultants.

In February 2002, the NHS International Fellowship Scheme was launched, to attract experienced surgeons and physicians from outside the United Kingdom for two-year fellowships, working in the NHS as consultants. The international fellowship scheme is very much a showcase project, which aims to enhance the reputation of the NHS as an employer abroad. The scheme aims to attract 450 fellows to NHS consultant posts over a three-year programme, mainly in clinical practice. It appears that a significant number of NHS trusts operate outside these schemes and contract commercial agencies regulated by the code of practice for NHS employers (outlined above). The Department of Health has indicated that it expects recruitment to focus on North America, the Middle East (aimed at recruiting expatriates), Australia and New Zealand. Considerations similar to the prohibition of nursing recruitment apply as well. The Department of Health also established a number of schemes in European countries, including Austria, Germany, Italy and Spain. These schemes generally involve recruitment fairs and seminars to advertise NHS posts and the benefits of working in the United Kingdom. Unfortunately, no accurate breakdown of the issue of work permits in specific occupations is available for 2001 and 2002.

Highly Skilled Migrant Programme

The Highly Skilled Migrant Programme (HSMP) was introduced in January 2001 as a Home Office pilot programme. The scheme is established on a point-scoring basis, with applicants needing to score 75 points in scoring areas covering educational qualifications, work experience, past earnings and achievements in their chosen field. Qualified medical general practitioners receive priority under the scheme. In its first year, there were approximately 2 500 applications, of which 53% were granted. Of the 47% refused, 30% were approved following reconsideration (Work Permits, UK). The scheme (sometimes disparagingly referred to as the Highly Paid Bankers Scheme following applications by redundant investment bankers in 2002) was criticised in its original form because it did not genuinely attract the skills the UK labour market needed. The scheme was revised in January 2003 and the allocation of points significantly amended, in particular, by increasing the points available for those with work experience, and revising the earnings thresholds applicable to individuals residing in the lowest income countries. The emphasis of the scheme is therefore now on work experience, and has reduced points available for those with exceptional and significant achievement in their field of work. Work Permits (UK) anticipate receiving 12 000 applications over the next year in the light of the change of criteria, which will open up the scheme to more applicants with significant work experience. The earnings threshold still requires applicants to be very high earners relative to average wages in the applicable home or residence country, in order to score points in the past earnings category. The intention of this change was to make the category more accessible for those earning their income in poorer countries.

In addition to meeting the 75 points requirement, applicants must also demonstrate that they are able to continue their work in their chosen field in the United Kingdom, and can support themselves and their families whilst in the United Kingdom. Applicants must also provide a written undertaking that they intend to make the United Kingdom their main home. The scheme provides a flexible route for individuals (rather than employers) to apply to come to the United Kingdom for work purposes, and enables participants to take employment, or self-employed work. It rewards those with significant past earnings and experience, and while not testing the labour market, requires the applicant to demonstrate reasonable prospects of securing work or establishing a business in the United Kingdom. The scheme also enables individuals to break out of the traditional distinct employment and business immigration categories, by allowing them to do both and work for a number of employers at any one time. Whilst not strictly relevant to labour migration, the HSMP has to some extent replaced the United Kingdom's cumbersome investment-linked business category.

Seasonal Agricultural Worker Scheme

The Seasonal Agricultural Worker Scheme (SAWS) originates from post-war arrangements to facilitate young people from across Europe to work in the United Kingdom during the main harvest periods. The scheme provides an additional source of labour to farmers from 1 May to 30 November each year, with a small number of additional periods to meet agricultural demands. There is a cultural element allowing participants to learn about UK culture and the English language, and to enjoy some recreational activities. Most participants are full-time agricultural students aged from 18 to 25, who often attend agricultural colleges in their home countries, mainly in Eastern Europe. Participants may only join the scheme once, but there is some flexibility which allows reliable workers who have worked in the past to return where they do not meet the criteria. Participants who are over 25 should only normally be allowed to return in supervisory roles, in a limited number of places. The scheme has approved operators (currently seven) the majority of which are farms recruiting labour for their own purposes. A Code of Practice covers aspects such as recruitment, accommodation, minimum pay and co-operation with the Home Office. The annual quota was 5 500 up to 1996 and, at the request of the operators and sector bodies, in 2001 increased substantially to 15 202. In 2001, the total number of SAWS participants reporting for work in the United Kingdom was 14 870. The larger participating countries were Poland (4 440), Lithuania (1 708), Bulgaria (1 779) and Ukraine (2 980).[2] The quota was raised to 20 200 in 2003 following demand from farmers for various additional kinds of seasonal labour. SAWS is a generic scheme which does not operate on a bilateral or reciprocal basis.

In May 2002 Work Permits (UK) published a review of the SAWS in order to make recommendations for improving the operation of the scheme and, in particular, with a view to extending the scheme to people aged over 25 and to encourage participants to return abroad after their stay in the United Kingdom. The consultation confirmed that it was estimated that between 4% and 10% of SAWS participants overstayed their visa. This did not take into account the significant number of participants coming from acceding countries who have rights to establish themselves in the United Kingdom under the provisions of the European Community Association Agreements. The review of SAWS 2002 was published in October 2002 and recommended that the scheme be retained and amended to extend the period of operation beyond May to November, to meet seasonal demands from the agricultural sector throughout the year. It also suggested retaining the annual quota of places to be determined by annual bids submitted by operators and statistics on shortages. The quota has again been increased to 25 000 despite requests from the Food and Farming Policy Commission to increase it to 50 000.

2.   *Source*: Ministry of the Interior, Immigration and Nationality Directorate (IND).

It was also recommended that the upper age limit be removed and that participants could take part in the scheme more than once, provided they did not breach immigration rules. It was also agreed to review the scheme, following the accession of new members to the European Union (EU) in May 2004. On 10 December 2002, the Foreign and Commonwealth Office announced that it would lift all immigration control on free movement for new EU citizens from acceding countries as of May 2004. As new EU citizens will no longer fall within the quota from that period, more than 50% of the current take-up would effectively be shifted further east to other countries, including Bulgaria and Romania, Russia, Ukraine and Belarus. It is anticipated that seasonal labour migration from acceding countries will continue, although at reduced levels.

Working Holidaymakers Scheme

The Working Holidaymakers Scheme (WHM) is a youth mobility scheme to enable young unmarried Commonwealth citizens aged 17 to 27 to visit the United Kingdom for a two-year period and to take up work incidental to their holiday. While other Commonwealth countries have similar schemes, it is non-reciprocal. The restrictions on the type of work to be carried out, are that participants in the scheme can only work 50% or less of the working holiday on a full-time basis, or part-time over the entire two-year period, as long as they take a holiday at some stage. Participants may not engage in business or pursue a career in the United Kingdom, or provide services as a professional sportsman or entertainer. Certain caveats to these rules are permitted to enable participants to teach (mainly primary school teachers), or take up posts as agency nurses as well as working on a temporary basis in a profession allied to medicine (including *locum* veterinarians). Working holidaymakers are not permitted to work in managerial positions as doctors or as general practitioners in medicine.

Approximately 96% of participants in 2000 were from Australia, Canada, New Zealand and South Africa. The discrepancy between admissions from poor and rich Commonwealth countries was recognised in the 2002 White Paper (for example, 17 000 applicants from Australia compared to 224 from Ghana and 25 from Sri Lanka, where the population sizes are very similar). A consultation document was issued in June 2002 to seek proposals to make the scheme more inclusive. The proposed changes included extending the scheme to include non-Commonwealth countries [mainly Central and Easter European Countries (CEECs)], reviewing the current age restrictions, relaxing the requirement that employment must be incidental to a holiday and allowing working holidaymakers to switch into work permit employment. In 2000, 38 500 people came to the United Kingdom as working holidaymakers, compared to 46 000 in 1999. Despite the significant number of working holidaymakers entering the labour market, there is no accurate information on the type of work they undertake and the periods for which they are employed in the relevant two-year period. The restrictions on employment are not enforced effectively and, because of the complex nature of the restrictions, cannot effectively be policed. The Home Office's view appears to be that there is evidence that working holidaymakers can help to alleviate recruitment difficulties, contribute to economic growth and reduce the demand for illegal work. It may be in the economic interests of the United Kingdom to fully enforce the current employment restrictions (Home Office, Immigration and Nationality Directorate, 2002).

Significantly, the main areas under review have been extending the scheme beyond the Commonwealth, and introducing a similar scheme for citizens from EU candidate countries. This proposal will most likely be abandoned in light of the United Kingdom's decision to lift restrictions on employment from the date of accession of these countries (1 May 2004). In addition, the Home Office is considering extending the maximum age to 30 years and increasing the period of time permitted for full-time work. This would open the scheme to all types of employment and allow some professional work (subject to restrictions on specific professions). What is clear from the review is that the Home Office is considering using the WHM scheme to address recruitment difficulties and skills shortages in the UK labour market. The emphasis is shifting away from the cultural exchange origins of the programme to one which is more focused on filling vacancies in the United Kingdom. The proposal contains suggestions that working holidaymakers should be provided with details of vacancies, regional shortages and recruitment difficulties, with the assistance of UK employers. Finally, the Home Office is also considering whether to formally allow working holidaymakers to switch into work permit employment whilst in the United Kingdom. The practice is at present not permitted under the Immigration Rules, although it is usually permitted on a discretionary basis.

Sectors Based Scheme

Work Permits (UK) introduced a new low-skilled work permit scheme on 30 May 2003. The Sectors Based Scheme (SBS) was established to deal with shortages in the food manufacturing and hospitality sectors, and to address problems with recruitment in fish, meat and mushroom processing, hotels and catering. An initial quota of 10 000 work permits per sector was introduced as of 30 May 2003. The scheme falls within the normal work permit scheme with reduced skills criteria for both the prospective employee and the level of the job. Employers will need to demonstrate that they have made efforts to recruit resident workers. Overseas nationals may only be issued work permits under the SBS if they are aged between 18 and 30 and want to take up those posts specified by Work Permits (UK). These types of jobs have been identified as hard to fill by resident labour and the categories have been agreed by Work Permits (UK), various sector representatives, Jobcentre Plus, the TUC and the CBI. All jobs must be advertised through the UK Jobcentre Plus Network as well as through the European Job Mobility Portal (EURES). There appears to be some flexibility in expanding the scheme when the quotas have been filled.

The scheme is clearly defined as a temporary migration programme. Permits will be issued for 12 months at a time and any applicants wishing to obtain a new work permit must leave the country for at least two months. The category does not lead to settlement in the United Kingdom, as it is clearly defined as a temporary work scheme. An employee may change jobs within the period of the work permit as long as the type of job is similar. The SBS marks a significant departure for the Work Permit Scheme, which has since 1972 prohibited the issue of permits for manual and low-skilled work.

Japan Exchange Scheme

On 2 February 2001, the Japan Youth Exchange Scheme was launched to enable Japanese nationals aged 18 to 25 (with a discretionary upper age limit of 30 years) to enter the United Kingdom for one year for a holiday, of which employment is only an incidental part. The scheme is similar to the WHM scheme, but is reciprocal and described as a bilateral arrangement. A Japanese national can take temporary work incidental to a holiday to supplement travel funds. A quota of 400 participants in each direction has been agreed. The scheme is operated outside standard immigration rules.

Conclusion

Under the heading of managed migration, the UK government has followed through its commitments on looking at ways of driving growth and productivity, while addressing shortages across the labour market. In 1999, the overall figure of those coming in under various routes of entry was 183 504 (Dobson *et al.,* 2001). In light of the increase in work permits granted, the introduction of the HSMP and the SBS and the increase in the SAWS quota, the figures for 2003 are likely to be in excess of 300 000.[3] The increased routes of entry for the highly-skilled and low-skilled, as well as the increased use of quotas, mark a significant change from previous practice.

The operation of the work permits scheme and the shortage occupation list in the IT and health sectors have effectively targeted recruitment at countries with the required skills pool. In the case of the IT sector, the increase in permits issued to Indian nationals appears to have been driven not by specific government-led recruitment initiatives, but by the operation of the global labour market. It remains to be seen whether this will be sustained in the future. With longer-term shortages in health, the shortage occupation list, together with specific initiatives aimed at recruiting nurses, in particular, have also led to significant increases in permits being granted to the Philippines. Despite the recruitment ban in developing countries, it is clear that migrants are self-selecting and nurses continue to apply personally for posts in the NHS, particularly from South Africa, Nigeria and Zimbabwe. The impact on the overburdened health systems in those countries can only be surmised.

At the other end of the labour market, new or expanded schemes to attract lower-skilled migrants to fill specific sector-based shortages will address ongoing problems, although there is evidence that it will not meet the government's aim of deterring irregular migration by providing legitimate entry routes (Lawrence, 2003). On 10 December 2002, the Foreign Secretary announced that the United Kingdom would grant full free movement rights to nationals of candidate EU countries upon accession. The announcement stated:

> "This decision is in the United Kingdom's interest. It will attract workers we need in key sectors and is part of our managed migration agenda. It will ensure they can work here without restrictions and not be a burden on the public purse. It makes sense financially, as we can focus resources on the real immigration problems, rather than trying to stop EU citizens enjoying normal EU rights. [...] We will provide safeguards. These will allow us to reintroduce restrictions in the event of an unexpected threat to a region or sector in the labour markets" (Foreign and Commonwealth Office, 2002).

The decision not to apply the transitional periods on free movement was clearly taken as part of the government's overall aims in managed migration. It remains to be seen what impact accession will have on the UK labour market.

---

3.   This projection is made on the basis that figures for working holidaymakers, domestic workers, au pairs and persons of UK ancestry will remain stable, that work permit grants for 2003 will fall by around 10% based on current refusal rates and that all quotas in the SAWS and SBS are filled.

BIBLIOGRAPHY

Department of Education and Employment (DfEE) (2000), *Outcomes of the Review of Work Permit Arrangements,* DfEE, London.

Department of Health (DH) (1999a), *Guidance on International Nursing Recruitment*, London.

DH (1999b), *Making a Difference: Strengthening the Nursing, Midwifery and Health Visiting Contribution to Health and Healthcare*, London.

DH (2001), *Code of Practice for NHS Employers Involved in the International Recruitment of Healthcare Professionals*, London.

Department of Trade and Industry (DTI) (1998), *Our Competitive Future: Building the Knowledge Driven Economy*, London.

Dobson, J., K. Koser, G. McLaughlan and J. Salt (2001), *International Migration in the United Kingdom*, Research, Development and Statistics (RDS) Occasional Paper, No. 75, Home Office, London.

Foreign and Commonwealth Office (FCO) (2002), "Jack Straw Announces the Extension of Free Movement of People Rights to EU Candidate Countries on Accession", FCO Press Release, 10 December 2002, available at *www.ind.homeoffice.gov.uk/filestore/FCO_press_release.pdf*.

H.M. Treasury (1999), *Stability and Steady Growth for Britain Pre-Budget Report*, The Stationery Office Limited, London.

H.M. Treasury (2000), *Budget 2000, Prudent for a Purpose: Working for a Stronger and Fairer Britain*, The Stationery Office Limited, London.

Home Office, Immigration and Nationality Directorate (2002), *Working Holidaymaker Scheme: Consultation Document*, Home Office, London.

Glover, S., C. Gott, A. Loizillon, J. Portes, R. Price, S. Spencer, V. Srinivasan and C. Willis (2001), *Migration: An Economic and Social Analysis*, RDS Occasional Paper, No. 67, Home Office, London.

Gott, C. and K. Johnston (2002), *The Migrant Population in the UK: Fiscal Effects*, RDS Occasional Paper, No. 77, Home Office, London.

Kempton, J. (ed.) (2002), *Migrants in the UK: Their Characteristics and Labour Market Outcomes and Impacts,* RDS Occasional Paper, No. 82, Home Office, London.

Laurance, J. (2003), "Nurses from Abroad Still Lured to UK Despite Ban", *The Independent,* 12 May 2003, London.

Lawrence, F. (2003), "The New Landless Labourers", *The Guardian*, 17 May 2003, London.

Nursing and Midwifery Council (NMC) (2003), "Overseas Poaching Still a Problem," available at *www.nmc-uk.org/nmc/main/news/overseasPoachingStillAProblem.html*.

The Times (2003), "Work Permit Inquiry", 12 May 2003, *The Times,* London.

Chapter 9

LABOUR MARKET MEASURES RELATED TO FOREIGN EMPLOYMENT IN IRELAND

by

Jerry J. Sexton

Economic and Social Research Institute, Dublin

Introduction

Apart from a longstanding arrangement with the United Kingdom, Ireland has substantive bilateral labour agreements with other countries.[1] In a multilateral context however, in accordance with the European Union (EU) treaty arrangements, nationals of the European Economic Area (EEA)[2] and of Switzerland are entitled to take up employment in Ireland without any requirement for work permits or working visas. Apart from those persons given official recognition as refugees, non–EEA citizens generally can obtain a legal means of employment in Ireland only through the state work permit or working visa systems.[3] The work permit programme is by far the most important. Over 40 000 new permits and renewals were issued in 2002; currently some 3 500 working visas (which are restricted to specified skilled occupations) are issued annually. Most of the content of this report is concerned with reviewing the larger work permit programme.

Arrangements with the United Kingdom

Before the details and the significance of this scheme are discussed, it is appropriate to comment briefly on the bilateral arrangements with the United Kingdom. Effectively, the combined area of Ireland and the United Kingdom forms a single labour market, with virtually complete freedom of movement between the two countries for the purpose of either work or residence. Apart from certain restrictions introduced during World War II, this has been the case since the foundation of the Irish state in 1922. Given these circumstances, it is hardly surprising that UK citizens constitute a significant proportion

---

1. Some bilateral schemes are associated with educational programmes or otherwise restricted to young people. Most significant of these is the bilateral Working Holiday Visa agreement with Australia, which is confined to persons less than 30 years old. In 2001-2002, nearly 11 000 such visas were issued to young Irish people by the Australian authorities.

2. The EEA comprises the member states of the European Union, along with Iceland, Liechtenstein and Norway.

3. However, non-EEA nationals who have permission to remain in Ireland as students are entitled to engage in casual employment (defined as up to 20 hours per week, or full-time during vacation periods) for the duration of their permission to remain. In these circumstances, a work permit is not required.

of the non-national component of the Irish labour force. Table 9.1 shows that in the first quarter of 2002, there were an estimated 100 000 non-nationals in the Irish labour force, of whom 40% were from the United Kingdom, 20% from other EEA states and an additional 40% from non–EEA countries. In earlier years, the proportion from the United Kingdom was much higher; the data show that it was more than 60% in 1998. However, among the groups distinguished, non-EEA nationals increased most rapidly in numbers in recent years, from 10 000 in 1998, to more than 40 000 in 2002. All of these immigrants entered the country through the work permit or working visa systems, mainly the former.

Economic background

Turning to the general economic context, the period 1998-2002 was for the most part a time of rapid economic growth. Table 9.1 shows that the Irish labour force increased by more than 200 000 between 1998 and 2002, a rise of nearly 13%. The unemployment rate fell sharply from 7.8% in 1998 to 3.7% in 2001, but increased again to 4.2% in 2002, as the pace of economic growth slowed and labour market conditions became less buoyant. During the five-year period concerned, the proportion of non-nationals in the Irish labour force increased from 3.3 to 5.5%. When viewed in absolute terms, this represents a rise of almost 50 000 between 1998 and 2002, thus comprising nearly one-quarter of the overall increase in labour supply during this time. This does not indeed reflect the full impact of immigration, bearing in mind that the migration inflows also have included significant numbers of returning Irish who had previously emigrated.

Work permits

Legal background: recent trends

The work permit programme, which is administered by the Department of Enterprise, Trade and Employment, was until recently based on the provisions of the 1935 Aliens Act (see section below on the Employment Permits Act). It applies to all engagements for financial gain involving non-EEA citizens, including those of short duration. The system is employer-based, and the initiative must be taken by the employer in the first instance to obtain the permit prior to the entry of the employee into the country. The application must relate to a specific job and to a named individual. The permits, which are issued for one year with the possibility of renewal, are intended to relate to posts that cannot be filled by Irish or other EEA nationals. Until recently, the Irish work permit system attracted little attention. The number of workers entering the country with such permits was small and did not change very much over the years. Many of those involved tended to be skilled, working in multinational enterprises, in the medical sphere or in a self-employed capacity in the catering area. However, Table 9.2 shows that the number of permits issued has escalated in recent years, rising from less than 6 000 in 1998 to more than 40 000 in 2002. The fact that this increase continued in 2002 is noteworthy, since by that time conditions in the Irish labour market had deteriorated significantly.

In recent years, about one-third of the work permits issued in any one year were renewed.[4] However, the most up-to-date figures available (for 2002) indicate that this proportion has increased to 45%. A notable feature of the 2002 data is that the number of new permits issued fell (to just under 24 000 compared with 30 000 in 2001), but renewals increased from 6 500 to 16 500, suggesting a tendency by employers to try to retain such workers rather than seek new permits. This is perhaps hardly surprising, in view of the more stringent conditions applied to the issue of new permits in 2002. While the recent influx of non-EEA workers has involved a diverse range of nationalities, Table 9.3 shows that the increases in the inflows for some nationality groups over the last few years have been particularly dramatic. The number entering from the Baltic States, for example, was only 17 in 1998 but had risen to almost 8 600 in 2002. For the same short period, the inflows from other Eastern European countries increased from about 500 to almost 14 000. Currently more than half of the total inflow of work permit holders comes from the Eastern European region. There have also been very large increases in the case of citizens of South Africa and the Philippines.

Table 9.4 contains a classification of work permits issued to non-EEA nationals according to the sector of activity. While all sectors recorded increases, the data show that in recent years, the most rapid increases have occurred in the agricultural sector, and activities associated with the catering and hotel industries. The figures for agriculture are quite phenomenal, indicating that the inflow of work permit holders (mainly from the Baltic States) into this sector increased from less than 100 in 1998 to over 6 200 in 2002. The nature of the large increase in the inflow of work permit holders in recent years, when viewed in parallel with the fact that many of the jobs involved relate to services or agriculture, suggests that those now entering under this system engage in mainly unskilled or semi-skilled work. This is in contrast to earlier periods when such immigrants tended to fill mainly skilled positions. In order to shed more light on this aspect, the Department of Enterprise, Trade and Employment has recently begun to classify the jobs associated with the work permit programme by occupation. While the information available thus far is limited, it does tend to confirm that the occupational profile of these jobs is weighted heavily towards the less skilled end of the labour market. Data compiled for the period from September to December 2002 (Table 9.5) indicate that more than 75% of the posts in question relate to unskilled or semi-skilled activities. Only some 12% involved managerial or professional functions and a similar proportion were engaged in skilled manual (craft) occupations.

There appears to have been widespread knowledge among potential immigrants of the employment opportunities in the Irish labour market over the past few years. The pattern of the inflows associated with work permits is influenced significantly by the manner in which contacts are made, frequently through intermediaries, such as recruitment agencies or groups of large employers (*e.g.* health authorities) who tend to target particular countries or regions. Once a flow from a particular source emerges, it tends to expand and become more established as a result of personal contacts among recently arrived workers, and their families and friends in the country of origin. Furthermore, employers associations have for some years been exerting

---

4.   The calculation of the proportion of work permits renewed in a particular year is based on the total issued or renewed in the previous year. It may be possible that some non-nationals whose permits have expired remain in the country and continue to work illegally, but no estimates of the extent of such activities are available.

pressure to allow increases in the number of work permits issued, as greater difficulties were encountered in recruiting workers at all skill levels. However, this scenario is now changing with the declining jobs growth in the Irish economy; hence the recent restrictions introduced by the Irish government on the issue of work permits.

Recent restrictions on the issue of work permits

In recent years, in view of the rising demand for labour, few obstacles were placed in the way of employers obtaining work permits. Indeed, under pressure from employer interests, some of the requirements that were previously in place were relaxed. With the deterioration in the labour market situation however, the conditions for obtaining such permits have been made more stringent. In early 2002, a requirement was introduced which stipulated that the National Employment and Training Authority (FÁS) has to be informed of the vacancies in question and that initially efforts must be made to fill such vacancies from FÁS jobseekers lists. A work permit will not be issued unless this procedure has been followed and FÁS provides a written confirmation that a permit is justified.[5] Furthermore the fees payable for obtaining work permits have significantly increased. The charge for a full 12-month permit is now EUR500, with reduced fees applying to permits covering shorter periods.

More recently in early April 2003, the Irish government indicated that, following consultation with FÁS, it will announce on a quarterly basis occupations which will be considered as ineligible for work permits. The list of ineligible occupational categories for the initial quarter, 9 April to 30 June 2003, which is quite extensive, is set out in Box 9.1. The list was drawn up following an analysis of the skills profiles of job seekers registered with FÁS, which were compared to the types of vacancies being registered by employers. The government and FÁS have indicated that they are satisfied that currently there is sufficient personnel available to fill vacancies arising in the occupational categories listed. Employers have however expressed reservations on this issue and have further concerns that in some instances they may be obliged to recruit personnel who may be less than willing to engage in the work involved. All work permit applications for eligible occupations will continue to be assessed, to ensure that every effort has been made to employ source EEA nationals. Furthermore, in considering future applications, preference will be given to those applications in respect of nationals from the EU accession states. This is in accordance with the provisions of the Treaty of Accession which was signed on 16 April 2003.

Working visas

The growth of the Irish economy in the second half of the 1990s resulted in shortages of skilled/qualified employees in particular areas such as information and computing technologies, construction, and across a broad range of medical, health and social care activities. In order to facilitate the recruitment of suitably qualified persons from non-EEA countries in these areas, a working visa scheme was introduced. This made it possible for prospective employees with job offers from employers in Ireland related to the designated occupations to obtain immigration and employment clearance in advance from Irish embassies and consulates. Applications for working visas were accepted for persons outside the country only. At present, the designated occupational categories are:

---

5.   These requirements do not apply to renewal applications.

information and computing technology professionals and technicians; architects, including architectural technicians/technologists; construction engineers and technicians; quantity surveyors and building surveyors; town planners; medical practitioners; registered nurses; dentists; and certain specified professional categories in the public health and social care sectors, such as radiographers, dieticians, psychologists, electrocardiogram technicians, etc. The list may be altered from time to time, depending on changing labour market conditions. A working visa is usually valid for two years. Holders of such visas are allowed to change their employers within the same skill category after arrival in Ireland, as long as they continue to have permission to work and reside in the country. As indicated earlier, currently some 3 500 visas are issued annually.

Box 9.1. Occupational sectors ineligible for work permits, from 9 April to 30 June 2003

- Clerical and administrative

- General labourers and builders

- Operator and production staff

- Sales staff (including retail sales, sales representatives and management/supervisory/ specialist Sales)

- Transport Staff (including drivers - bus, coach, car, taxi, fork-lift and heavy machinery, etc)

- Childcare workers (including nursery/crèche workers, child minders, etc.)

- Hotel tourism and catering (including reception staff and barpersons)

- Craft workers (including aircraft mechanic, bookbinder, bricklayer, cabinet-maker, carpenter/joiner, carton-maker, fitter-construction plant, electrician, instrumentation craftsperson, fitter, tiler-floor/wall, heavy vehicles mechanic, instrumentation craftsperson, metal fabricator, motor mechanic, IT-network administration, originator, painter/decorator, plumber, printer, refrigeration engineer, sheet-metal worker, tool-maker, vehicle body repairer, wood machinist).

Employment Permits Act 2003

The purpose of the Employment Permits Act is primarily to facilitate the granting of free access to the Irish labour market to nationals of the new EU accession states as of May 2004. Basically this provides that the requirement for work permits and working visas will not apply in the case of the employment of nationals from these states after EU enlargement. However, it also allows the Minister for Enterprise, Trade and Employment to re-impose the requirement for employment permits for these nationals, if the labour market is experiencing or is likely to experience what is termed a disturbance.[6] This provision is in accordance with the national measures permitted in the transitional period up to 2010, as set out in the Treaty of Accession.

---

6.   In this context the term "disturbance" is defined as in the Treaty of Accession. This can arise when a (non-accession) member state "undergoes or foresees disturbances on its labour market which could seriously threaten the standard of living or level of employment in a given region or occupation". The member state may, in these circumstances, request the Commission to state that the application of Articles 1 to 6 of Regulation (EEC) No 1612/68 (which deals with freedom of movement for workers) be wholly or partially suspended in order to restore to normal the situation in that region or occupation. A (non-accession) member state may, in urgent and exceptional cases, suspend the application of Articles 1 to 6 of this Regulation, followed by a reasoned *ex-post* notification to the Commission.

The act also incorporates a provision whereby, for the first time, the requirements for employment permits in respect of non-nationals working in Ireland are set out in primary legislation, together with penalties for non-compliance by both employers and employees. The latter remedies a defect in the earlier legal basis on which the employment permit system operated. Until the new legislation was enacted, an employer could not be charged with employing a person not entitled to work in the state without an employment permit. On the basis of the figures set out above, it is expected that granting free access to the Irish labour market to nationals of accession states after EU enlargement will result in a reduction of about one-third in the number of work permits currently issued. However, this could be significantly larger, depending on the degree to which demand for labour switches to accession country personnel.

Conclusion

The consensus view of most analysts is that the Irish economy derived considerable benefits from the large inflows of foreign workers which occurred in the final years of the 1990s. Against a background of unprecedented growth levels, labour demand rose sharply and towards the end of the decade significant labour shortages had emerged, not only for qualified personnel but also across the entire skills spectrum. Were it not for the availability of foreign labour, severe bottlenecks would have arisen in many areas of the labour market, thus impeding overall expansion. Furthermore the migration inflows also contributed to a moderation in wage trends, which in turn served to preserve competitiveness – a vital factor in a relatively small open economy.[7]

With regard to the latter issue, there were concerns about exploitation, especially in relation to work permit holders who are mainly engaged in unskilled occupations and are generally prepared to accept lower than average wages. The fact that increasing numbers of work permits continued to be sought in 2002 when private sector employment ceased and unemployment began to rise intensified the debate concerning this issue.

The current deterioration in economic conditions has, as indicated, caused steps to be taken to restrict migration inflows from non-EEA States. Nevertheless, few are advocating a closed door policy, because even with the expectation of more moderate growth rates, there is likely to be a continuing need for immigrant labour, in view of the changes in the population age structure. Furthermore, the stock of Irish emigrants abroad has fallen, thereby reducing the possibilities of augmenting labour supply from this source. Future inflows will not however be on the scale of those that occurred over the past number of years.

Finally there is clearly a need for a more planned policy approach to non-EEA immigration, in place of the *ad hoc* responses which have been characteristic of recent years. Apart from regulating inflows, such policies should ensure that a balance is struck between the competitive objective and the need to provide adequate protection to immigrant workers. It would be desirable that the introduction of a more managed system involve assessments of the likely volume and skill profiles of Ireland's residual labour needs, following expansion of the European Union.

7.　　It is of interest to note that a recent analysis provided evidence which indicated that immigration of skilled workers into Ireland in the mid-1990s did give rise to a moderation in wage growth. See A. Barrett, J. Fitz Gerald and B. Nolan (2000), *Earnings Inequality, Returns to Education and Immigration into Ireland*, Centre for Economic Policy Research, Discussion Paper No. 2493, London.

Table 9.1. **Labour force by nationality, 1998-2002**

Thousands

Nationality	1998	1999	2000	2001	2002
Irish	1 567	1 630	1 682	1 700	1 728
All non-nationals	53	58	64	82	100
United Kingdom	*33*	*34*	*34*	*38*	*39*
Other EEA	*11*	*13*	*16*	*18*	*19*
Non-EEA	*10*	*10*	*13*	*26*	*41*
Total labour force	1 621	1 688	1 746	1 782	1 827
Unemployment rate (%)	7.8	5.7	4.3	3.7	4.2

Source: Central Statistics Office, Quarterly National Household Survey.

Table 9.2. **Total work permits issued and renewed, 1998-2002**

	1998	1999	2000	2001	2002
Permits issued	3 830	4 602	15 735	29 961	23 759
Permits renewed	1 886	1 660	2 271	6 485	16 562
Total	5 716	6 262	18 006	36 446	40 321
Percentage renewed	42.0	29.0	36.3	36.0	45.4

Note: The percentage renewed is calculated on the basis of the total for the previous year.

Source: Department of Enterprise, Trade and Employment.

Table 9.3. **Work permits issued and renewed by nationality, 1998-2002**

Country, Region	1998	1999	2000	2001	2002
			Total		
United States and Canada	1 645	1 075	1 851	1 470	1 096
Australia	312	347	768	1 098	1 116
India	446	390	644	757	845
Japan	248	191	176	205	197
Pakistan	224	254	468	821	840
Philippines	63	156	991	2 472	3 255
South Africa	178	352	637	2 305	2 273
Baltic States	17	285	3 351	8 346	8 594
Other EU accession countries	223	480	2 322	4 984	5 131
Other Eastern Europe	292	495	2 351	6 662	8 562
Other countries	2 068	2 237	4 447	7 326	8 412
Total	**5 716**	**6 262**	**18 006**	**36 446**	**40 321**

Note: The EU Accession States comprise the Baltic States, Cyprus, the Czech Republic, Hungary, Malta, Poland, the Slovak Republic and Slovenia.

Source: Department of Enterprise, Trade and Employment.

Table 9.4. **Work permits issued and renewed by sector, 1998-2002**

Sector	1998	1999	2000	2001	2002
Agriculture	70	449	2 980	5 714	6 248
Industry	705	414	1 750	3 119	3 094
Services	4 941	5 399	13 276	27 613	30 979
Medical, Nursing	620	720	1 360	2 252	2 883
Catering	607	694	3 920	9 129	10 306
Education	298	304	370	480	610
Domestic	59	80	200	521	941
Entertainment/Sport	264	246	771	1 142	874
Other Services	3 093	3 355	6 655	14 089	15 365
Total	**5 716**	**6 262**	**18 006**	**36 446**	**40 321**

Source: Department of Enterprise, Trade and Employment.

Table 9.5. **Work permits issued and renewed by occupation,
September to December 2002**

Occupation	Permits issued	
	Total	%
Agricultural	1 325	10.7
Managers etc.	297	2.4
Professionals	697	5.6
Associate professionals	495	4.0
Clerical	160	1.3
Craft occupations	1 435	11.6
Plant operatives	551	4.4
Sales occupations	356	2.9
Catering occupations	1 725	13.9
Personal and protective	1 192	9.6
Other (mainly unskilled) occupations	4 189	33.7
Total	**12 422**	**100.0**

Source: Department of Enterprise, Trade and Employment.

PART III

ASSESSING NEW OPPORTUNITIES FOR LABOUR MIGRATION

Chapter 10

RECRUITMENT OF FOREIGN LABOUR IN GERMANY AND SWITZERLAND

by

Thomas Liebig

Research Institute for Labour Economics and Labour Law
and Department of Economics, University of St. Gallen, Switzerland

Introduction

A comparison between the Swiss and German migration policies might not seem very straightforward at first, even though the two countries are neighbours and share many structural features (*i.e.* economic, institutional, linguistic and cultural). After all, Switzerland continuously pursued a policy of labour immigration throughout the entire post-war era. Germany, however, in 1973 stopped recruitment of persons outside of the European Economic Area (EEA) and this policy still applies in principle. Also, despite being neighbours, their geographical position is somewhat different. Germany is closer to Eastern Europe, that is, to countries where wages (adjusted for purchasing power) are a fraction of those in Germany. Despite the high income level in Switzerland, the gap in wages *vis-à-vis* its neighbouring countries (*e.g.* France, Italy) is not so wide. However, prior to 1973, both countries had very similar policies, as they relied heavily on the recruitment of foreign workers. This recruitment was mainly based on bilateral agreements, as neither country had colonial links to rely on, unlike Belgium, France, the Netherlands and the United Kingdom. In addition, despite having relatively high immigration rates, neither country ever defined itself as an immigration country. Furthermore, both countries are currently in the process of a major restructuring of their immigration systems.

If the current policy proposals are enacted, the two countries will have again quite similar approaches. Both will have free movement of persons with EEA member states and, regarding non-EEA countries, there will be a focus on highly-qualified permanent immigrants. Furthermore, both countries will (generally) have quotas and labour market testing, as well as special provisions for specialists and investors. In fact, as will be argued below, and despite very different developments and backgrounds, policies relating to foreigners in Germany and Switzerland have been steadily converging since the 1980s. Differences in the treatment of non-EEA nationals will remain noteworthy, principally in two areas. First, Germany envisages a channel which allows qualified foreign labour to immigrate, independent of actual job offers, whereas labour immigration in Switzerland will remain based on labour market demand. Second, Germany is expected to remain open to permanent settlement by temporary workers, whereas this will generally be avoided under the new Swiss scheme. In any case, even though the background and the institutional setting in both countries have many unique features, both countries could benefit from each other's experiences because they are likely to face similar challenges in the future. A series of expert interviews were conducted in Switzerland, and the results have been included in the analysis below. The first section of this chapter presents a background of the labour recruitment policy in both countries. The chapter then provides a comparative assessment of both systems and points to some common future challenges. The final section summarises the findings and provides conclusions.

Country-specific background

Germany

Historical overview

Germany was the only country in Western Europe to experience massive immigration flows after 1945. In the broad sense of the word, it is the second most important immigration country in the OECD, after the United States, even though Germany did not define itself as a country of immigration until 2000. A particularity of German post-war immigration is that one out of every two immigrants was of German origin. Immediately after the war, a first wave of ethnic immigrants entered Germany as either refugees from the eastern part of the country or expelled persons from the former German territories. With the construction of the Berlin Wall, this ethnic immigration stopped rather abruptly. Since the late 1990s, a surge of German ethnic immigrants have come from Eastern Europe. To accommodate the rising labour demand of the prospering economy, Germany conducted a series of recruitment agreements.[1] As in most other Western European countries, this recruitment lasted until the recession of the early 1970s, and recruitment was banned in November 1973. This ban on recruitment did not lead to the intended decline in the foreign population. Instead, it had the opposite effect, by creating an incentive for family migration. The new policy ruled out future legal re-immigration, so many temporary immigrants decided to stay in Germany and encouraged their spouses and children to join them. Family-related migration was also fostered by a provision that child assistance would only be given to children raised in Germany.

These were far from being the only adverse effects caused by the halt in recruitment. The closing of the borders for labour immigration also gradually began to foster asylum migration, as this remained for many foreigners the only legal way to enter Germany.[2] Non-labour immigration into Germany accelerated drastically in the 1990s: between 1991 and 1999, nearly 10 million foreigners (including *Spätaussiedler* or ethnic Germans from Eastern Europe, asylum seekers and refugees) entered the country. These migration flows, however, were mainly based on entitlements due to constitutional rights,

---

1.   The first bilateral recruitment agreements were signed prior to the construction of the Berlin Wall. The first country was Italy in 1955, as it seemed clear that the European integration process was just beginning and would imply some form of freedom of movement sooner or later. Further recruitment agreements were signed with Greece and Spain (1960), Turkey (1961), Morocco (1963), Portugal (1964), Tunisia (1965) and the former Yugoslavia (1968). For an analysis of German guest worker recruitment, see Werner (2001a).

2.   In the early 1980s, Germany even offered emigration bonuses for guest workers who were willing to leave the country.

humanitarian obligations or international law. They were thus neither adapted to labour market needs, nor subject to control. The only major channel for legal immigration with specific reference to labour market needs after 1973 was for nationals of the member states of the European Community (EU) and some other countries from which massive immigration was not a concern.[3]

In 1991, Germany reorganised several special schemes within the framework of a new immigration law, although this was still done in a very restrictive and fragmentary way. Regulations were created for particular labour shortages in specific sectors such as speciality restaurants, as well as other important exceptions concerning contract workers, seasonal workers, guest employees (not to be confused with the former guest workers) and cross-border commuters. Since 2000, information and communication technology (ICT) workers may also work in Germany on a temporary basis. Although limited in scale and scope, this Green Card programme paved the way for a new immigration law.

Current developments: from the Green Card to a new immigration law in Germany

Despite the various forms of (temporary) labour immigration outlined above, until recently, immigration was mainly associated with asylum. Only a small elite discussed the need for labour migration into Germany. Indeed, the discussion of labour migration was destined to be theoretical until the end of the millennium, as the break in the recruitment of foreign workers was not seriously questioned. With unemployment rates at almost 10% in the late 1990s, labour immigration seemed unthinkable. At the same time, however, unemployment and vacancy rates were both particularly pronounced. By the end of 1999, more than 10% of all firms claimed that the lack of skilled labour hampered their development (Magvas and Spitznagel, 2000, p. 4). The supposedly strategic ICT sector seemed to be especially affected. It has been argued that Germany began the 21st century with a lack of about 70 000 ICT workers; some estimates calculated that there would be an additional demand of up to 350 000 as early as 2002.[4]

In this context, Chancellor Gerhard Schröder announced in his opening speech to the world's largest computer fair, CeBIT, in February 2000 in Hanover, the launch of a German Green Card programme for foreign ICT workers. As of August 2000, up to 20 000 ICT specialists from countries outside of the EEA would be allowed to work in Germany for a maximum of five years, provided that they have a tertiary level ICT degree, or earn at least EUR51 000 per year in Germany. As long as the wage is above a certain threshold (EUR39 600 in the western and EUR32 700 in the eastern part of Germany), there would be no test on wage conditions.

The first results of the Green Card programme have been mixed. On the one hand, employers are generally content with the administration of the programme, and studies have indicated important spillovers (Bundesministerium für Arbeit und Sozialordnung 2002). On the other, the programme did not attract the high numbers of applicants that

---

3. Today, there are specific provisions which allow for facilitated labour immigration from the following countries: Andorra, Australia, Canada, Cyprus, Israel, Japan, Malta, Monaco, New Zealand, San Marino, Switzerland and the United States. Turkish citizens also have some additional rights, due to their country's associated status with the European Union.

4. See, for example, Fuchs (2000), and the critique in IZA (2001, p. 16).

were originally expected, and only 9 614 Green Cards were issued up to December 2002. Furthermore, Indian computer scientists, who were originally seen as the main target group of the programme, did not seem very attracted by the Green Card (see for example Werner, 2001b, p. 323). Instead, more than 42% of all Green Cards were issued to people from Central and Eastern Europe. From an EU integration perspective, a large share of nationals from the candidate countries was desirable. Yet, the share of Polish and Hungarian nationals was well below expectations, whereas applications from countries such as Romania exceeded the expected level.

The rise and fall of the German Green Card (in December 2002, only 117 new Green Cards were issued) points to the drawbacks of focusing on a particular occupation that is temporarily in high demand. It has also highlighted groups with high recruitment potential for Germany: people from Central and Eastern Europe and foreign students. About 15% of all Green Cards were issued to foreign IT students already in Germany (Zentralstelle für Arbeitsvermittlung, 2003). Despite some shortcomings (*e.g.* maximum stay limited to five years, restrictions on occupational mobility) the programme has two advantages. First, the federal employment office provides a virtual job placement service, by matching potential foreign employees with German employers. Second, there is no wages testing if a specified legally fixed wage threshold is met. Both provisions are likely to lower transaction costs considerably.

Despite its rather limited quantitative impact, the Green Card served as the trigger for the immigration debate in Germany. It virtually put an end to the 1973 break in recruitment. In September 2000, half a year after the Green Card announcement, the Independent Commission on Migration to Germany was established by the Minister of the Interior. Its task was to develop a proposal for an integrated framework for all categories of migration to Germany (*i.e.* encompassing both labour and humanitarian migration). In its final report in July 2001, the commission recommended a re-definition of Germany as an immigration country, with several channels of labour immigration to Germany.[5] According to the proposal, short-term immigration for a maximum of five years should tackle temporary shortages in the labour market. Young highly skilled foreigners, as well as entrepreneurs with a viable business plan, would be able to enter the country as permanent immigrants. With the exception of entrepreneurs and so-called top achievers, labour immigration should be subjected to annual quotas which would be set by a newly formed migration council. Top achievers, who are mostly highly-skilled scientists and business executives, would benefit from simplified entry rules for a temporary stay, with the prospect of permanent settlement. Although all the other groups would need an employment offer in Germany, they would have the possibility of applying for a permanent residence permit via a points system. In addition, it was envisaged that additional students and apprentices would be attracted into the German training and education system.

In the meantime, political parties have also presented proposals for a new immigration policy. With regard to labour immigration, the various propositions were quite similar. There is a consensus that selective labour immigration is necessary, and that particularly highly-qualified workers, scientists, entrepreneurs and other groups should be given permanent resident status immediately. Differences among the proposals are mainly with respect to family reunion, integration, and refugee and asylum policies. The current

---

5.   For details of the recommendations, see Independent Commission on Migration to Germany (2001).

draft of the law largely follows the commission's proposals in the area of labour migration. It contains *inter alia* a drastic simplification of the complex current system of permits: there will only be one temporary and one permanent permit. The permits would establish both right of residence and permission to work. In some areas, the draft appears more liberal with respect to labour immigration than the commission proposals (see Davy, 2002, for a comparison). For example, whereas the commission's proposals envisage a quota for temporary immigration, to reduce labour shortages, no such provision exists in the draft of the law. Furthermore, in some special cases of pronounced shortages, individual labour market testing may not be necessary. These temporary migrants would not need to be eligible under the points system for permanent immigration, to obtain a permanent residence permit. Finally, the draft of the law envisages permanent residence for highly skilled top achievers, whereas the commission had only planned for a facilitated transfer from a temporary to a permanent residence permit for these groups. Chart 10.1 summarises the commission's proposals and the government draft for a new immigration policy in Germany.

On 22 March 2002, the upper chamber of the German parliament (*Bundesrat*) passed the law in a way that raised constitutional objections. In December 2002, the German Federal Constitutional Court declared the process unconstitutional. At the time of writing, the law is being debated again in the parliament. Regardless of the ultimate outcome, any new immigration framework will be clearly more transparent and more focused on labour market aspects than the current system.

Institutional setting for labour immigration

Since the 1973 break in recruitment, residents from countries without preferential status, in principle, can only obtain a work permit for a maximum duration of three months. Consequently, unlike Switzerland, Germany does not have specific residence permits tailored to labour immigration. The German framework for foreigners, which relies on an extensive permit system, is parallel to the Swiss system, although it appears much more complex and opaque. Up to 2004, six categories with varying degrees of rights can be distinguished. For labour immigration, two separate permits are required: one establishing a right of residence, and the other granting permission to pursue employment. Accordingly, both the Office of Immigration and local employment offices have a say in labour immigration. In general, neither office can issue a permit without the consent of the other. The present framework of labour immigration is laid out in the current Foreigners Act (*Ausländergesetz*) and in three ordinances: the Ordinance on the Residence for Work Purposes (*Arbeitsaufenthalteverordnung*), the Ordinance on Exceptions from the General Recruitment Break (*Anwerbestoppausnahmeverordnung*) and the Ordinance on Work Permits (*Arbeitsgenehmigungs-verordnung*). An important feature of the policy on foreigners in Germany is the different labour market treatment accorded to foreigners, depending upon their permit category. The resulting complexity is enhanced even further by the fact that the recruitment ban applies only in principle. The labour immigration framework thus contains a host of different provisions for special groups of persons, occupations and areas, along with country-specific agreements and corresponding quotas. Although the exceptions are numerous, they are all of very limited scope, thus contributing to the complexity of the system.

An important element of the current immigration policy is the number of bilateral agreements with Central and Eastern European countries (CEECs), which establish several forms of temporary immigration for work purposes.[6] These bilateral agreements serve mainly as a tool to foster co-operation between the CEECs and Germany, by strengthening the links between them. Whereas CEEC workers and their respective economies profit by gaining some knowledge of the German market and techniques, German companies also may benefit by establishing contacts and, potentially, better access to the CEEC markets. Therefore, these agreements do not have an exclusive labour market focus. They are also seen as a means of gradually integrating the CEECs into the European labour market in the wake of EU enlargement. Furthermore, they aim both to limit the migration pressure from these countries and to direct it into legal channels. There are four different channels for the temporary legal labour immigration from the CEECs: seasonal workers, contract workers, guest employees and cross-border commuters.[7]

Under the seasonal worker scheme for classified seasonal businesses, more than 200 000 people have temporarily worked in Germany every year in recent years. Seasonal workers may stay in Germany for a maximum of nine months.[8] More than 90% work in agriculture and an additional 5% in the hotel and catering industry. The programme is heavily dominated by Polish workers, who represent about 90% of all seasonal workers. Recruitment is not based on intergovernmental recruitment agreements. Instead, the employment of these workers is mediated through agreements between the Central Placement Office of the Federal Employment Agency and the source countries.

Perhaps the most interesting channel for legal migration is the contract worker scheme (Table 10.1). Based on intergovernmental bilateral recruitment agreements, employees from foreign companies may work in Germany as contract workers. Some of these agreements existed even prior to the Eastern European transformation process, although they were very limited in scope. Bilateral contract worker agreements contain country-specific quotas which may be adapted according to the labour market situation in Germany. During their stay in Germany, contract workers remain employed by the foreign company but provide their services to German companies in Germany. The foreign company acts as a sub-contractor for a German firm. The duration of residence is limited to two or three years. Originally, the contract worker scheme was considered to be a panacea (for the remainder of this paragraph, refer to Reim and Sandbrink, 1996. First, it enables the temporary and flexible recruitment of foreign workers to take place, due to quotas adjusting to the German labour market situation. Second, recruitment is the responsibility of the sending countries, meaning that there is no onerous individual labour market testing conducted in Germany. Due to the political focus of the programme, any labour market testing is done mainly after recruitment. As will be seen below, this stands in contrast to the Swiss approach, where individual labour market testing, and verification of work and living conditions, are mainly completed before recruitment. Third, co-operation between Germany and the CEECs is fostered, offering new opportunities for both areas. Fourth, the integration of the CEECs into the European labour market is enhanced, and the supposed immigration pressure from these countries is conducted into

---

6.   Bilateral agreements have been conducted with Albania, Bosnia and Herzegovina, Bulgaria, Croatia, the Czech Republic, Estonia, Hungary, Latvia, Lithuania, FYR Macedonia, Poland, Romania, Slovenia, the Slovak Republic, Turkey and the former Yugoslavia.

7.   For an overview, see Ausländerbeauftragte (2001) and Fröhlich (2002).

8.   The seasonal worker scheme is thus quite similar to its (former) Swiss counterpart (see below).

legal channels. However, this last effect should not be overestimated, as the contract worker scheme has been fairly limited in scale and scope (Table 10.2).[9]

Like other forms of temporary labour immigration, the payment of foreign contract workers is subject to the standard wage in Germany and taxed there. However the important difference lies in that social security contributions are paid according to the regime of the source country. Given the high level of social security contributions in Germany, this can result in a cost advantage of more than 20% to employers and workers, and has given rise to an intense debate about the potential for distortion of competition (see for example Sieveking *et al.*, 1998). There has also been concern that this scheme acts as a gateway to illegal employment in Germany, particularly in the construction industry, which accounts for the majority of contract workers (see for example the report of the Deutscher Bundestag, 1996). As abuses mounted and the labour market situation deteriorated, the quotas were lowered substantially, and a fee of about EUR1 000 per employee was introduced. Along with other restrictions, and the poor labour market conditions in Germany, these changes led to a sharp reduction in the number of workers entering Germany by means of the contract worker scheme, from about 95 000 in 1992 to approximately 47 000 in 2001.

The third temporary labour channel is the guest employee agreement, which is aimed at allowing skilled people to work in Germany to obtain supplementary specific training. They are allowed to work in Germany for a maximum of 18 months. Despite the fact that there is only a small annual quota of 10 250 people for this purpose, it is far from being fully used. In 2001, less than 6 000 foreigners entered Germany as guest employees. This is mainly attributed to the fact that German employers are not willing to employ foreigners for temporary training purposes only.

The fourth temporary labour channel is open to the special group of cross-border commuters. Although their permits are not limited in time, they can only work in pre-defined border regions and generally have to return to their home country on a daily basis. More than 85% of all cross-border commuters come from the Czech Republic.

Switzerland

Historical overview

A tight labour market has been a marked feature of the Swiss economy since the end of World War II. Unlike other European countries, Switzerland's economy remained intact, leading to an immediate economic boom after the war. In 1948, Switzerland was one of the first European countries actively to recruit foreign workers, by signing a recruitment agreement with Italy. As the competition for guest workers with countries like Germany intensified, Switzerland had to revise its 1948 recruitment agreement with Italy in 1964, giving more rights to Italians living in Switzerland (*inter alia*, provisions which facilitated permanent residence and family reunion).[10] Unlike other Western

---

9.   Reim and Sandbrink (1996) argued that different motives dominated in different periods. Initially, the contract worker scheme was mainly aimed at fostering economic co-operation and tackling labour shortages. In the 1990s, however, foreign policy considerations dominated.

10.   During this period, the traditionally strong migration relationship with Italy had been further strengthened. In 1960, Italians accounted for almost 60% of all foreigners in Switzerland. In the following years and decades, the relative and absolute number of Italians steadily declined. A similar tendency has later been observed in the case of Portugal and Spain, with whom bilateral recruitment agreements were also concluded. The continuing integration in the

European countries such as Germany, Switzerland did not have public recruitment agencies. Instead, recruitment was organised by the employers themselves (Körner, 1990, p. 68).[11] Like other countries, Switzerland thought that the excess labour demand and the corresponding immigration would be temporary, which resulted in a lenient immigration policy and a massive influx of foreign workers. This situation led to rising xenophobia and foreign labour was deemed responsible for growing inflationary pressures.[12] In 1963, Switzerland began to control labour immigration gradually by introducing a ceiling on the stock of foreigners per firm. In 1970, the Swiss government introduced a global quota, which placed an upper limit on the number of new foreigners allowed to enter the country. As a result, Switzerland was one of the first Western European countries to restrict labour immigration.

Compared to Germany, the policy change associated with the introduction of the 1970 quotas was much more gradual. Yet, it still led to an immediate reduction in the number of foreign workers, which fell further with the 1973 global recession. At that time, Switzerland did not have mandatory unemployment insurance. Thus many foreigners who did not enjoy social protection left the country. By doing so, the foreign workers served as a buffer in the labour market: despite a reduction of the overall workforce of 8% (one of the highest drops compared to other OECD member countries), the unemployment rate never reached 1% (Sheldon, 2001). However, as time passed, the quota system became less and less capable of controlling immigration. *Inter alia*, the right to family reunion and the births of foreign children led to a steady growth in the foreign population.

At the end of the 1980s, the environment in which Swiss immigration policy operated changed dramatically (Wimmer, 2001). First, the future free movement of persons with the EEA implied that a large number of immigrants would no longer be subject to control. Initially, Switzerland had intended to join this economic zone and, more recently, signed a group bilateral agreements, to allow gradually the free movement of workers. Second, in marked contrast to the situation in the 1970s, the economic downturn of the early 1990s led to a drastic increase in unemployment, which affected foreign workers in a disproportionate way. Foreigners no longer seemed to serve as cyclical buffers. Third, the number of asylum seekers increased dramatically. Finally, the geographical origin of the foreigners diversified, with an increasing proportion coming from outside EEA countries. The combination of these developments threatened the public's acceptance of the existing Swiss immigration policy.

To tackle these challenges, the Swiss government introduced the three circles model in 1991. According to this concept, immigrants from the EEA were granted preferential status (first circle). If labour demand could not be met by immigrants from these countries, nationals from the Australia, Canada, New Zealand and the United States could be recruited (second circle). All other countries were included in the third circle. Workers from this last group of countries could thus only be employed as a final resort. Officially, the distinction between the second and the third circle was justified by defining the

---

European Community seemed to lower the attractiveness of Switzerland as a receiving country for foreigners from these countries.

11.   Even today, social partners (*i.e.* employers' associations and labour unions) in several sectors maintain recruitment and associated training facilities abroad.

12.   At the time, it was assumed that a halt in immigration would have limited growth and inflation; see Mahnig and Piguet (2003, p. 70 onwards).

countries of the second circle as traditional recruitment sources, which would imply that people from these countries would integrate more easily. One of the main results of the three circles model was that recruiting new former Yugoslavian nationals, who accounted for almost 15% of all foreigners at that time, became nearly impossible. Additionally, seasonal permits were restricted to EU and EFTA nationals, and the recruitment policy became gradually restricted to highly qualified foreigners, particularly for permanent immigration from non-EEA countries. Overall, the new model marked a fundamental break with the past immigration policy.

The distinction made between the second and the third circle, which was based mainly on cultural grounds and integration ability, was criticised as being discriminatory (see *Eidgenössische Kommission gegen Rassismus,* 1996).[13] In response, the three circles model was changed to a dual recruitment system in 1998, which differentiates only between EEA and non-EEA nationals. Since 1998, employers who want to recruit persons outside the EEA need to prove not only that they could not find domestic workers for the vacancy, but also that they could not recruit people from EEA countries. This has significantly reduced applications for permits for people from non-EEA countries.

Current developments: bilateral agreements and a new foreigners law

The single most important change in Swiss policy on foreigners is the establishment of freedom of movement of persons with EEA member countries. Together with the economic situation and dramatically rising unemployment (for Swiss standards), immigration has always been a key issue in the Swiss stance towards European integration, which dominated the public debate in the early 1990s.[14] Although most experts agree that the fears of drastically rising immigration from EEA countries will not materialise,[15] these worries can be partly explained by Switzerland's geographical situation, the number of EEA nationals in Switzerland and the overall attractiveness of Switzerland as a place to work. In 1980, more than 80% of all foreigners were nationals of the EEA. Since then, their share has steadily declined and now seems to have stabilised slightly below 60%.[16]

Despite these fears, the free movement of workers is now part of a package of seven agreements (bilateral agreements) between Switzerland and the EU member states.[17] The European Union insisted that free movement be introduced in the package deal, which also provides substantial advantages to the Swiss economy in other areas.

---

13. It should be noted, however, that many EU member states have a system that also differentiates among non-EU foreigners. In Germany, for example, the break in general recruitment *inter alia* does not apply to foreigners from the Australia, Canada, Japan, Israel, New Zealand, Switzerland and the United States.

14. Indeed, the fear of a massive influx of EU workers was one of the reasons for Switzerland's refusal to join the EEA in 1992.

15. There is an almost unanimous view among experts that free movement of persons with the European Union will not lead to a major influx of workers. Indeed, instead of threatening the employment prospects of low-skilled workers, free movement might considerably diminish the high charges made by certain highly skilled professions that are currently sheltered from competition. See, for example, Straubhaar (1999).

16. The current figure (56.4% in 2002) is still well above that of most EU member states. In Germany, for example, EU citizens account for only about 25% of all foreigners. Furthermore, it is worth noting that the highest absolute increase in the foreign population was among Germans (in 2002 +8 384 and in 2001 +7 834), while the greatest decrease was among Italians (in 2002 -5 721 and in 2001 -5 665).

17. For a detailed description of the agreements, see Bundesrat (1999).

Overall, the agreements are a substitute for Switzerland joining the EEA, but they are less far-reaching and less dynamic than membership, thereby providing more autonomy to Switzerland. The lack of dynamism is already posing problems regarding the recognition of social security provisions, an area which is still evolving among EU member states. As the recognition of social security provisions in Switzerland often lags behind developments in EU member states, Switzerland's system is becoming increasingly complex and opaque. Furthermore, it is unclear how Switzerland will adapt to EU enlargement. Whichever path Switzerland chooses, the currently low immigrant stocks from the CEECs indicate that their future inflow may be rather small, as the necessary networks among these foreigners are not in place.

Swiss voters approved the bilateral agreements package in May 2000. The first steps regarding the liberalisation of labour immigration of EEA nationals were taken in June 2002, and full freedom of movement will be introduced by 2007. In light of this fundamental change, an overhaul of the entire immigration policy is under way, and a new foreigners law for non-EEA nationals is envisaged. Unlike Germany, Switzerland did not opt for an integrated migration law additionally covering non-labour immigration, such as asylum and refugee immigration.

As a first step towards the reform of the immigration law, the Ordinance on the Restriction of the Number of Foreigners (*Verordnung über die Begrenzung der Zahl der Ausländer*) underwent a major change in July 2002. Like the new law, the revised ordinance is limited to non-EEA nationals. It only applies to EEA nationals, if it provides them with better treatment than under the bilateral agreements, which is generally not the case. Seasonal permits, one of the most problematic features of the Swiss immigration system (see below), were abolished. Currently, four main categories of labour immigration permits can be identified. These apply to both EEA and non-EEA nationals, but the former group benefits from more favourable treatment.

- *Cross-border commuter permits* for gainful employment of people resident in neighbouring countries. These permits are not subjected to quota. Their validity is for one year and they are renewable.

- *Short-term residence permits* are granted to people who are offered employment in the country, originally for no more than 12 months, although the permit may be extended for an overall duration of no more than two years. Originally, this category was intended to relieve excess demand for the seasonal permits, and was limited to six months. It has gained importance in recent years, and has now completely replaced the seasonal permit system. Short-term permits are intended to tackle shortages on a project-like basis, such as in the ICT sector. They are subject to an annual quota, unless they are issued for less than four months.

- *Annual residence permits* entitle foreigners to live and work in Switzerland for one year. These permits have become gradually restricted, mostly to highly-qualified workers (with the exception of EEA residents). Authorities generally renew the annual permits each year, although a legal claim on renewal exists only in certain cases. Annual permits are subject to a quota if, and only if, they are granted for the first time. Once issued, the annual permits may be renewed each year, indefinitely. Most importantly, a change in the labour market situation (*i.e.* periodic unemployment) cannot be used to justify the refusal of an extension. Indeed, once foreigners have obtained an annual permit, they are considered to be part of the domestic labour market. Thus, in more than 90% of the cases, the permit will be renewed if the foreigner applies for an extension. Some permits, however, are tied to a particular occupation and/or are only valid for a specific time, without the option of renewal.

- *Settlement permits* are granted to people who have resided in Switzerland without interruption for five (EEA and US nationals) or ten years (all other nationals). Only the EEA and US nationals group, however, has an entitlement to such a permit, based on agreements with the countries of origin. People holding settlement permits are treated like Swiss nationals in the labour market, but do not have any political rights. Their residence is not limited and cannot be tied to any conditions. While holders of the other residence permits are generally taxed at source, this treatment does not apply to those with a settlement permit.

As mentioned earlier, a new law on foreigners is currently being developed. Its scope will be limited to non-EEA nationals, because it supplements the policy for foreigners established by the bilateral agreements. In effect, the draft law puts many of the recent changes in the immigration system, already introduced by means of ordinances onto a firmer legal footing. The key features of the current policy (*i.e.* quota system, priority of domestic labour, proof of workplace, control of wages and working conditions) will remain, but the basic changes in the legal system for non-EEA nationals can be summarised by the following two points. First, there will be higher entry barriers for foreigners, but they will have more rights and freedom once they enter Switzerland. Second, the distinction between temporary and permanent immigrants will better defined than in the past, and changes in status, generally, will be avoided. This new scheme also implies improvements in the legal position of permanent immigrants.

One of the key changes of the reform is the simplification of the permit system. According to the draft, short-term residence permits linked the stay to a particular purpose (especially project-related activities). As is currently the case, these permits may be extended for one year, but there is no legal entitlement to an extension. After that time, a new temporary permit will only be issued after the foreigner has spent a specified amount of time outside Switzerland. The draft also envisages allowing family reunion for temporary residents, which is not possible under the current system. Although this provision is not intended to introduce an entitlement to foreigners, it has been harshly criticised by those who fear that family reunion will be a first step towards permanent residence. This is particularly the case for the majority of non EEA immigrants who are likely to enter Switzerland by means of the short-term residence permit. It should also be noted that the short-term residence permit is already attractive for certain sectors of the economy. When the permit expires, the employer is not obliged formally to dismiss the foreign worker if there is no longer a need for the post, or if the employee does not match up to expectations.

The hurdles to obtaining an annual permit will be set higher than in the past. It is envisaged that a system of discretion-guiding legal requirements (*ermessensleitende Gesetzesbestimmungen*) will be introduced. The main guiding principle, both for the annual and the short-term permit, is the national economic interest of Switzerland, a very vaguely defined concept. Whereas there is some consensus that the annual permit should remain restricted to qualified labour, a similar constraint on the short-term permit is still being discussed. To obtain an annual permit, the foreigner should also possess the characteristics that support lasting integration into the Swiss labour market: qualification, occupational adaptability, knowledge of languages and age. How these criteria are interpreted and weighted, however, is likely to remain within the discretion of the cantonal authorities. The new law will thus remain relatively flexible.

Certain restrictions may be added to the current draft regarding the annual permit. After five years, permit holders have a legal claim to an extension, provided they have not committed any serious crime against the *ordre public* and are not dependent on welfare services. Currently, the authorities have more discretion in denying an extension. After an additional five years, the foreigner has the right to claim a settlement permit (again subject to the above-mentioned *ordre public* reservation). Even though the authorities already issue settlement permits under these circumstances, the associated legal changes will significantly improve legal certainty for immigrants. These changes are very controversial, because they curtail the rights of the cantons. The fundamental principle underlying these marginal yet important changes indicates that the longer foreigners stay in Switzerland, the more they become increasingly attached and integrated there (see also Niederberger, 2001). Their legal status should therefore be improved as time passes, which is in the interest of both the foreigner and the receiving country. If the length of stay becomes the only determining factor for permanent residence, the actual selection process has to occur before foreigners enter Switzerland. These provisions seem to serve the interests of immigrants and Swiss society: the former have a clear idea of how to obtain permanent settlement and Swiss authorities maintain some control, which is important for public acceptance and helps to prevent abuses.

Exceptions to these policies can be made for investors, business persons, scientists, athletes, artists and specialists, provided they have the necessary financial means and that their presence does not interfere with the national economic interest. As a consequence of the changes outlined above, the line separating the different categories of permits will be drawn quite clearly, in contrast to the system envisaged by Germany, where temporary migrants may eventually settle permanently. The Swiss short-term residence permit is issued only for a limited time, but the annual permit will provide a clear prospect of obtaining permanent settlement. However, it should be noted that the status change from a temporary to a permanent permit is not completely ruled out in Switzerland. Temporary migrants may qualify for an annual permit, but they are generally not given preferential treatment and have to fulfil all the requirements for an annual permit.

Institutional setting for labour immigration

The most remarkable feature of the Swiss immigration policy is its extensive quota system, which aims to strike a balance between the interests of the employers, on the one hand, and rising xenophobia on the other.[18] Once a year, the Swiss government sets a quota for the following year. The quota is set by taking past experiences and the current economic and labour market situation into account. Part of the yearly quota for each category remains with the federal government, though the bulk is at the discretion of the cantons. The quota for each canton is determined by a complex system, taking into account *inter alia*, the population, industrial structure and GDP per capita. As a rule, the

18.   The global quota was introduced as a reaction to a popular initiative that aimed to restrict the share of foreigners in each canton to 10%. On 7 June 1970, the initiative, which contained drastic measures that would have violated the basic human rights of foreigners (it implied *inter alia* a forced return of approximately 200 000 foreigners), was rejected by only a slim margin. For a detailed analysis of the impact of xenophobia on Switzerland's migration policy, see for example Mahnig and Piguet (2003). See also Koopmans and Kriesi (1997) for a comparative study of Germany and Switzerland in this regard.

federal quota is mainly complementary to that of the cantons, for example, in cases where the interests of several cantons are affected, such as the opening of a new large-scale factory.

Nevertheless, only about 20% of all foreigners entering Switzerland in the last decade were subject to quotas. As in Germany, family reunion, and refugee and asylum seeker flows cannot be limited in number, due to international obligations and humanitarian considerations. An additional restriction on the ability of quotas to control immigration effectively has been the entitlements related to a status change, which are a particular feature of Swiss immigration policy. Generally speaking, seasonal permits can be transformed into annual permits if the foreigner has worked in Switzerland for a total of 36 months during four consecutive years. This permit transfer is not subject to quotas, and represents an entitlement if the conditions were met. The seasonal permit statute, which was abolished in June 2003, allowed the temporary immigration of foreigners for employment in classified seasonal jobs for a maximum of nine months, after which they had to leave the country again, but could later re-enter. In the main, the construction industry, hotels, restaurants, agriculture and forestry were categorised as seasonal businesses. About 35% of all seasonal workers subsequently obtained annual permits, which considerably hampered control of immigration (De Wild, 1999).[19]

The seasonal permit promoted a substantial influx of labour immigration into the low-skilled seasonal sectors. Not surprisingly, the foreign population is over-represented at the bottom end of qualification levels. More than a third of all foreigners have completed only compulsory education, compared to less than 20% of the Swiss. However, highly-skilled workers are also over-represented compared to Swiss nationals. For example, about 40% of all privately-employed scientists are foreigners, which suggests that the foreign labour supply is mainly complementary to the domestic labour supply (Haug, 1995). The seasonal permit is thus likely to have had a negative impact on the economy as a whole. Indeed, there is convincing evidence that growth and structural change have been negatively affected by the resulting large scale of low-skilled migration.[20] In addition, the recession of the early 1990s has led to growing unemployment in this group.

Wide-scale recruitment of low-skilled seasonal workers is not the only factor which is likely to have hampered structural change. This could also have been affected by the allocation of annual quotas among cantons and the corresponding restrictions on mobility. In fact, a large part of labour allocation takes place outside the market (see, for example, Mahnig and Piguet, 2003). Another fundamental feature of the immigration policy is the priority given to residents (*Inländervorrang*). New foreign workers may only be recruited if the employer proves that appropriate workers cannot be found in the domestic labour market.[21] This proof of resident priority may increase transaction costs considerably. However, for those occupations in high demand and with very limited domestic supply, cantonal authorities do not require strict proof, as it is assumed that no person with similar qualifications can be found in the domestic labour market. In addition to labour

---

19.   Furthermore, the transfer from an annual permit to a settlement permit occurs, as outlined above.

20.   See Schwarz (1988), who studied the economic impact of the employment of foreigners in Switzerland.

21.   This proof generally requires advertisements of the vacancy in newspapers, and reporting to the local employment office.

market testing, employment conditions (*i.e.* work and living) are examined, to avoid labour dumping.[22]

In a study on the recruitment of foreign workers in Switzerland, Kuster and Cavelti (1999) outlined how flexibility in the Swiss immigration law allows for varying cantonal practices according to the needs of their respective industries. In their comparative study of recruitment practices in four cantons and across four industry sectors, they point to important regional differences. This seems to be most pronounced in the hotel and catering industry. In the canton of Basle city, for example, widespread use of cross-border commuter permits facilitated the recruitment of German and French nationals. For Zurich, which is not located near the Swiss border, temporary permits were issued continuously. This supplied the hotels with a steady flow of foreign workers, but settled foreigners had to be repeatedly replaced by new migrants, once the former group's permits expired. Likewise, asylum seekers played on important role.[23] It is important to note, however, that asylum seekers obtain special permits and are not part of the regular labour immigration system. Finally, in the canton of Graubünden, where labour demand in the hotel industry was largely seasonal (with peaks in winter and summer), most workers in that sector were foreigners with a seasonal permit.

In the existing labour migration framework, bilateral approaches are limited to the trainee agreements.[24] Similar to the German guest employee programme, foreigners may work in Switzerland as trainees, to improve their language and vocational skills if they have finished their formal education, and are between 18 and 30 years old (for some countries, 35). Switzerland has concluded trainee agreements with 30 countries, since 1946. So far, about 53 000 foreigners have entered Switzerland under the programme, and more than 36 000 Swiss have worked abroad in the partner countries. In addition to the personal benefits to the people involved, the programme aims to strengthen ties between Switzerland and participating countries. The proportion of total labour migration flows is fairly limited (Table 10.3). This is also the case for nationals from the CEECs who make up a significant portion of the trainees, but who do not profit from the favourable treatment given to EEA nationals entering through main labour migration schemes. The share of trainees out of total labour immigration for each CEEC has never exceeded 10%.

Comparative analysis

The unemployment of foreigners is more than twice as high as that of the national population in both Germany and Switzerland, even though the levels and the composition of the respective foreign populations differ substantially (Table 10.4). Regarding the levels, the share of the foreign population in the total population is more than twice as

---

22. The test of employment conditions is also applied during the first three renewals of the annual permit. After three renewals, the cantonal industry and labour offices are no longer involved in the process.

23. Indeed, asylum immigration seems to have been gradually replacing the seasonal permit as a means of recruitment of low-skilled foreigners, see Kuster and Cavelti (1999), and Piguet and Wimmer (2000).

24. Furthermore, Switzerland has concluded bilateral agreements with the purpose of mutually improving labour market access for, and the legal status of, their citizens and foreign nationals. The most recent agreement, a Memorandum of Understanding with Canada, was implemented in May 2003.

high in Switzerland compared to Germany.[25] As far as the composition is concerned, both the sectoral and the ethnic concentrations of foreigners are more pronounced in Switzerland. Perhaps the most striking difference is the fact that the share of nationals from EU member states is much higher in Switzerland than in most EU countries (including Germany), despite the fact that Switzerland is not a member country. These facts point to the particularly strong impact of networks in Switzerland, especially among Italian nationals. Strong network effects, which were fostered by the 1973 recruitment break for foreigners outside the European Community, also explain the high share of Turkish nationals in Germany. It is noteworthy that this latter group is among the least integrated in the German labour market, which gives a negative bias to data on foreigners in Germany. Turkish nationals face considerably higher unemployment rates than the average foreigner, and this is partly due to their very low educational attainment level and relatively uncertain legal status. Even excluding Turkish nationals, the (relative) labour market participation of foreigners is higher in Switzerland than in Germany. This seems to be a result of the fact that Swiss immigration policy has been much more labour-market focused than that of its neighbour.

Regarding highly-skilled immigration, there is a striking parallel between both countries. Contrary to common belief, Switzerland and Germany already have similar legal provisions for the immigration of highly-skilled non EEA nationals, even though the Swiss regulations remain more liberal. In Germany, highly skilled foreigners may already immigrate on an exceptional basis, if their employment is in the public interest (though this is generally interpreted rather strictly). In Switzerland, if the new law is introduced, national economic interests will be the guiding principle for skilled immigration.

Important parallels can also be drawn in the area of integration. Giugni and Passy (2003) have argued that the lack of integration of former guest workers in both countries might have gradually evolved into a self-fulfilling prophecy. In their view, Switzerland and Germany define themselves as national communities, based on each country's specific ethnic-cultural background. Foreigners are considered to be temporary guest workers, who do not need to be integrated. Together with stringent citizenship laws, this has had the effect of fostering the organisation of foreigners into ethnic-cultural networks, which has further hampered integration. Nevertheless, there are also noteworthy differences between the two countries. In Switzerland, the term law on foreigners traditionally is equivalent to labour immigration, whereas in Germany quite the opposite seems to be true. Non-economic migration (*e.g.* asylum and refugee flows, family reunification) has dominated Germany's policy on foreigners in past decades. In both countries, however, the respective policies on foreigners are increasingly evolving into migration policies. In Switzerland, the federation and several cantons have recently renamed from the Foreign Office to the Office of Immigration.[26]

Likewise, Germany is about to introduce an immigration law which will partly replace the current foreigners law.[27] These nominal changes seem to point to an

---

25. It should be noted that ethnic Germans from Eastern Europe, who account for a substantial share of the population, are not considered to be foreigners.

26. Since May 2003, the Federal Aliens Office now is called the Federal Office for Immigration, Integration and Emigration.

27. Furthermore, the former Federal Government's Commissioner for Foreigners' Issues has been renamed the Federal Government Commissioner for Migration, Refugees and Integration since October 2002.

underlying awareness in both countries that permanent immigration, and the associated need for integration, have not only become a reality, but are also increasingly viewed as a necessity (see also Wicker, 2003). Consequently, both countries have recently relaxed their citizenship laws, or are in the process of doing so. In Germany, the reform of the citizenship law was tackled prior to the immigration law, whereas in Switzerland both laws are currently in the process of revision.[28] Furthermore, the drafts of the new immigration laws in both countries put more emphasis on integration. The new German law envisages special integration courses that intend to familiarise immigrants with the German language, culture, and the political and legal systems. Until recently, integration in Switzerland was solely within the discretion of the cantons and local authorities, which led to many different approaches. Since 2001, the federal government supports these efforts with federal grants.

In both countries, there are important regional differences in the implementation of immigration laws and regulations. In Switzerland, the strong federalist tradition assigns an important role to the cantons in immigration policy, as they have to apply and interpret immigration law. Differences in application can be attributed to a host of factors specific to each canton, including the relative importance of export-oriented sectors, the presence of multinational enterprises, the political orientation of the cantonal government, its administration of foreigners and the regional unemployment rate. Although the differences are somewhat less overt in Germany, regions still retain some flexibility. For example, exceptions from the recruitment halt can be made if the migrants are highly qualified and their employment is considered to be in the public interest. The state labour office of Baden-Württemberg, for example, has interpreted this provision in such a way that the public can assume that the foreigner earns more than EUR39 000 annually.

In this context, it is interesting to compare the arguments that were made in both countries concerning the introduction of a points system.[29] Unlike Germany, Switzerland does not envisage the introduction of a points system in its new law on foreigners (Liebig, 2002). In Switzerland, the major arguments in favour of a points system were increased transparency and standardisation in the immigration system. Yet, a points system would limit the success with which interest groups could put pressure on the authorities. At the same time, the lack of flexibility of a points system was considered to be the main obstacle to its implementation. In particular, it was argued that a points system would unduly limit the necessary discretion for special cases and would not easily adapt to new developments. This intrusion into the authorities' discretion was deemed unacceptable by parliament and the public, particularly since Switzerland never defined itself as a country of immigration. The arguments put forward in Germany were somewhat different. Generally, the points system was praised for its accuracy and supposedly high level of acceptance. However, it was recognised that the system's lack of flexibility and undesirable distribution effects might pose obstacles to its implementation.

---

28. In Germany, a new liberalised citizenship law has been applied since 2000. It was established prior to the Green Card programme. In Switzerland, a revision of citizenship law is still in the legislative process. Currently, citizenship provisions are mainly cantonal and show a very diverse picture: in some cantons, fees amounting to several thousands of Swiss francs for receiving citizenship. Furthermore, citizenship is often denied arbitrarily and the minimum length of stay requirements in any given canton differs greatly (from two to twelve years).

29. For the arguments in the German debate, see *e.g.* Munz and Ochel (2001, p. 109 onwards). For Switzerland, see Bundesamt für Ausländerfragen (2000, p. 11).

The most pronounced differences regard the countries' approaches to the temporary immigration of non-EEA nationals, as proposed in their respective new immigration laws. In Switzerland, temporary immigration will be limited to skilled foreigners and their permanent settlement will generally be prevented. The German draft legislation remains somewhat more flexible with both issues. Both countries relied heavily on bilateral agreements for labour recruitment in the 1950s and 1960s. Today, Germany still utilises these agreements, whereas Switzerland's bilateral agreements play a negligible role. In both countries, bilateral agreements have served political objectives, such as strengthening the ties between the countries involved. In interviews conducted for the preparation of this study, the Swiss partners almost unanimously rejected the idea of (re-)introducing bilateral schemes. Overall, the Swiss authorities, companies and social partners are satisfied with the present system and see no need to introduce new recruitment schemes, as this might jeopardise the current consensus on migration policy. In addition, the discussion on the three circles model showed a resistance to the introduction of schemes that favour some non-EEA countries to the detriment of others. Finally, Swiss employers fear that bilateral agreements might lead to more rather than less obstacles to migration. The consensus on bilateral agreements for Switzerland appears to be that the potential risks greatly outweigh the possible benefits. Nevertheless, it should be noted that bilateral approaches could also have important advantages. *Inter alia*, they allow for tailor-made migration policies that are adapted to both the needs of the host and source countries. Signatory countries do not compete for migrants in high demand, as migration is perceived as a process from which both sides may benefit. Furthermore, the involvement of government agencies might lower transaction costs for both sides by overcoming information asymmetries, assisting in job searches and possibly even lowering transportation and settlement costs.

Government involvement using bilateral agreements could also play a role in countering possible wage discrimination against foreigners, although its existence is difficult to prove and often disputed. De Coulon *et al.* (2003) analysed wage differentials between Swiss citizens and foreign nationals. After controlling for socio-demographic characteristics, they found evidence of a strong correlation between a foreigner's legal status and the size of the wage gap, in that the more unstable the legal status, the larger the gap. Notably, education abroad seemed to provide much lower returns than the Swiss equivalent. Bilateral recruitment agreements might be able to lower this gap, for example by setting means of acknowledging education equivalencies, especially if the wage gap is due to information asymmetries. Likewise, bilateral agreements could promote integration and public acceptance.

On the other hand, by channelling migration into country-specific frameworks, migration flows related to bilateral agreements tend to be subjected to political considerations rather than to market forces. This hampers transparency and possibly structural adjustment. Furthermore, as the German agreements with the CEECs have shown, the allocation of quotas is often arbitrary and is prone to unexpected changes. This could lead, in turn, to discrimination.

Future challenges

Perhaps the greatest challenge for labour recruitment in the future is related to skill shortages. Since the 1990s, shortages of skilled workers, particularly in the ICT sector, are seen as obstacles to growth and immigration is considered as one way to meet these needs (see for example European Employment Observatory, 2001). Although shortages in the ICT sector have considerably declined in the past two years, skill shortages are likely to reappear, reinforced by growing demographic and fiscal pressures as well as by skills-biased structural changes (which demand a relatively highly-skilled workforce). The resulting labour demand is particularly pronounced in developed countries, which specialise in industries with an intensive use of skills. Since both Germany and Switzerland have comparative advantages in the production of very skill-intensive goods and services, they should be concerned about an emerging competition for highly-skilled immigrants. Furthermore, with ongoing international integration, the ease of entry for foreign professionals is increasingly becoming a decisive location factor for firms.

Many OECD countries have already opened their labour markets to highly-skilled migrants and several have even taken active measures to attract them. For example, in the Netherlands, highly-skilled foreigners benefit from a 30% income tax discount for ten years[30] and, in the United States, highly-skilled immigrants are exempt from income tax for the first three years (OECD, 2001). Likewise, in several OECD countries, tax incentives for stock options have been introduced, which were partly motivated by the aim of attracting internationally mobile labour (Liebig, 2001). In contrast, several features of the Swiss and German tax and benefit systems discriminate against immigrants. In Switzerland, holders of an annual permit are generally taxed at source, which leads to a higher tax burden vis-à-vis domestic labour. In Germany, temporary immigrants have to pay social security contributions, but often cannot benefit from the system in the same way as Germans, (e.g. as is the case with unemployment benefits). To a lesser degree, the inequity even applies to highly-skilled immigrants. In principle, unemployed holders of a German Green Card, for example, are entitled to unemployment benefits, but local practices may treat them less favourably than Germans in a comparable situation. Tax and social security provisions that tend to discriminate against immigrants result from the traditional view, which believes in an unlimited supply of immigrants. This view is also pronounced in the legal framework. The new law on immigration to Germany still focuses largely on the selection of appropriate migrants and the same holds true for Switzerland. However, it is not the selection of immigrants that is likely to be the key challenge of foreign labour recruitment in the 21st century, but attracting highly-skilled migrants to work, for example, in Germany rather than in another OECD country.

At the same time, there is growing concern about brain drain from the sending countries. Although the notion of brain drain is heavily disputed in migration literature,[31] adverse effects on sending countries cannot be ruled out. Bilateral agreements might help to alleviate these effects, as they can take into account the respective interests of both sending and receiving countries. Even in the new systems, Germany and Switzerland still adhere to the shortages principle, that is, immigration is viewed as a means of tackling (temporary) shortages in certain sectors. This approach is much more apparent in Switzerland. Other countries, however, have recently abolished this principle, given its doubtful economic impact. Canada for example, since 2002 no longer gives preference to people with skills that are temporarily in high demand. Instead, immigrants are chosen based on their human capital (i.e. their general skills) and their prospects for a lasting integration into both society and the labour market irrespective of specific sectors or

---

30.   See Mahroum (2001), who also provides other examples.

31.   See for example the overview in Regets (2001).

occupations. The Swiss approach of allowing temporary non-EEA immigration on the basis that the foreigner is skilled can be interpreted as the middle ground in this regard.

Another challenge arises from the imminent EU integration, which seems to deter immigration from other important OECD countries like the United States and Canada. Germany has reacted to this challenge by giving preferential treatment to nationals from these countries. Switzerland officially abandoned this practice with the introduction of the dual recruitment system, but some cantons still give preference to these OECD countries over other non-EU countries. However, the discretion of the cantons in this regard is fairly limited and the preference appears mainly as a result of more knowledge about the educational standard in OECD countries (*i.e.* lower information asymmetries). A final important challenge is related to emigration and secondary migration flows. This area is not the subject of much research, despite the fact that it is generally acknowledged to be a major problem. Particularly noteworthy is the fact that Germany has had negative migration surpluses with the European Union, the United States and Switzerland in recent years. German emigrants to countries like Switzerland tend to be relatively skilled and this might point to a growing brain drain from Germany. Until recently, this problem has been largely neglected in the migration debate.

Emigration and secondary migration are also important from another perspective. It is sometimes implicitly assumed that it is advisable to limit the inflows of foreigners at a certain level, vaguely defined as the integration capacity. In Switzerland, this notion is apparent in the quota system and in the Ordinance on the Restriction of the Number of Foreigners. The current debate in Germany often assumes that a net inflow of around 300 000 foreigners would be an implicit upper limit.[32] However, neither net nor gross immigration figures alone are appropriate measures in the highly questionable debate on what constitutes capacity. All things being equal, the gross inflow of 800 000 foreigners will have a fundamentally different effect whether in a country of high or low (or even nil) emigration. The gross inflow of foreigners into Germany during the second half of the 1990s was estimated at between 600 000 and 800 000. Emigration, however, was only slightly lower in 1997 and 1998, while net flows were negative. Yet, focusing solely on net figures is also questionable, given that gross migration flows affect integration-related needs. In principle, Germany needs to assimilate more than 600 000 new foreigners per year, even though many are likely to leave the country in subsequent years. It is important to take into consideration the interaction between net and gross immigration figures to measure integration needs.

Summary and conclusions

Despite the fact that Switzerland and Germany at the outset have extremely different backgrounds, the current reforms in these countries share many common features. Immigration is increasingly being viewed as inevitable to ensure future growth and the stability of social security systems. For this reason, permanent immigration is not only facilitated for skilled and highly-skilled foreigners, but also is increasingly tailored to them. Nonetheless, tax and social security provisions in Switzerland and Germany remain relatively unfavourable to foreigners (compared to nationals) unlike in other OECD countries. This could become a decisive disadvantage for Switzerland or Germany if competition for skilled migrants emerges in the future. Although Switzerland currently

---

32.   See for example the scenarios in Börsch-Supan (2002).

appears quite attractive to highly-skilled migrants, it cannot be taken for granted that this will hold true in the future. Other countries are increasingly offering better opportunities and more liberal immigration frameworks, as indicated by the steady increase in the mobility of highly-skilled workers.

Non-discrimination between foreigners and nationals should not be limited to fiscal aspects. A new perspective on integration is needed as well. For example, the relaxation of relatively strict citizenship laws not only fosters integration, but also promotes stronger links with the host country, often at the expense of links with the source countries.[33] This position might also be in the strategic interest of the host country, if the expected competition for skilled migrants materialises. On the other hand, future cohorts of highly-skilled migrants might have less of a need for integration than past migrant cohorts.[34] Improved integration would be in the vital interest of host countries, as it leads to the development of human capital specific to the host country. Policy makers should realise that increased integration also presents a better national picture to foreigners, prevents secondary migration of desired migrants and helps lower psychological costs related to high immigration as perceived by nationals. Both Switzerland and Germany are undergoing increased efforts to promote integration.

Less skilled immigration is generally considered of a temporary nature in both countries. The movement from temporary (for the less skilled) to permanent immigration might soon become nearly impossible in Switzerland. In Germany, the break in recruitment of low-skilled labour, in principle, will continue to exist after the new law is voted. Instead of focusing on preventing the settlement of temporary immigrants as in Switzerland, an alternative would be to provide temporary migrants with an opportunity for permanent settlement. The system would value the preceding (partial) integration of these migrants into the labour market and host society while avoiding any automatic change of status. However, past experiences concerning the transfer from a low-skilled seasonal permit to a permanent permit were particularly discouraging for Switzerland.

Despite the reliance on bilateral recruitment in both countries until the 1970s, and to a considerable degree today in Germany, there seems to be a clear trend away from the geographical selection (bilateral recruitment) to qualification-based recruitment (see also Fibbi, 2003). This trend is likely to continue, as the EU enlargement process consists of many countries presently included in Germany's bilateral framework. Given the ongoing technological and structural changes which demand a relatively highly-skilled workforce, a system like the Swiss one (*i.e.* not distinguishing among different countries of origin) is more neutral. Yet, important lessons can also be drawn from the German experience. It would be premature to conclude from some of the problems associated with the contract worker scheme that bilateral agreements are generally flawed. The negative effects of the contract worker scheme are not due to failures or abuses in the administration of the source countries, but instead are mainly associated with its hybrid legal character and sectoral focus. In fact, bilateral agreements might be an example of how future highly-skilled migration could develop to benefit all involved parties, in the wake of emerging competition for highly-skilled labour. Bilateral approaches are based on the insight that migration can be beneficial for both sending and receiving countries. They are thus

---

33.   This is particularly pronounced in Germany, as dual citizenship is generally avoided.

34.   For example, Fibbi (2003, p. 579) raises the question whether traditional migration concepts like integration and assimilation are still adequate for highly-skilled migrants.

intrinsically concerned with brain exchange, not with the traditional brain drain *versus* brain gain dichotomy. What is needed is a market-neutral, brain exchange approach to recruitment that takes into account increasing competition for highly-skilled migrants, growing migration pressure from less skilled migrants and fears of massive brain drain from sending countries. Although bilateral approaches are not a panacea, they should not be dismissed from the outset.

BIBLIOGRAPHY

Ausländerbeauftragte (2001), *Migrationsbericht der Ausländerbeauftragten*, Beauftragte der Bundesregierung für Ausländerfragen, Berlin and Bonn.

Börsch-Supan, A. (2002), *Labour Market Effects of Population Ageing,* Mannheim Institute for the Economics of Ageing Discussion Paper, No. 11-2002, Mannheim.

Bundesamt für Ausländerfragen (2000), *Schlussbericht der Arbeitsgruppe Bürgerrecht,* Office fédéral des étrangers, Berne

Bundesministerium für Arbeit und Sozialordnung (2002), *Monitoring des IT-Sofortprogramms*, Berlin.

Bundesrat (1999), *Botschaft zur Genehmigung der sektoriellen Abkommen zwischen der Schweiz und der EG.,* Schweizerischer Bundesrat, Bern.

Bundesrat (2002), *Botschaft zum Bundesgesetz für Ausländerinnen und Ausländer,* Schweizerischer Bundesrat, Bern.

Davy, U. (2003), "Das neue Zuwanderungsrecht: Vom Ausländergesetz zum Aufenthaltsgesetz", *Zeitschrift für Ausländerrecht und Ausländerpolitik*, No. 5/6, pp. 171-177.

De Coulon, C. and M. Florez (2002), *Rapport SOPEMI pour la suisse,* Federal Aliens Office, Bern.

De Coulon, D., J.-M. Falter, Y. Flückiger and J. Ramirez, (2003), "Analyse der Lohnunterschiede zwischen der schweizerischen und der ausländischen Bevölkerung", in H.-R. Wicker, R. Fibbi, and W. Haug (eds.), *Migration und die Schweiz*, Seismo, Zurich, pp. 275-301.

De Wild, D. (1999), *Entstehung der ausländischen Erwerbsbevölkerung in der Schweiz: Eine Markow-Betrachtung. Forschungsstelle für Arbeitsmarkt- und Industrieökonomik*, Basel.

Deutscher Bundestag (1996), *Achter Bericht der Bundesregierung über Erfahrungen bei der Anwendung des Arbeitnehmerüberlassungsgesetzes - AÜG - sowie über die Auswirkungen des Gesetzes zur Bekämpfung der illegalen Beschäftigung,* BillBG, Bonn and Berlin.

Eidgenössische Kommission gegen Rassismus (1996), *Stelllungnahme der Eidg,* Kommission gegen Rassismus zum Drei-Kreise-Modell des Bundesrats über die schweizerische Ausländerpolitik, Bern.

European Employment Observatory (2001), *Labour Shortages and Skills Gaps*, European Employment Observatory, Birmingham.

Feldgen, D. (2003), "Zugang zum Arbeitsmarkt nach dem Zuwanderungsgesetz", *Zeitschrift für Ausländerrecht und Ausländerpolitik*, No. 4, pp. 132-139.

Fibbi, R. (2003), "Nachwort", in H.-R. Wicker, R. Fibbi and W. Haug (eds.), *Migration und die Schweiz*, Seismo, Zurich, pp. 577-587.

Fröhlich, B. (2002), *SOPEMI-Bericht 2002 über internationale Wanderungen*, Federal Ministry of Economics and Labour, Berlin.

Fuchs, F. (2000), "Rekrutierung von IT-Fachkräften. Bitte komm zu mir!", *NetworkWorld*, Vol. 23.

Guingi, M. and F. Passy (2003), "Staatsbürgerschaftsmodelle und Mobilisierung der Immigranten in der Schweiz und in Frankreich im Hinblick auf politische Gelegenheitsstrukturen", in H.-R. Wicker, R. Fibbi and W. Haug (eds.), *Migration und die Schweiz*, Seismo, Zurich, pp. 109-138.

Haug, W. (1995), *Vom Einwanderungsland zur multikulturellen Gesellschaft. Grundlagen für eine schweizerische Migrationspolitik*, Swiss Federal Statistical Office, Bern.

Independent Commission on Migration to Germany (2001), *Structuring Immigration – Fostering Integration*, Independent Commission on Migration to Germany, Berlin.

IZA (2001), "Die Nachfrage nach internationalen hochqualifizierten Beschäftigten", *Ergebnisse des IZA International Employer Surveys 2000*, IZA, Bonn.

Koopmans, R. and H. Kriesi (1997), *Citizenship, National Identity and the Mobilisation of the Extreme Right: A Comparison of France, Germany, the Netherlands and Switzerland*, Wissenschaftszentrum Berlin für Sozialforschung, Berlin.

Körner, H. (1990), *Internationale Mobilität der Arbeit: Eine empirische und theoretische Analyse der internationalen Wirtschaftsmigration im 19. und 20. Jahrhundert*, Wissenschaftliche Buchgesellschaft, Darmstadt.

Kuster, J. and G. Cavelti, (1999), *Rekrutierung ausländischer Arbeitskräfte*, Seco Publikation Arbeitsmarktpolitik, No. 2, Staatssekretariat für Wirtschaft, Bern.

Liebig, T. (2001), *Is There a "Tax Penalty" on Stock Options in Germany?*, Discussion Paper, No. 73, Research Institute for Labour Economics and Labour Law, St. Gallen.

Liebig, T. (2002), *Switzerland's Immigration Experiences: Lessons for Germany?*, Discussion Paper, No. 75, Research Institute for Labour Economics and Labour Law, St. Gallen.

Magvas, E. and E. Spitznagel (2000), "Arbeitskräftemangel – Bremse für Wachstum und Beschäftigung?", *IAB Kurzbericht*, No. 10, 14 July, Institute for Employment Research of Federal Employment Services, Nuremberg.

Mahnig, H. and E. Piguet, E. (2003), "Die Immigrationspolitik der Schweiz von 1948 bis 1998", in H.-R. Wicker, R. Fibbi and W. Haug (eds.), *Migration und die Schweiz*, Seismo, Zurich, pp. 65-108.

Mahroum, S. (2001), "Europe and the Immigration of Highly-skilled Labour," *International Migration*, No. 39 (5), pp. 27-43.

Munz, S. and W. Ochel. (2001), *Fachkräftebedarf bei hoher Arbeitslosigkeit. Studie im Auftrag des Bundesministeriums des Inneren*, Ifo Institute, Munich.

Niederberger, J. (2001), "Von der "Wiederentfernung" zur Integration: Kommentar zum Entwurf eines neuen Ausländergesetzes", *Schweizerische Zeitschrift für Politikwissenschaft*, No. 7(1), pp. 112-118.

OECD (2001), *Employment Outlook*, OECD, Paris.

Piguet, E. and A. Wimmer (2000), "Les nouveaux 'Gastarbeiter'? Les réfugiés sur le marché du travail Suisse", *Journal of International Migration and Integration*, No. 1 (2), pp. 233-257.

Regets, M. (2001), *Research and Policy Issues in Highly-skilled International Migration: A Perspective with Data from the United States*, IZA Discussion Paper, No. 366, Bonn.

Reim, U. and S. Sandbrink (1996), *Die Werkvertragsabkommen als Entsenderegelung für Arbeitnehmer aus den Staaten Mittel- und Osteuropas,* ZeS Working Paper, No. 12/96, Zentrum für Sozialpolitik, Bremen.

Renner, G. (1995), "Aufenthaltsrechtliche Grundlagen für Arbeitserlaubnis und Sozialleistungen", *Zeitschrift für Ausländerrecht und Ausländerpolitik*, Vol. 1, pp. 13-22.

Schwarz, H. (1988), *Volkswirtschaftliche Wirkungen der Ausländerbeschäftigung in der Schweiz*, Rüegger, Chur.

Sheldon, G. (2001), "Foreign Labour Employment in Switzerland: Less Is Not More", *Schweizerische Zeitschrift für Politikwissenschaft*, No. 7 (1), pp. 104-112.

Sieveking, K., U. Reim, and S. Sandbrink (1998), "Werkvertragsarbeitnehmer aus osteuropäischen Ländern – politische Konzepte und arbeitsmarktpolitische Probleme", *Recht in Ost und West*, No. 42 (5), pp. 157-166.

Straubhaar, T. (1999), "Integration und Arbeitsmarkt: Auswirkungen einer Annäherung der Schweiz an die Europäische Union", *BWA Schriftenreihe Beiträge zur Wirtschaftspolitik*, Nr. 3, Bundesamt für Wirtschaft und Arbeit, Bern.

Werner, H. (2001a), *From Guests to Permanent Stayers? From the German "Guestworker" Programmes of the Sixties to the Current "Green Card" Initiative for IT Specialists*, IAB Labour Market Research Topics, No. 43, Federal Employment Services, Nuremberg.

Werner, H. (2001b), "The Current 'Green Card' Initiative for Foreign IT Specialists in Germany", *International Mobility of the Highly Skilled,* OECD, Paris, pp. 321-326.

Wicker, H.-R. (2003), "Einleitung: Migration, Migrationspolitik und Migrationsforschung", in H.-R. Wicker, R. Fibbi and W. Haug (eds.), *Migration und die Schweiz,* Seismo, Zurich, pp. 12-62.

Wimmer, A. (2001), "Ein helvetischer Kompromiss: Kommentar zum Entwurf eines neuen Ausländergesetzes", *Schweizerische Zeitschrift für Politikwissenschaft*, Vol. 7(1), pp. 97-104.

Zentralstelle für Arbeitsmarktvermittlung (2003), *Arbeitsmarkt-Information für qualifizierte Fach- und Führungskräfte – Informatikerinnen und Informatiker*, Zentralstelle für Arbeitsvermittlung der Bundesanstalt für Arbeit, Bonn.

Zimmermann, K. *et al.* (2001), *Fachkräftebedarf bei hoher Arbeitslosigkeit*, Report for the Independent Commission on Migration to Germany, IZA, Bonn.

Table 10.1. **Bilateral contract worker agreements signed by Germany**

Country	Duration of employment	Sectors	Annual quota 2002	Total	Quota take-up rate
Hungary	Up to 2-3 years (managers 4)	Mainly construction	7 060	12 432 (1992) 14 449 (1993) 8 890 (1994) 9 165 (1995) 8 993 (1996) 5 813 (1997) 5 036 (1998)	89% (1992) 106% (1993) 67% (1994) 71% (1995) 129% (1996) 87% (1997) 96% (1998)
Poland	Up to 2-3 years (managers 4)	Construction, installation, restoration and other (*e.g.* power industry, iron and steel processing)	22 950	24 423 (1996) 21 104 (1997) 16 942 (1998) 18 243 (1999) 18 537 (2000) 21 905 (2001) 21 193 (2002)	84.6% (1999) 91.8% (2000) 95.4% (2001)
Slovak Republic	Up to 2-3 years (managers 4)	Construction	1 400	1 250 (1996) 1 206 (1997) 943 (1998) 1 348 (1999) 1 545 (2000) 1 268(2002)	Almost fully utilised
Czech Republic	Up to 2-3 years (managers 4)	Agriculture, forestry, viniculture, entertain-ment and hotel trade, juke joints and construction.	4 000	1 947 (1996) 1 439 (1997) 1 060 (1998) 1 366 (1999) 1 445 (2000) 3 010 (2002)	50%-70% (average)
Bulgaria	Up to 2-3 years	Construction	2 500	989 (1996) 1 229 (1997) 688 (1998) 1 402 (1999) 1 724 (2000) 1 710 (2002)	80% (average)
Bosnia-Herzegovina	Up to 2 years, extension to 3 years (managers 4)	Construction	n.d.	682 (1996) 511 (1997) 687 (1998) 966 (1999) 884 (2000) 1 860 (2002)	n.d.
Former Yugoslavia	Up to 2 years, extension to 3 years (managers 4)	Mainly construction	n.d.	Not implemented before 2001 2 650 (2002)	n.d.

Table 10.1. **Bilateral contract worker agreements signed by Germany** *(cont.)*

Latvia	Up to 2 years, extension to 3 years (managers 4)	Mainly construction	n.d.	179 (1996) 274 (1997) 167 (1998) 178 (1999) 195 (2000) 410 (2002)	n.d.
Croatia	Up to 2 years, extension to 3 years (managers 4)	Mainly construction	n.d.	4 375 (1996) 3 604 (1997) 2 780 (1998) 3876 (1999) 5 136 (2000) 5 140 (2002)	n.d.
Former Yugoslavian Republic of Macedonia	Up to 2 years, extension to 3 years (managers 4)	Mainly construction	n.d.	194 (1996) 112 (1997) 185 (1998) 253 (1999) 335 (2000) 530 (2002)	n.d.
Romania	Up to 2 years, extension to 3 years (managers 4)	Mainly construction	n.d.	15 (1996) 966 (1997) 2 631 (1998) 3 901 (1999) 5 239 (2000) 4 270 (2002)	n.d.
Slovenia	Up to 2 years, extension to 3 years (managers 4)	Mainly construction	n.d.	974 (1996) 680 (1997) 660 (1998) 657 (1999) 536 (2000) 1 210 (2002)	n.d.
Turkey	Up to 2 years, extension to 3 years (managers 4)	Mainly construction	n.d.	1 591 (1996) 1 429 (1997) 1 103 (1998) 1 267 (1999) 1 296 (2000) 5 920 (2002)	n.d.

n.d.: Not defined.

Table 10.2. **Bilateral agreements and immigration into Germany, 2001**

Country	Contract workers		Guest employees		Seasonal workers[2]	Total bilateral only	Total permanent
	Quota[1]	Actual	Quota	Actual			Non-German[3]
Albania	..	..	1 000	..	..	..	1 417
Bosnia-Herzegovina	1 860	1 148	..	..	..	1 148	12 817
Bulgaria	1 710	1 861	1 000	776	1 349	3 986	13 295
Croatia	5 140	5 211	..	..	6 157	11 368	13 861
Czech Republic	3 040	1 398	1 400	796	2 913	5 107	11 298
Estonia	..	..	200	7	..	7	914
Hungary	7 060	7 263	2 000	1 124	4 783	13 170	17 421
Latvia	410	217	100	85	..	302	2 145
Lithuania	..	..	200	110	..	110	3 508
FYROM	530	451	..	..	..	451	5 421
Poland	22 950	21 979	1 000	858	243 405	266 242	79 650
Romania	4 270	3 728	500	514	18 015	22 257	20 328
Russian Fed.	..	..	2 000	78	..	78	36 554
Slovak Republic	1 590	1 488	700	964	10 054	12 506	11 424
Slovenia	1 210	716	150	16	264	996	2 605
Turkey	5 920	1 420	..	..	..	1 420	54 587
Former Yugoslavia	2 650	103	..	..	..	103	28 349
Subtotal	58310	46 983	10 250	5 328	286 940	339 251	315 594
Other	..	..	..	..	..	..	369 665
Grand total	58 310	46 983	10 250	5 328	286 940	339 251	685 259

FYROM: Former Yugoslav Republic of Macedonia.

1. Permit procedures do not ensure that the quota is strictly adhered to. It is thus possible that the influx of workers exceeds the respective country quota.
2. There are no quotas for seasonal workers.
3. Permanent immigration presented here excludes immigration in the context of bilateral agreements, but includes non-labour immigration. Furthermore, immigration of ethnic Germans is not included.

Source: Fröhlich (2002), SOPEMI-Bericht 2002 über internationale Wanderungen, Federal Ministry of Economics and Labour, Federal Statistical Office Germany, Berlin; author's calculations.

Table 10.3. **Trainees and labour immigration in Switzerland, 2002**

Country	Annual quota	Stagiaires	Permanent labour immigration [4]	Temporary labour immigration	Total labour immigration	Share of stagiaires (of total labour)
Argentina	50	9	77	78	155	5.81%
Australia	50	14	153	237	390	3.59%
Austria	150	7	1 442	9 509	10 951	0.06%
Belgium	100	1	374	1 385	1 759	0.06%
Bulgaria	100	88	61	983	1 044	8.43%
Canada	200	44	375	579	954	4.61%
Czech Republic	100	80	115	870	985	8.12%
Denmark	150	4	184	702	886	0.45%
Finland	150	4	131	354	485	0.82%
France	500	102	3 047	12 617	15 664	0.65%
Germany	500	210	8 242	34 446	42 688	0.49%
Great Britain	400	4	1 418	3 539	4 957	0.08%
Hungary	100	56	164	791	955	5.86%
Ireland	200	6	111	289	400	1.50%
Italy	50	---[1]	2 724	17 956	20 680	---
Luxembourg	50	2	33	64	97	2.06%
Monaco	20	---	---	---	---	---
Netherlands	150	2	539	1 710	2 249	0.09%
New Zealand	20	7	58	109	167	4.19%
Norway	50	5	79	129	208	2.40%
Philippines	50	---[2]	70	181	251	---
Poland	150	61	139	2 315	2 454	2.49%
Portugal	50	---	4 614	38 753	43 367	0.00%
Rumania	150	148	84	1 883	1 967	7.52%
Russia	200	11	195	1 360	1 555	0.71%
Slovakia	100	113[3]	72	1 487	1 559	7.25%
Spain	50	3	687	3 205	3 892	0.08%
South Africa	50	3	78	71	149	2.01%
Sweden	100	8	327	744	1 071	0.75%
United States	200	23	830	1 048	1 878	1.22%
Subtotal	4 190	1 015	24 981	126 500	163 817	0.62%
Other	---	---	6 978	9 519	16 497	---
Grand total	4 190	1 015	31 959	146 913	180 296	---

1. Agreement currently not in operation.
2. Agreement implemented in 2003.
3. As long as the total quota is not filled, permits for trainees may be granted even if the country's quota for trainees is exceeded.
4. To facilitate comparison, and in contrast to official statistics, all immigrants with a short-term permit (including those with a duration of more than 12 months) were included in temporary labour immigration. Note that if trainees obtain a short-term permit, *i.e.,* they are included in temporary labour immigration as depicted above.

Source: Swiss Federal Office of Immigration, Integration and Emigration; author's calculations.

Table 10.4. **Comparative statistics, 2002**

	Switzerland	Germany
Average unemployment rate	3% (entire population) 6% (foreigners)	9% (entire population) 18% (foreigners)
Share of foreigners in the population	21%	9%
Gross labour market participation rate[1]	60% (foreigners) 56% (entire population)	40% (foreigners) 41% (entire population)
Sectors with the highest share of foreigners[2]	Metal processing (55%); hotel and catering (46%); electrical machines (45%); chemical industry (39%); construction (36%)	Hotel and catering (22%); metal processing (14%); automotive (14%)
Relative share of largest country groups among foreign population	Former Yugoslavia (24%); Italy (21%); Portugal (10%); Germany (9%); Spain (6%); Turkey (5%)	Turkey (26%); Former Yugoslavia (15%); Italy (8%); Greece (5%); Poland (4%)
Relative share of nationals from EU Member state as proportion of total foreign population	56%	25%

1. Data is from 2001.
2. Figures are not directly comparable as they are based on different measurements. For Switzerland, relative shares are calculated based on two different data sources and could therefore be biased on the high side.

Source: Federal Statistical Office Germany; Federal Employment Service Germany; Swiss Federal Office for Immigration, Integration and Emigration; Swiss Federal Statistical Office; Swiss Central Foreigner Registry; de Coulon and Florez (2002), "Rapport SOPEMI pour la Suisse", Federal Aliens Office, Bern; author's calculations.

Chart 10.1. **Proposals for a new immigration system in Germany**

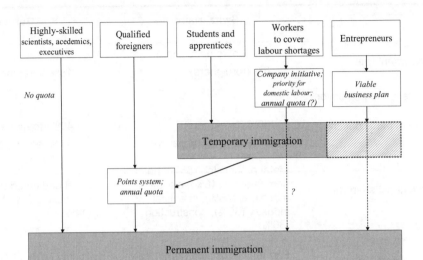

Chapter 11

FIGHTING FOR THE RIGHTS OF MIGRANT WORKERS: THE CASE OF THE PHILIPPINES

by

Stella P. Go

De La Salle University, Philippine Migration Research Network

Introduction

Over the last 30 years, the welfare and human rights issues confronting the overseas employment programme of the Philippines have increasingly put pressure on government to take concrete steps to ensure that overseas Filipino workers are adequately protected in their countries of destination. One of the ways in which the Philippines has tried to overcome the disadvantages experienced by Filipino workers abroad and to promote their well-being is by entering into bilateral, regional and multilateral arrangements. The government has taken the lead in various international forums to promote migrants' rights. In the Asia-Pacific Economic Cooperation Forum (APEC), the Philippines has spearheaded the move to have members of this group of nations establish migrant protection standards.

The issue of the welfare and protection of its workers abroad looms large in bilateral relations with other countries, particularly in Asia and the Middle East where an estimated 80% of all its overseas workers are deployed. The Migrant Workers and Overseas Filipinos Act of 1995 mandates that the "State shall deploy overseas Filipino workers only in countries where the rights of Filipino migrant workers are protected". The government recognises the existence of any of the following measures as a guarantee on the part of the receiving country that overseas Filipino workers will be protected and that their rights are upheld:

- Existing labour and social laws protecting the rights of migrant workers.

- Signatory to multilateral conventions, declarations or resolutions relating to the protection of migrant workers.

- Concluded a bilateral agreement or arrangement with the government protecting the rights of overseas Filipino workers.

- Taking positive, concrete measures to protect the rights of migrant workers.

However, negotiating formal bilateral labour agreements, including memoranda of understanding (MOU), memoranda of agreement (MOA), maritime agreements and social security agreements (SSA) for the protection and welfare of Filipino workers, has been an extremely tedious and difficult undertaking. Among the most common arguments raised by many receiving countries for their reluctance, if not outright refusal, to enter into any formal agreement with the Philippines is that overseas Filipino workers are subject to the same laws and regulations as nationals; consequently, they do not need any special attention. Labour receiving countries have also argued that since the terms of employment are negotiated by the overseas Filipino workers and private employers or agencies, they do not want to get involved. Moreover, they are concerned that entering into a formal agreement with the Philippines would open the floodgates to proposals for similar agreements from other sending countries, which they are reluctant to entertain. As a result, all that the Philippines obtained from most host countries are informal assurances that Filipino workers will be treated fairly and given the utmost protection. While this remains the case, the Philippines will continue its efforts to forge bilateral agreements with other countries. The number of bilateral labour, social security and maritime agreements into which the Philippines has successfully entered into over the last 30 years attests to the difficulty of such an undertaking.

Bilateral labour agreements

Today, overseas Filipino workers can be found in about 180 countries in the world. Since the overseas employment programme began in 1974, however, the Philippines has successfully forged bilateral labour agreements with only 12 countries: 11 labour receiving countries and one labour sending country (Table 11.1). It is significant to note however, that the Philippines has not been able to enter into such agreements with the largest labour-receiving countries of overseas Filipino workers, particularly Saudi Arabia and Japan.

The bilateral labour agreements between the Philippines and other countries may be classified into two broad categories: i) the labour recruitment and special hiring agreements, and ii) the labour, employment and manpower development agreements. The labour recruitment agreements focus on the terms and conditions of the employment and recruitment of Filipino workers or the exchange of trainees. Bilateral agreements with Norway, the United Kingdom, Papua New Guinea, Chinese Taipei and Switzerland are largely recruitment agreements. Specific terms and conditions are outlined in the agreements with Norway and the United Kingdom (regulating the recruitment of Filipino health professionals), Sweden (for the exchange of Filipino professional and technical trainees) and Papua New Guinea (employment of Filipino workers under a non-citizen employment contract). The memorandum of understanding between the Philippines and Chinese Taipei implements a special hiring simplicity that allows employers in Chinese Taipei to hire Filipino workers directly without the intervention of manpower agencies. The agreement also includes the commitment of both parties to advance the interests of the employers as well as of the Filipino workers.

On the other hand, the labour, employment and manpower agreements with Libya, Jordan, Qatar, Iraq, Kuwait and the Commonwealth of Northern Marianas Islands (CNMI) contain the following essential features:

- The promotion and strengthening of areas of co-operation in the field of labour, employment and manpower development.

- The exchange of information on relevant research, technical expertise and other matters that would enhance employment promotion and labour administration in both the Philippines and the labour receiving country.

- The enhancement of the welfare and protection of the rights of Filipino workers in accordance with the labour laws in the receiving country.

- The establishment of a joint committee composed of members from the Philippines and the receiving country to carry out a periodic review of the agreement and its implementation.

Since 1974, most of the efforts of the Philippine government have been directed towards pursuing bilateral labour agreements with labour receiving countries. A significant development in 2003 was the signing of a bilateral labour agreement between the Philippines and Indonesia, another labour sending country. This agreement is significant because it is the first successful attempt by the Philippines to try to co-ordinate the efforts of other labour sending countries in the region towards promoting the welfare of migrant workers and protecting their rights. The agreement identifies the following priorities for joint initiatives and co-operation:

- Promotion and protection of the welfare and rights of migrant workers of both countries.

- Training and certification of migrant workers.

- Provision of legal aid for the protection of the rights of migrant workers.

The agreement includes various forms of co-operation such as the exchange of information, materials, experience, experts and staff. Also included are the development of collaborative training, joint research and development, joint efforts to promote and protect the welfare and rights of workers and to provide legal assistance for the protection of the rights of workers. A steering committee composed of senior officials of both countries is to be established which meet at least once a year to review the MOU and co-ordinate the implementation of programmes. Joint working groups will also be established in receiving countries through the respective embassies or labour offices of the Philippines and Indonesia to promote and protect the welfare and rights of their migrant workers. These joint working groups are to meet regularly and to pursue programmes on-site in close co-operation with the steering committee.

The implementation of this agreement between the Philippines and Indonesia will be interesting to monitor since it may serve as a test case for the viability and the effectiveness of collaboration between sending countries, in order to increase the pressure they can jointly bring to bear on receiving countries with a view to protecting the welfare and rights of their migrant workers. However, negotiating bilateral labour agreements with other sending countries in the Asian region is just as difficult as negotiating with labour receiving countries. Since they see the Philippines as a major competitor for the overseas labour market, they are reluctant to enter into any agreement with the Philippines that would, for instance, standardise work contracts of migrant workers, including wages and benefits, for fear that they would lose out in the competition with overseas Filipino workers.

As of March 2003, bilateral labour agreements have been proposed to a number of countries in the following regions: Asia-Pacific (seven countries), the Middle East (five), Europe (four) and Africa (two). However, Saudi Arabia, Israel, Lebanon, Brunei and South Korea have declined to enter into the proposed agreements (Table 11.2). Although Japan has not explicitly declined the proposed labour agreement officially presented to it in 1988, it has not acted on the proposal. This inaction has been construed by many as an implicit refusal. Similarly, there are currently four proposed bilateral labour agreements with Malaysia:

- Memorandum of agreement on the supply of Filipino workers to Malaysia (1987).

- Memorandum of understanding on a Special Hiring Programme for Malaysia (1995).

- Memorandum of understanding and Co-operation Against Trafficking in Women and Children (2000).

- Memorandum of agreement on Filipino Employment in Malaysia (2002).

No agreement has been reached yet on any of the above points, due to disagreements between the Philippine and Malaysian governments on various points in the proposed agreements.

Bilateral social security agreements

In the area of social security, the Philippines has also only been able to forge bilateral agreements with eight countries: Austria, Belgium, Switzerland, Canada and the province of Quebec, France, the United Kingdom, the Netherlands and Spain (Table 11.3). The salient features of the treaties include:

- Mutual assistance between the Philippines and the other country in the field of social security: members who are covered or beneficiaries may file their claims with the designated liaison agencies of the Philippines or the other country, which will provide help to facilitate the processing of claims.

- Equality of treatment: a Filipino covered by social security, including his/her dependants and survivors, shall be eligible for benefits under the same conditions as the nationals of the other country.

- Export of social security benefits: a Filipino shall continue to receive his/her benefits wherever he/she decides to reside (in the Philippines, the contracting country or a third country).

- Summation: quantifying membership periods in both the host country and the Philippines (excluding overlaps) and adding them together to determine eligibility for benefits.

- Pro-rated payment of benefits: both the host country and the Philippines shall pay the share of the benefit due from their respective systems, in proportion to the actual contributions or qualifying periods.

In 2000, the Social Security System of the Philippines reported that 260 Filipino claimants were granted benefits, 192 (74%) of whom were from Canada, following the implementation of the agreements. Through the Social Security System, the Philippines continues to pursue bilateral social security agreements with the host countries of overseas Filipino workers. Currently, there are proposed social security agreements with Cyprus, Denmark, Germany, Greece, Israel, Italy, Libya, the United States and Sweden.

Bilateral maritime agreements

In maritime transport, the Philippines has also been actively negotiating bilateral agreements to protect the interests of the Filipino shipping industry in general and Filipino seafarers in particular. The Philippines is the largest supplier of seafarers in the world. About 200 000 Filipino seafarers work on board international vessels, representing 20% of actively employed seafarers in ocean-going vessels. Japan is the biggest employer of Filipino seafarers accounting for an estimated 25% of the 200 000 Filipino seamen deployed yearly. The Philippine government's efforts at negotiating have resulted in the signing of bilateral maritime transport and merchant shipping agreements with eight countries, namely Iran, Cyprus, Liberia, Bangladesh, Vietnam, Norway, the Netherlands and Brunei (Table 11.4). The most salient feature of these maritime agreements is the promotion of co-operation between the two countries in the field of merchant shipping or maritime transport and related activities through:

- The exchange of information on maritime transport or merchant shipping policies, regulations, training, and legislation.

- The enhancement of maritime training, licensing, and certification to improve the competence of ships' officers and seafarers.

- The promotion and enhancement of seafarers' welfare.

- According both countries in the agreement most favoured nation status under which ocean carriers of one country are given the same rights and privileges extended by the other country to its flag-carriers.

- The establishment of joint commissions to review the implementation of the agreements and to discuss any other shipping or transport matters of mutual interest.

Currently, there are a number of proposed bilateral maritime agreements with other countries such as Chinese Taipei, Germany, France, Romania, Panama, Cuba, India, Italy, Saudi Arabia and Spain (Table 11.5). On the other hand, the Philippines has been more successful in forging bilateral agreements on the recognition of Filipino seafarers' certificates under Regulation 1/10 of the 1978 International Convention on Standards of Training, Certification and Watchkeeping for Seafarers (STCW), which establishes the minimum standards for the training and performance of seafarers deployed in vessels engaged in both overseas and domestic shipping. In 1995, the STCW was amended and specified the implementation of new requirements for the training and education of seafarers, apart from additional responsibilities for ship owners and operators. Regulation 1/10 of the amended STCW requires a bilateral agreement between seafarer sending and seafarer accepting countries for the recognition of seafarers' certificates of competencies. Under the amended STCW, which took effect on 1 February 2002, seafarers could not be hired to work on board ocean-going vessels if their countries of origin were not on the International Maritime Organization (IMO) White List and not covered by bilateral agreements.

The Philippines is on the IMO White List and the government has been fast-tracking its bilateral negotiations with countries employing Filipino seafarers on board their flag-carrying vessels to ensure the continued employment of its seafarers overseas. Since 2000, the Philippines has signed bilateral agreements on the recognition of seafarers certificates with 29 countries (Table 11.6).

Conclusion

In an era of increasing globalisation and trade liberalisation, the one significant exception to free markets today has been the free movement of people. Few bilateral and multilateral agreements exist for international migration and the absence of any protection under the law has led to exploitation and abuse of many migrant workers, Filipinos included. While many receiving countries claim to believe in free markets, including labour markets, they use highly restrictive and bureaucratic regulations to control cross-border labour migration, particularly of unskilled workers. The Philippine government has pursued diplomatic efforts at the bilateral level to promote the welfare of its migrant workers abroad and to protect their rights. Although progress in this area has been slow because of the reluctance of labour receiving countries to enter into formal agreements, the Philippines has been persistent in its efforts and has had some success.

It is worth noting, however, that the bilateral labour and social security agreements that the Philippines has successfully concluded and that those which are still pending are not with any of the countries where the largest numbers of overseas Filipino workers can be found. Saudi Arabia, where the greatest number of overseas Filipino workers are employed, has refused invitations for formal discussions on bilateral labour agreements with the Philippines. A draft labour agreement with Japan, initiated in 1988, has never been pursued despite efforts on the part of the Philippines to push negotiations forward. South Korea has also declined to enter into any bilateral labour agreement. Even more disappointing are the attempts to forge similar agreements with the country's ASEAN partners like Singapore, Malaysia and Brunei. Singapore and Brunei have declared that they are not interested in entering into a formal labour agreement with any country, while bilateral negotiations with Malaysia are bogged down by differences in opinion.

Similarly, the bilateral shipping agreements that the Philippines has entered into do not include Japan, which employs the largest proportion of Filipino seafarers. Bilateral agreements on the recognition of Filipino seafarers' certificates of competencies are the only agreements that have been more successful. These agreements have been less contentious and have been concluded with greater dispatch. Although the constraints upon forging bilateral agreements are numerous and difficult to overcome, it is encouraging to note that the Philippine government is persevering in its efforts at getting the international community to take a more co-operative stance towards international migration. The list of proposed bilateral labour, shipping and social security agreements drafted by the Philippines remains long. It can be expected that negotiations will be tedious and extended; however, the Philippine government remains optimistic.

Since arriving at formal labour agreements with receiving states is difficult, the Philippines has taken a multi-pronged approach in the promotion of the well-being of its overseas workers. It has tried alternative arrangements, such as in the case of Singapore, where the Philippines drafted a proposed memorandum of understanding with private agencies in 1995. The Philippines has also used other international channels to promote the welfare and protection of its workers. These include international bodies and multilateral conventions, declarations and resolutions. It has initiated and supported United Nations (UN) declarations and statements on labour migration. It has signed, adopted and ratified UN documents related to migrant worker protection and welfare (Gonzalez, 1998). It has:

- Ratified the 1990 International Convention on the Protection of the Rights of all Migrant Workers and Members of their Families.

- Initiated Resolution 37/7 on Violence against Women Migrant Workers and successfully lobbied the 38th Session of the UN Commission on the Status of Women to pass it.

- Endorsed the Statement by the Refugee and Migrant Women's Caucus to the UN Fourth World Conference on Women in Beijing in 1995.

Unfortunately, very few countries have recognised and abided by these UN guidelines. Apart from the Philippines, only 21 countries have ratified the UN Convention on the Protection of the Rights of all Migrant Workers and Members of their Families. Moreover, the Philippines and Sri Lanka are the only Asian countries to have done so. Of the ten other countries that are non-ratified signatories to the convention, Bangladesh is the only Asian signatory. Interestingly, all three of these countries are labour sending countries in Asia. Aside from initiating and backing UN declarations and statements on labour migration, the Philippines has also endorsed many International Labour Organization (ILO) conventions and recommendations and has also actively incorporated them into proposed bilateral agreements. These include the following (Gonzalez, 1998):

- Convention 19 on Equality of Treatment for National and Foreign Workers on Accident Compensation.

- Convention 97 on Migration for Employment.

- Convention 143 on Migration in Abusive Conditions and the Promotion of Equality of Opportunity and Treatment of Migrant Workers.

- Conventions 118, 157 and 165 on Social Security for Migrant Workers.

- Recommendation 86 on Migration for Employment.

- Recommendation 100 on the Protection of Migrant Workers in Underdeveloped Countries and Territories.

- Recommendation 151 on Migrant Workers.

- Recommendation 167 on the Maintenance of Social Security Rights.

The task of government however does not end with the signing of bilateral agreements. Since diplomatic discourse can sometimes be broad and ambiguous, formulating clearer and more specific implementing guidelines has become imperative. However, once these agreements have been signed and the implementing guidelines have been drawn up, the biggest challenge facing Philippine government personnel and their counterparts from other countries is monitoring the agreements' implementation and the enforcement of violation sanctions. Since these tasks are not easy, it is important that both countries willingly commit manpower, financial and other institutional resources to back up these agreements. Moreover, governments must also ensure that the implementing agencies have not only adequate resources but also the institutional capabilities to fulfil their tasks effectively.

The Philippine government should also pursue more vigorously its efforts at forging bilateral agreements with other labour sending countries in the Asian region. By doing so, it will be in a better position to promote the welfare of migrant workers in the region and protect their rights by strengthening not only its own bargaining power, but also that of other labour sending countries. Perhaps such a move is a first step towards realising the proposal made by the Department of Labour and Employment (DOLE) at the OECD forum in May 2001 to set up an international co-operation network to regulate migration and promote the welfare of migrant workers, including overseas Filipino workers.

BIBLIOGRAPHY

Gonzalez, Joaquin L. III. (1998), *Philippine Labour Migration*, Institute of Southeast Asian Studies, Singapore.

Maritime Industry Authority (various years), *Accomplishment Reports*.

Table 11.1. **List of countries with signed and existing bilateral labour agreements, March 2003**

Region/Country	Year signed	Title
Asia-Pacific		
Chinese Taipei, China	2001 and 2002	Memorandum of Understanding on the Special Hiring Programme for Chinese Taipei between the Manila Economic and Cultural Office in Taipei and the Taipei Economic and Cultural Office in the Philippines
Indonesia	2003	Memorandum of Understanding between the Department of Labour and Employment of the Republic of the Philippines and the Department of Manpower and Transmigration of the Republic of Indonesia concerning Migrant Workers
Papua New Guinea	1979	Memorandum of Understanding between the Governments of the Philippines and Papua New Guinea
Commonwealth of Northern Marianas Islands	1994, amended 2000	Memorandum of Understanding between the Department of Labour and Employment of the Republic of the Philippines and the Department of Labour and Immigration of the Commonwealth of the Northern Marianas Islands
Middle East		
Qatar	1981	Communiqué between the Ministry of Labour and Employment of the Republic of the Philippines and the Ministry of Labour and Social Affairs of the State of Qatar
	1997	Agreement between the Government of the Republic of the Philippines and the State of Qatar Concerning Filipino Manpower Employment in Qatar
Jordan	1981	Memorandum of Understanding between the Minister of Labour and Employment of the Republic of the Philippines and the Ministry of Labour of the Hashemite Kingdom of Jordan
	1988	Agreement on Manpower between the Government of the Republic of the Philippines and the Government of the Hashemite Kingdom of Jordan
Iraq	1982	Memorandum of Agreement Relating to the Mobilisation of Manpower between the Republic of the Philippines and the Republic of Iraq

Table 11.1. **List of countries with signed and existing bilateral labour agreements, March 2003** *(cont.)*

Kuwait	1997	Memorandum of Understanding on Labour and Manpower Development between the Government of the Republic of the Philippines and the Government of Kuwait
Europe		
United Kingdom	2002	Recruitment Agreement between the Government of the Republic of the Philippines and the Government of the United Kingdom of Great Britain and Northern Ireland
Switzerland	2002	Agreement between the Government of the Republic of the Philippines and the Swiss Federal Council on the Exchange of Professional and Technical Trainees
Norway	2003	Agreement between the Philippine Overseas Employment Administration (POEA) and The Directorate of Labour (Aetat) Norway on Transnational Co-operation for Recruiting Professionals from the Health Sector to Positions in Norway
Africa		
Libya	1979	Agenda for Co-operation in the Fields of Labour Employment and Manpower Development between the Republic of the Philippines and the Socialist People's Libyan Arab Jamahiriya

Source: Marketing Division, Philippine Overseas Employment Administration.

Table 11.2. **List of countries with proposed bilateral labour agreements, as of March 2003**

Region/Country	Year proposed	Title	Status
Asia-Pacific			
Brunei	1987	Memorandum of Agreement on the Mobilisation of Manpower	Declined
Japan	1988	Memorandum of Agreement on the Mobilisation of Manpower	Has not been acted upon by Japan
Lao People's Democratic Republic	2002	(not available)	Initial draft is being prepared
Macau	2000	Republic of the Philippines - Macau Agreement on the Supply of Workers	Draft is still with the Philippines
Malaysia	1987	Memorandum of Agreement on the Supply of Workers	No agreement has yet been Reached on any of the proposals
	1995	Memorandum of Understanding on the Special Hiring Program for Malaysia	due to conflicting views
	2000	Memorandum of Understanding on Cooperation Against Trafficking in Women and Children	
	2002	Filipino Manpower Development in Malaysia	
Palau	1997	Memorandum of Understanding on the Mobilisation and Conditions of Employment of Filipino Workers in Palau	No agreement has yet been reached
South Korea	1996	Memorandum of Understanding on the Technical Transfer Program	Declined
Middle East			
Israel	1999	Memorandum of Understanding on Labour and Manpower Development	Declined
Saudi Arabia	1988	Memorandum of Understanding on Labour	Declined
Oman	1992	Memorandum of Agreement on the Mobilisation of Manpower	No agreement has yet been reached
Lebanon	1997	Bilateral Manpower Agreement	Declined

Table 11.2. **List of countries with proposed bilateral labour agreements, as of March 2003** *(cont.)*

Jordan	2001	(not available)	No agreement has yet been reached
Africa			
Egypt	2001	(not available)	No agreement has yet been reached
Libya	1996	Memorandum of Agreement on Manpower Cooperation and Social Security	No agreement has yet been reached
Europe			
Belgium	1988	Memorandum of Understanding between the Department of Foreign Affairs, the Philippine Overseas Employment Administration and the Bureau of Immigration on the Deployment of Filipino Workers to Belgium	Draft is still with the Philippines
Cyprus	1997	Agreement on Manpower	Draft is still with the Philippines
Greece	1989	Memorandum of Agreement on Labour	Draft is still with the Philippines
Netherlands	2000	(not available)	Draft is still with the Philippines

Source: Marketing Division, Philippine Overseas Employment Administration.

Table 11.3. **Countries with signed and existing bilateral social security agreements, April 2003**

Country	Year signed	Title
Belgium	2001	Convention on Social Security between the Republic of the Philippines and the Kingdom of Belgium
Switzerland	2001	Agreement on Social Security between the Republic of the Philippines and the Swiss Confederation
Netherlands	2001	Agreement between the Republic of the Philippines and the Kingdom of the Netherlands on the Export of Social Insurance Benefits
Canada	1999	Agreement on Social Security between the Republic of the Philippines and Canada
Quebec	2000	Understanding on Social Security between the Republic of the Philippines and Quebec
France	1990	Social Security Convention between the Philippines and France
Spain	1988	Convention on Social Security between the Philippines and Spain
United Kingdom	1985	Convention on Social Security between the United Kingdom of Great Britain and Northern Ireland and the Philippines
Austria	1980, amended 1982 and 2000	Convention between the Republic of the Philippines and the Republic of Austria in the Field of Social Security

Source: Social Security System, Philippines.

Table 11.4. **Signed and existing bilateral agreements on maritime transport and merchant shipping, 25 April 2003**

Country	Year signed	Title
Iran	1975	Agreement between the Government of the Republic of the Philippines and the Government of Iran on Merchant Shipping
Cyprus	1984	Agreement between the Government of the Republic of Cyprus and the Government of the Republic of the Philippines on Merchant Shipping
Liberia	1985	Memorandum of Understanding on the Employment of Seafarers
Bangladesh	1989	Agreement between the Government of the People's Republic of Bangladesh and the Government of the Philippines on Merchant Shipping
Vietnam	1995	The Philippines-Vietnam Merchant Maritime Shipping Agreement
Norway	1999	Republic of the Philippines-Norway Agreement on Maritime Transport
Netherlands	2000	Republic of the Philippines (Department of Transport and Communication) - Netherlands (Ministry of Transport, Public Works and Water Management) Memorandum of Understanding on Maritime Transport
Brunei Darussalam	2002	Republic of the Philippines - Brunei Darussalam Agreement on Maritime Transport

Source: Maritime Industry Authority, Department of Transport and Communications.

Table 11.5. **Proposed bilateral agreements on maritime transport and merchant shipping, 25 April 2003**

Country	Year proposed	Title
Germany	2002	Agreement on Maritime Shipping between the Republic of the Philippines and the Government of the Federal Republic of Germany
France	1999	Agreement on Merchant Shipping between the Republic of the Philippines and the Republic of France
Romania	2001	Agreement on Merchant Shipping between the Republic of the Philippines and the Government of Romania
Panama	1999	Agreement on Merchant Shipping between the Republic of the Philippines and the Government of Panama
Cuba	2002	Agreement on Maritime Transport between the Republic of the Philippines and the Government of Cuba
India	2002	Memorandum of Understanding on Maritime Transport between the Republic of the Philippines and the Republic of India
Italy	2000	Agreement on Maritime Shipping between the Government of the Republic of the Philippines and the Government of Italy
Spain	2003	Agreement on Maritime Shipping between the Government of the Republic of the Philippines and the Government of Spain
Malaysia	2003	Agreement on Merchant Shipping between the Government of the Republic of the Philippines and the Government of Malaysia

Source: Maritime Industry Authority, Department of Transport and Communications.

Table 11.6. **List of countries with signed and existing bilateral agreements on the recognition of seafarers' certificates**

Under regulation 1/10 of the 1978 International Convention on Standards of Training, Certification and Watchkeeping for Seafarers (STCW), as amended in 1995[1] as of 25 April 2003

Country	Date signed
Ireland	25 April 2003
Dominican Republic	25 April 2003
Switzerland	12 March 2003
Kuwait	10 November 2003
Cambodia	2 October 2002
Indonesia	16 September 2002
Panama	3 April 2002
Malaysia	31 July 2002
Luxembourg	28 June 2002
Australia	21 June 2002
Belize	5 June 2002
Liberia	5 June 2002
Italy	26 March 2002
Barbados	22 April 2002
Sweden	29 January 2002
Isle of Man	11 January 2002
Malta	11 January 2002
Antigua and Barbuda	12 December 2001
Norway	19 November 2001
Hong Kong, China	29 October 2001
Marshall Islands	8 October 2001
Vanuato	26 September 2001
Cyprus	13 September 2001
Bahamas	10 September 2001
Singapore	25 August 2001
Brunei	23 August 2001
Denmark	3 August 2001
Netherlands	31 May 2001
Japan	21 January 2000

1.   Regulation 1/10 of the 1978 International Convention on STCW, as amended in 1995, requires a bilateral agreement between seafarer sending and seafarer receiving countries for the recognition of a seafarer's certificate of competencies for his/her continued employment on board international vessels. This took effect on 1 February 2002.

Source: Maritime Industry Authority, Department of Transport and Communications.

Chapter 12

SEASONAL LABOUR MIGRATION IN THE LIGHT OF THE GERMAN-POLISH BILATERAL AGREEMENT

Marek Okólski[1]

Director, Centre of Migration Research,
Faculty of Economics, University of Warsaw

Introduction

Bilateral agreements on the employment of migrant workers are not a novelty in Poland. Since the 1970s Polish workers have left to work in other countries in accordance with official inter-governmental arrangements. By the same token, since 1990 movements in the reverse direction have been possible. The Polish government has long been interested in promoting the employment of Poles in other countries. Until 1989 however from the point of view of Poland, the principal advantage of labour export was the offsetting of trade imbalances by channelling foreign currency earned by migrants back to the home country. The official flows of migrant workers were governed by rules specific to particular projects rather than subject to general, long-term regulation. The majority of the workers exported from Poland consisted either of posted employees of Polish sub-contracting companies or of labour specially recruited to work in their foreign outlets. Although this did not require bilateral agreements, by the very nature of the political system in Poland and of the state itself, this kind of foreign employment was subject to inter-governmental co-ordination.

Nevertheless, Poland concluded a number of bilateral agreements, notably with the former German Democratic Republic (GDR) (1988) and the former Czechoslovakia (1984). Mention might also be made of the only agreement concluded by Poland with a Western country (in 1979), that is, with the Federal Republic of Germany (FRG). The agreement concerned the employment of Polish posted workers mainly hired to assemble and run-in machinery imported by Germany from Poland, or by Poland from Germany. The significance of labour exports within the framework of bilateral agreements has been declining over time. Whereas in 1983 as much as 43% of the stock of Polish workers were officially employed abroad (81 300) in that category, in 1989, the share was only 9% (out of 158 000).

---

1.   In drafting parts of this chapter (from the "Polish Seasonal Workers" section on), the author drew upon a preliminary research report *Polish Workers in the Labour Markets of the European Union at the Turn of the Century* (Institute for Social Studies, Warsaw, 2003) edited by W. Lukowski, especially from chapters by A. Fihel, P. Kaczmarczyk, E. Kepinská and L. Tanajewski.

A new chapter was initiated in 1990 when a host of related documents were signed by representatives of the governments of Germany and Poland: five bilateral agreements pertaining to the employment of contract workers, guest workers, cross-border workers, students and seasonal workers.[2] Between 1990 and 2001, 18 additional agreements were concluded with 15 countries, of which seven are member states of the European Union (EU) and six are Central and Eastern European countries (CEECs). In contrast to the 1980s the main component of labour exports (*i.e.* the flow of regular migrant workers) in the 1990s was the transfer of workers under bilateral agreements. It is estimated that by the year 2000, 85% of Polish residents legally working abroad had found employment through bilateral agreements. The principal aim of government involvement in the export of labour changed as well. It now concerned protecting the rights of Polish workers in foreign countries and at the same time alleviating labour market imbalances in Poland.

Employment under bilateral agreements signed by Poland

In mid-2003 as many as eight bilateral agreements (out of 19 valid agreements) were considered to be inactive, of which six were with the CEECs. That is, all the agreements so far signed by Poland with those countries are non-active. Interestingly, these non-active agreements co-existed with high levels of worker flows through other channels, mainly to informal labour markets. For instance, out of an estimated several hundred thousand citizens of the Ukraine who found employment in Poland in 2001, only 3 158 worked legally, that is more than 90% were illegal workers. Moreover, none of the legally employed persons had been contracted in accordance with the provisions of the bilateral agreement signed by both countries in 1994.

In 2002, the 13 active agreements enabled close to 300 000 Polish workers to be employed in a foreign country. Although this constituted a tiny fraction of Poland's labour force, Polish migrants came to be the predominant temporary workers in the European labour market. It should be noted however that more than 80% worked seasonally on the basis of the German-Polish agreement. A clear majority of the remaining agreements made only a symbolic contribution.[3] If the primary purpose of a bilateral employment agreement was to facilitate the orderly transfer of labour between contracting countries, then it would be legitimate to say that in the case of Poland, only one agreement (*i.e.* concerning seasonal workers and signed with Germany) has been a clear success story. In contrast, many other agreements seem to have failed to attract either large numbers of employees to potential receiving countries, or employers to recruit in potential sending countries.

The bilateral agreement on seasonal employment between Germany and Poland

The bilateral agreement between Germany and Poland on seasonal workers has been by far the most important agreement on migrant workers ever entered into by Poland,

---

2.   In 1996, yet another agreement, regarding the holiday training of Polish workers, was concluded between Germany and Poland.

3.   For instance, although the guest worker programme agreed upon between Germany and Poland in 1990 set a very modest annual quota of 1 000 persons (from Poland), since 1995, that limit has never been reached (*e.g.* 575 in 1998, 776 in 2002). The case of the on-the-job training programme of 1990 with France seems even less successful. The annual number of Polish participants here has varied between 44 and 289 despite the ceiling of 1 000. The impact of agreements concluded with Belgium (1990) and Switzerland (1993) has been even less significant with the annual number of workers benefiting from the agreements never exceeding 100.

even though it is strikingly simple in form. The declaration, expressed in an act signed on 8 December 1990 by the Ministers of Labour of Germany and Poland confirmed the significance of the bilateral agreement concluded earlier that year (concerning guest workers and contract workers). Additionally, it made it possible for Polish citizens to take up employment in Germany as cross-border workers and seasonal workers and to carry out work designed for students. While the employment of guest workers and contract workers, including posted workers and those in project-linked employment, has been subject to separate detailed agreements (and subsequent amendments), the case of seasonal workers has been dealt with only by that single document, and to be more precise, by just two sentences. Section Four of the declaration stipulates that: "As of 1991, Polish citizens are free to take up employment in the Federal Republic of Germany as seasonal workers for a period of up to three months a year,[4] according to the procedure elaborated by the labour organisations of both states. This employment is not designed for specific sectors of economic activity,[5] but it is subject to labour market analysis before its execution".

The procedures in the declaration were almost instantly agreed upon and put into operation. They turned out very to be simple and transparent. In short, German employers take the initiative in offering a seasonal job to a citizen of Poland. Job offers, which can be personally addressed or non-nominative and are subject to the authorisation of a local labour office in Germany. The German labour office then sends the authorised offers to local labour offices in Poland, who either pass job offers to specific workers or in the case of non-nominative offers, undertake to recruit appropriate individuals. A duly authorised job offer almost automatically gives a Polish citizen the right to a special German work permit visa, and consequently opens the way to seasonal employment in Germany. The only administrative cost an employee has to bear is the German visa fee, which in 2002 was EUR25-30,[6] or EUR12.50 for students.

When the Polish government signed the bilateral agreement on seasonal employment in Germany, it was claimed this agreement would be a tool for the government's labour market policy. A document, *Premises of the Programme on Alleviating the Consequences of Unemployment* (Polish Ministry of Labour and Social Policy, April 1991), suggested that bilateral employment agreements have been included in the arsenal of state instruments for combating unemployment. Specifically, it stated that in 1991 "around 50 000 Poles were due to go to Germany for seasonal work and that the contracts were regionally allotted (by the Polish labour authorities) according to the regional level of unemployment". This approach has been refined and reaffirmed in another document by the Polish Ministry of Labour and Social Policy (*Migration and the Internationalisation of the Labour Market*) issued in October 1994. While the document claimed that access to foreign labour markets was generally expected to boost the professional and language skills of Poland's labour force and to increase its familiarity with the operations of a market economy, seasonal employment was seen as a means of alleviating the negative effects of unemployment.

The implementation of the migration programme for seasonal work to Germany was carried out rapidly. In the first year the bilateral agreement became operative (1991) more than 60 000 persons were covered (68 516 authorised job offers arrived from Germany).

---

4.   An exception is employment in the exhibition sector where the upper limit has been fixed at nine months.

5.   After 1993 seasonal employment in the construction industry was excluded from this provision.

6.   Depending on whether it covered a single or multiple journeys.

The following year that number approximately doubled. The bilaterally-established administrative procedures seemed to work efficiently, as the proportion of job offers not taken up by Polish workers quickly diminished and ultimately fell to a fairly negligible level. It was at 12.5% in 1991, 6% to 8% in 1992-1994, 4% to 6% in 1995-1998 and fell below 4% in 1999-2002. Altogether, the period 1991-2002 saw uninterrupted growth in the number of job offers and the number of Poles actually taking up seasonal employment in Germany.[7] The latest available figure is for 2002: 282 830 offers and about 272 000 actual contracts. By and large, Poland has become the main source of foreign labour for German agriculture and over time has been able to strengthen her dominant position.[8]

From the very start of the programme, agricultural farms were the principal employers but initially (1991-1993), their share in the total seasonal employment of Polish migrants declined (from 79.1% to 68.9%),[9] mainly at the expense of firms in the construction industry (a rise from 8.7% to 15.3%). Since 1994 a constant increase in the importance of agricultural employment has been observed, and in 2000 its proportion stabilised at the remarkably high level of 95%. Two other sectors continued to play a role, albeit a smaller one – exhibitions and hotels – each with a relatively stable share (especially since 1998) of the total, around 2%. Over time, the seasonal employment of Polish workers has become more and more sector-homogeneous. For instance, in the early and mid-1990s an important sub-sector of agriculture proved to be viticulture which at its height in 1996, attracted as many as 16.7% of all seasonal workers from Poland. In the late 1990s the number of job offers from that sector however started to decline very markedly, and in 2000-2002, only a handful of Poles (4 to 6 persons a year) found employment in viticulture. Also, ultimately, the share in forestry (2.8% of the total at its height), restaurants (0.5%) and all other sectors (12.4%) has become negligible. All this suggests that after a decade of operations, Polish seasonal workers in Germany have effectively been crowded out of other areas of work and are employed only on farms.

Polish seasonal workers

Two sources may be used to describe the characteristics of the population of migrants who worked seasonally in Germany under the relevant bilateral agreement: a complete register of job offers arriving in Polish labour offices from Germany and special surveys conducted by research institutes. The data used in the following description comes from the current Ministry of Economy, Labour and Social Policy (which in 2001 incorporated the former National Labour Office) and from a study carried out in 2002 and 2003 by the Institute for Social Studies of the University of Warsaw (ISS).[10] Most migrants are males

---

7. The only exception was observed in 1994, when there was a decline in the total number of workers by around 15 000 or 11%, which was entirely due to the exclusion of the construction industry from seasonal employment (a drop from 22 751 in 1993 to 436 in 1994).

8. For instance in 2000 German agriculture employed 26 400 foreign residents of the FRG and 263 800 seasonal foreign workers. The proportion of Poles in the latter figure was 87%.

9. These figures include employment in viticulture and forestry. The proportion of the former in agriculture was around 20% and of the latter around 1.5%.

10. The study included a national survey of persons who from 1998 to 2000 were employed in Germany as seasonal workers and a series of in-depth interviews with selected migrant workers, experts in Germany and Poland, and German entrepreneurs who employed Polish seasonal workers. In the survey, the pool from which the sample of all executed job offers was drawn amounted to 500 000 persons and the size of the sample actually analysed was 804. The study was pursued with financial support from the Polish Government Committee of Scientific Research; certain aspects of the questionnaire were included at the request of the OECD Secretariat.

(two-thirds of the total). Typically, they are in their mid-thirties (the median age was 37). Half of these persons have a job in Poland (41.2% have permanent jobs)[11] and a large majority (77.2%) are married. Over time however the migrant population is ageing: the median age at the time of a migrant's first seasonal job, usually in the first half of the 1990s, was 31, and the proportion of migrants below the age of 25 was considerable (27.2%), much higher than at the time of the study (9.1%). Migrants' skills and educational attainment are rather low: nearly 60% did not complete secondary education and they typically (47.7%) ended up with a three-year vocational school certificate.[12]

By and large, the only aim of seasonal migrants working in Germany is to supplement their household income with additional earnings. Almost all of the migrant's money is distributed between current consumption (including the purchase of durables) and the repayment of debts. Few migrants (around 15%) are able to make future-oriented expenditures (supplementing the purchase of an apartment, paying tuition in educational institutions, savings and investing in financial assets, investing in an enterprise). On the other hand, only a minority of migrants were found to be living below the poverty line. For a large part of the population of migrants who participated recently in the seasonal employment programme (1999-2001) the work in Germany seems to be a fairly stable source of income over time. As many as 74% of migrants had worked there seasonally at least twice and 38% had done so at least five times. This last figure is high because nearly 30% of these persons only started to migrate to Germany for seasonal employment during the period 1999-2001. In order to increase their earnings from this source, some households send more than one person abroad at a time. Furthermore, certain migrants work in Germany illegally between their consecutive spells of migration for officially approved seasonal work. The ISS study found that 16% of migrant workers travelled at least once to Germany after their last seasonal job, and one in four of them worked informally. Moreover, 52% of all past migrants planned their next migration for legal seasonal work for within the following two years, and 22% of them expressed their intention to travel for an individually arranged job (two-thirds of whom stated an intention to do seasonal work).

Migrants generally originate from peripheral regions of Poland, half of them from urban areas composed mainly of small or medium-sized towns. If seasonal migrants are categorised according to their principal administrative district of origin (49 in total),[13] it is evident that they were initially, in 1991 and the subsequent two to three years, recruited from metropolitan or highly urbanised areas, such as Wroclaw, Katowice, Warsaw, Walbrzych, Poznan and Krakow. A smaller number originated from much less urbanised areas where as a rule, the majority of the population lived in villages such as Chelm, Ciechanow, Skierniewice, Wloclawek and Sieradz. In the highly urbanised areas, the

---

11.   A quarter of all seasonal migrants are unemployed and another quarter are inactive in Poland.

12.   More striking however is the fact that 11.1% of migrants apparently have completed tertiary education. This by any standards means that these persons were considerably over-qualified for the jobs available under the bilateral agreement.

13.   This administrative division was in existence until 1997, when the 49 districts were re-organised into 16 large regions. However, the National Labour Office presents statistical data on migration for seasonal work using the old divisions until 2001 (comprising 49 districts).

unemployment rate was generally lower than the national average, whereas it was higher in the less urbanised areas.[14]

The situation has changed substantially over time. Between 1991 and 2001, the overall number of seasonal migrants rose by a factor of 3.8. Districts with relatively low levels of urbanisation and a relatively high unemployment rate witnessed a very large increase in migration for seasonal work (*e.g.* Zamosc by 11.6 times, Rzeszow by 10.7, Kielce by 7.1 and Olsztyn by 6.7). Districts with a relatively high level of urbanisation and relatively low unemployment recorded less significant changes (*e.g.* in Wroclaw the numbers dropped by a factor of 2.5, Katowice by 1.9, Poznan by 1.2 and Warsaw by a striking drop of 40%). This suggests that after what may be called an exploratory or pioneering period, seasonal work migration to Germany has become more beneficial for inhabitants of the less developed regions of Poland and less beneficial for people from relatively well-off regions.

It might also be mentioned that from the very beginning of the programme, German employers knew precisely who they wanted to employ as Polish seasonal workers. The number of non-nominative job offers arriving in Poland was invariably very low and never exceeded 2 000 (or 1.5% of all job offers). To illustrate this, in 1992 at least 60 000 new seasonal workers came to Germany from Poland, but only 931 non-nominative job offers were available in that period. It seems to be an indisputable fact that employers had contact with workers prior to their employment. In any case for a large number of employees, this suggests that they had previously been seasonal workers in the German labour market. Prior to 1991 practically no opportunities existed for the legal employment of Polish residents in Germany, so it might be argued that those persons had worked there illegally. Therefore the bilateral agreement on seasonal employment concluded in 1990 between Germany and Poland may have redirected many thousands of Poles from the informal to the formal labour market in Germany.

The ISS study attempted to verify this hypothesis. It turned out that three-quarters of migrants who worked in Germany in 1998-2000 had visited foreign countries even before 1991, the year in which the bilateral agreement came into effect. About 41% had visited Germany, of whom 17% had been gainfully employed during a visit and an additional 13% had earned money as petty traders.[15] Moreover, a quarter of migrants whose first official seasonal work took place in 1991 or 1992 earned money in Germany before the bilateral agreement was signed. Finally, it may be mentioned that a large majority of seasonal workers are involved in a migration network linking three major groups: German employers, past migrants from Poland and potential migrants from Poland. Nearly 40% of past migrants were active in such a network and stated that they had helped a family member or a friend to obtain a seasonal job in Germany. Two-thirds of former migrants did this more than once.

Work in Germany

The regions which hosted the largest numbers of seasonal workers from Poland were: Bavaria (20%), Nordrhein-Westfalen (17.5%) and Baden-Württemberg (16%), followed

---

14.   A number of exceptions to this however were observed from the very beginning. For instance the districts of Kielce, Konin and Opole were major participants in seasonal migration in spite of their relatively low level of urbanisation and a moderate unemployment rate.

15.   Among those who met the bilateral agreement minimum age of 18 at the time the agreement became effective, 44% had visited Germany before and one-third of these stated that they had earned money during a visit.

by Hamburg, Hessen and Rheinland-Pfalz (altogether 26%). As mentioned earlier, from the onset of the programme agriculture was the main sector attracting migrants from Poland. Between 1999 and 2001 three agricultural areas were open to Polish seasonal workers in Germany: horticulture (mainly asparagus and tobacco), fruit growing and viticulture. Almost 85% of all jobs were provided in these areas. Poles were mainly employed as vegetable, fruit or flower pickers (64%) or performed relatively more specialised functions in plant-growing (15%), sorting fruit or vegetables (5.5%) or storage (3%). Other functions which were less frequent (*e.g.* laundry or kitchen help, cleaning, loading/unloading of goods, etc.) as a rule required relatively less skills.[16] All in all, these jobs are very simple; they do not require any professional skills and do not offer workers any opportunities to improve their qualifications. Moreover, the specific organisation of work by employers generally involves nationally homogeneous teams,[17] which reduces the possibility of migrants learning German. In fact, a knowledge of German, let alone proficiency, is irrelevant for the large majority of Polish workers. Sixty-two per cent of migrants do not know any German and claim that this has never interfered with their work. Firms (mainly agricultural farms) that offered jobs to Polish seasonal migrants were relatively small: 55.5% of migrants worked in firms with up to 25 employees and of those two-thirds were firms with 6 to 25 employees. Only 17.8% were employed on big farms with more than 100 workers.

While the average duration of a single employment contract remained constant between 1991 and 2001 (between 7 and 8 weeks), the intensity of work and the level of wages changed substantially over time. The average net wage rate as estimated by employees themselves tended to decrease after 1994, from DEM7.55 per hour to DEM7.05 per hour (in 2000), in contrast to the trend in the gross wage rate.[18] On the other hand, daily and weekly working hours are on the rise. For instance, the average number of hours per week increased from 52.9 hours in 1992 to 62.3 hours in 2000, and the average number of hours per working day in the same period increased from 8.95 hours to 10.15 hours. It is likely that seasonal migrants from Poland worked longer, in order to compensate for declining real wage rates.

German employers and experts[19] almost unequivocally point to the positive aspects of having easy access to the seasonal employment of Polish labour. They hardly mention the related disadvantages. Because of insufficient labour supply in local labour markets, the hiring of foreign labour for seasonal work has become an economic necessity for employers, who generally believe that the specific institutional features of the German-Polish arrangement (the bilateral agreement and the associated administrative procedures) are a necessary condition for the benefits acquired by German firms. However, it is believed that the seasonal employment programme owed its success less to an efficient bureaucracy and the low cost of official recruitment, than to a smooth functioning of the informal hiring of labour, that is through the networks controlled by the leaders of various

---

16.   It is noteworthy that only 0.1% of migrants worked as head of a team, whereas during their first seasonal employment in Germany, this proportion was as much as 1.1%.

17.   For instance on average, 78% of Poles worked on horticultural farms, 73% in fruit growing/picking and 72% in exhibitions. Between 1991 and 1997, on the whole that share has been growing constantly (40% to 73%) and from 1997 to 2001 remained relatively stable at a very high level.

18.   On average it decreased between 1994 and 1997 (from DEM8.38 to DEM7.82 per hour) and then increased to DEM9.05 in 2000. The gross wage here is that which is fixed in an employment contract and the net wage is that actually paid to a worker after various deductions, including the cost of accommodation arranged by the employer.

19.   Experts in the ISS study are usually the representatives of employers associations.

migrant teams.[20] One of the major consequences of the arrangement is said to be the elimination of incentives to employ workers illegally. In praising the overall institutional arrangement, employers also emphasize the need for a reduction of bureaucracy on the part of local German labour offices and a wider relaxation of the three-month limit of employment.[21] This would apparently lead to an additional 100-150 000 seasonal workers being brought in from Poland. To explain the fact that Poles are the most sought after seasonal workers in Germany, employers refer above all to the well-developed Polish migrant networks mentioned above, the relatively high productivity of Polish workers in German firms, as well as the very strong motivation and high flexibility of those workers.[22]

A preliminary assessment

Main reasons for the success of the programme

Migration for seasonal work under the German-Polish bilateral agreement has been steadily growing. In 2000 in as many as 50 of the local administrative units (county, in Polish *powiat*) or 13% of the total, at least 3% of the workforce was seasonally employed in Germany. In turn, by and large, those migrants were able to fill an acute labour shortage in a segment of the German labour market. This alone would be enough to consider the programme to be a success. The programme has been working efficiently both because of its institutional simplicity and its low costs. Administrative procedures are not burdensome and are rapidly completed. Fees paid by the workers and employers are only symbolic and the costs borne by the administration are relatively low. However, bilateral agreements concluded by Germany with several other CEECs at about the same time and on similar terms as that with Poland have not resulted in any significant migration for seasonal work from these countries.

The success in the Polish case, compared to other CEECs, stems not just from appropriate institutional arrangements but from the interplay of two complementary factors. One feature largely missing in the case of CEE countries other than Poland seems to be that of well-developed migrant worker networks. The second is that Polish seasonal workers have a currently privileged position relative to for example, Bulgarians, Romanians or Slovaks. This position may have its origins in the fact that prior to 1990 Polish citizens travelled widely internationally, which remains fairly unique among the former Soviet bloc countries. It was this factor which proved conducive to large-scale clandestine work by the Poles in Germany in the 1980s and to the establishment of networks of informal contacts between Polish migrants and German employers.

---

20. This method of contracting seasonal workers is said to bring about various advantages such as the possibility of selecting workers according to desired personal characteristics (sex, age, strength, loyalty and sometimes even marital status). Neither employers nor employers' representatives indicated that knowledge of German was relevant for migrants.

21. The present regulations compel many employers to recruit annually at great cost two or three shifts of seasonal workers from Poland, because a season in the case of their enterprises extends from four to nine months a year. As mentioned above, only in the exhibition sector are contracts of up to nine months currently allowed.

22. Bearing in mind the relatively short duration of a typical employment contract and the rather low ratio of German to Polish wages, migrants from Poland are strongly motivated not only to be productive but also to work as many hours a day (and days a week) as possible.

Fulfilment of policy goals in Poland

In the implementation of the bilateral agreement, the Polish government had only a narrow margin within which to actively pursue its major policy aim, that is, giving regions with very high unemployment priority in access to job offers arriving from Germany. The fact that an overwhelming majority of offers were addressed to specific persons prevented Polish authorities from having any direct influence on the economic mobility of the workforce, and especially from helping the unemployed. The spontaneous development of the programme however exerted a systematic influence on the labour market in Poland. First of all, a trend was observed toward including more unemployed workers and less employed workers in the programme. In contrast to the initial three to four years of the programme, the later period showed a growing positive correlation on a local level between local job opportunities and the intensity of migration to Germany for seasonal work. This can be illustrated by Map 1, which presents the number of seasonal migrants as a proportion of all economically active persons for each local administrative unit in 2000. A striking conclusion is that nearly all units displaying a relatively high proportion of seasonal migration to Germany were remote from Poland's major economic growth areas and employment centres, such as Warsaw, Katowice, Gdansk, Poznan and Lodz. The ISS study also revealed the fact that the units with the highest proportion of that specific migration flow were affected by particularly high unemployment.

There is, however, another conclusion which emerges from the study. An analysis of the various migration flows of seasonal migrants to Germany by labour force status (employed, unemployed and inactive) suggests a considerable outflow (12.3%) from employment to unemployment between the migrant's first and second migration. For some migrants, this seems to be a conscious strategy of searching for the greater flexibility required of seasonal workers. With subsequent migrations, however, the probability of status change dramatically diminishes. A plausible interpretation might be that repeat migrations tend to preserve the *status quo* and limit the chances of unemployed and inactive migrants becoming employed. It was found that this trend is, to a large degree, dependent on the general labour market situation in Poland, which means that a deteriorating situation characterised by high and rising unemployment rates reduces the probability of flow from unemployment to employment.

Impact on the regularity and legality of employment in Germany

In the 1980s many Polish temporary migrants worked illegally in Germany. The ISS study suggests that a significant proportion of migrants who were employed between 1991 and 2001 under the bilateral agreement had been illegal workers in Germany prior to 1991. In other words, the bilateral agreement has helped transfer many Poles going to work in Germany from the informal to the formal economy. In the 1991-2001 period the incidence of illegal employment among persons who migrated for authorised seasonal work seems to have been very low. About 2% of seasonal workers from Poland overstayed in Germany after the expiry of their contract.[23] A similarly small proportion (4%) migrated to Germany for illegal employment after completing a season of employment there.

This kind of migration between prior and subsequent authorised seasonal jobs, however, is rare. In other words, migrants who have the chance to be legally employed in Germany, even though the duration of the majority of the contracts is very short, might be

---

23.   This estimate however may be considerably biased as it does not count migrants who discontinued their contracts in Germany before 1998, some of whom may have done so to work illegally.

effectively discouraged from seeking employment informally. It should be noted, moreover, that whilst performing their legal contracts, seasonal migrants worked overtime (more hours a day or more days a week than specified in their contracts) or had an extra job with a different employer. Almost 58% worked overtime and about 5% had an extra job, in both cases depending on whether the seasonal worker concerned had undertaken several previous seasonal contracts.

Costs and benefits for individual migrants: short-term and long-term perspectives

Migrants evaluate rather highly their general level of personal satisfaction with seasonal work in Germany. Only 12.3% expressed dissatisfaction. Surprisingly, migrants who were employed in Poland have a higher rate of satisfaction with their experience than those who have been unemployed or economically inactive in Poland. This might partly be attributed to different expectations and to the functions which the money saved in Germany plays for the three groups of migrants. For migrants with a job in Poland, it is mainly supplementing other often far more important earnings and permitting the purchase of non-essential consumer goods, whereas for the reminder the main function is, as a rule, to finance necessities (*e.g.* purchase of food stuffs, current payment for utilities). On the other hand, because of a higher degree of relative deprivation, the expectations of the unemployed, housewives, pensioners and the like who seek seasonal employment in Germany are probably considerably higher than those who have a job in Poland.

In addition, migrants generally feel that their family economic situation improves as a result of seasonal work in Germany although only 17.3% report a significant improvement. Indeed in objective terms, migrants savings actually transferred to Poland are very important in household budgets. The ISS study revealed that seasonal workers saved on average per annum EUR1 100 (net) in recent migration,[24] which amounted to around 18.5% of average annual household (net) income in 2000. In other words, every euro earned by each household member in Poland during the year was, on average, supplemented by as much as EUR0.23 brought in by a migrant (which was earned over a tiny fraction of the year). On the other hand, taking a long-term perspective, pecuniary incentives related to seasonal work in Germany have been gradually diminishing. Despite an increasingly heavy workload in Germany between 1991 and 2000, the net nominal amount of money transferred to Poland remained stable. In the same period however nominal wages and the cost of living in Poland continued to increase steadily.

In contrast, the change in the labour market situation in Poland, especially since the end of 1998, has become an increasingly important stimulus to seasonal migration. A structural job deficit in Poland affecting mostly the young, the low-skilled and the inhabitants of peripheral areas, makes seasonal work in Germany one of the few viable employment opportunities for many people. In a way, seasonal employment in Germany has become a buffer during the hard times of Poland's transition to a market economy. In the longer run, the growing dependence of an increasing number of Poles on seasonal employment in Germany might be a factor in their lasting social and economic marginalisation. During their work in Germany, Polish migrants do not acquire new skills or even German language proficiency. Moreover, some migrants are unemployed upon their return to Poland in between contracts abroad; they are increasingly out of touch with local labour market requirements and their skills are becoming outdated.

---

24. The actual average amount of money transferred to Poland in 2000 was 27% higher than this (approximately EUR1 400). The difference stemmed from the costs borne prior to migration (*e.g.* visa, travel, canned or dried food, sometimes health insurance or other items).

Map 12.1. **Polish seasonal workers in Germany in 2000 by administrative unit of origin**

(as percentage of all economically active persons in a given unit; figures in bracket denote the actual numbers of units of local administration)

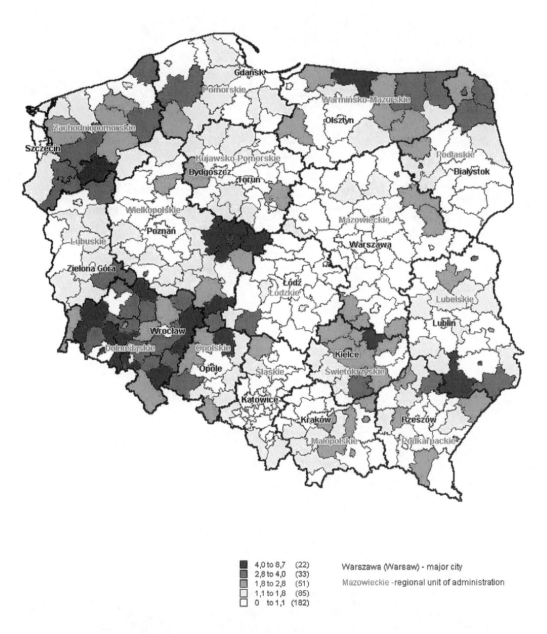

■	4,0 to 8,7	(22)
▓	2,8 to 4,0	(33)
▒	1,8 to 2,8	(51)
□	1,1 to 1,8	(85)
□	0 to 1,1	(182)

Warszawa (Warsaw) - major city

Mazowieckie - regional unit of administration

Source: The ISS study.

Chapter 13

RECRUITMENT OF NURSES IN ROMANIA BY THE FRIULI-VENEZIA-GIULIA REGION IN ITALY

by

Jean-Gabriel Barbin

President, Association Balkans Pays de la Loire

In 2002, the Autonomous Region of Friuli-Venezia-Giulia created a programme to recruit registered or general nurses from Romania to supplement the region's shortage estimated at 2 000 nurses. In the framework of this programme, the region formed an association under Romanian law, the *Association de Préparation et de Perfectionnement Professionnel* (APP), to improve the quality of recruitment, which remains under the region's political responsibility. This non-profitmaking organisation is a consortium of its representative body in Bucharest, Centrum, a major trade union, *Le Bloc National Syndical* and Balkans Pays de la Loire (a French nongovernmental organisation with a medical and cultural purpose). APP has three principal roles regarding the implementation of the recruitment programme: to evaluate candidates, to prepare successful candidates for expatriation and, if necessary, to participate in retraining individuals. From the onset, this programme made it possible to identify certain characteristics of this socio-professional category in Romania.

- The skills levels of nurses vary widely across the country, for the same age range, in the regions, and even in the same hospital.

- The recent unemployment of several hundred nurses, due to restructuring of the hospital system (bed closures).

- A large share (35%), during the first series of interviews, of highly-specialised nurses willing to work abroad as general nurses, due to the difficulty of their work and the professional risks against which they were poorly protected.

- The majority of nurses were from hospitals.

The programme was also able to clarify three points. First, the monthly Romanian salary, in euros, after 15 years of service, is ten times less than the net salary of an entry-level nurse in Italy. Moreover, the savings possible by a Romanian nurse working in Italy are equivalent to the cost of a house in the home country. Second, the lack of guarantees that nurses will find employment after working for one year abroad has been the subject of recent measures (especially fiscal ones) taken by the Romanian government to provide them with an incentive to return. Third, post-baccalaureate education for a nursing degree is composed of a three-year cycle in the private education sector.

The programme's implementation also confirmed the importance of five programme elements. The first requirement regards facilitating the procedure for expatriation in both the Romanian and the Italian administrations. Delays in the receiving country are mostly due to problems of diploma recognition, which are not addressed in an efficient and secure manner. The second element is the need to facilitate flows among several groups: nurses who are just finishing their training, unemployed nurses who wish to find new work, nurses who are looking to work abroad and the nursing vacancies, especially in specialised posts, resulting from the emigration flows of these nurses. The third point regards the importance of having an on-site capacity to evaluate the professional abilities of candidates. This is the only way to guarantee quality of care. A concrete evaluation of skills cannot be determined from an administrative case-by-case recognition of diplomas or by signing a bilateral agreement on equivalencies. Fourth, it is particularly valuable, not only for efficacy but also for the utmost protection of patients, to prepare workers for emigration so that they integrate quickly on a socio-professional level. Finally, it is critical that the sending country also benefits from emigration within this occupational category. The programme must consider several elements simultaneously: responding to the receiving country's needs, protecting workers' rights and preventing the sudden void of highly-specialised nurses in the sending country (associated with high training costs).

These five elements confirmed that it was absolutely critical to provide support to the temporary recruitment programme by developing a co-operation programme that focuses both on initial training and re-training. This programme would include the following components:

- *Trainee posts (with a student status)*: These practical and non-theoretical training posts would occur in the receiving country. The training would be in addition to the regular three-year curriculum in Romania. Romanian nursing schools could offer this additional training year, without making it mandatory to students. These internships would facilitate a concrete evaluation of the trainee and, for example in the case of France, could lead to a temporary permit allowing work as a salaried employee in the receiving country.

- *Contract posts for the purposes of training*: Based in the receiving country, these posts could retrain registered or general nurses. Contract posts could also fill vacancies in speciality nursing fields and could be offered to registered or general nurses either at the beginning or upon completion of their temporary employment contract.

- *Professional training posts*: These posts, based in the sending country, would be specifically designed for retraining chiefly unemployed nurses and could be sponsored with European funds.

In conclusion, these types of programmes are best tested in a regional framework. Regions offer certain flexibility in the programme's implementation and provide a distinct advantage to monitor effectiveness. These recommendations could help to partially offset labour shortages in areas which are particularly affected during holiday periods and at the same time facing the pressure of high tourism. In addition, the observations from this programme also hope to best prepare these employees for their imminent ability to move across the enlarged European labour market.

CONCLUSIONS

by
Martine Durand

Deputy Director, Directorate for Employment, Labour and Social Affairs, OECD

The main aim of the Montreux Seminar was to offer participants an opportunity to exchange and obtain information on bilateral labour agreements and other forms of recruitment of foreign workers. In my view, the Seminar fully achieved its aim. Some very informative papers were drafted for this Seminar and the debates on how all the procedures operate and compare, how they are evaluated and how they are likely to develop were particularly interesting and stimulating.

The discussions illustrated the wide range of situations to be found across the OECD area. Bilateral labour agreements are part of a long tradition in some member countries, such as Germany and Switzerland, which was the first to sign such agreements as early as 1890. In others countries they are more unusual and are put to very different uses. They now cover only a small share of employment-related migration and of migration flows in general. Finally, some countries such as Canada, Australia and New Zealand have little experience of bilateral agreements, while others like the United States or the United Kingdom have opted to develop other employment-related migration programmes.

That being so, I should like to pose three questions that summarize the conclusions reached during the seminar debates: What exactly are the objectives of bilateral labour agreements? Are such agreements effective in achieving those objectives? Are there other ways of achieving the objectives? I should like to address each of these questions individually, and hopefully add some input for discussion.

What are the objectives of bilateral labour agreements?

It was clear that the objectives of bilateral labour agreements are many and various, but not necessarily mutually exclusive.

From the *receiving country* standpoint, the primary aim is to meet labour market needs by facilitating short-term or medium to long-term adjustment. In the first case, the agreements cover temporary migrants, including seasonal workers, and are more specifically concerned with demand for low-skilled labour. In the medium to long-term, however, the agreements focus more on skilled workers to tackle the more structural labour shortages (*e.g.* in information and communication technology, or healthcare).

Host countries also have recourse to bilateral agreements in order to manage migration and combat or curb illegal migration. Some agreements, particularly those on temporary workers, pursue that objective. Others also seek to promote the longer-term integration of immigrants.

Receiving countries may also wish to promote economic links with a number of countries. The aim here, via migration, is to promote the regional economic integration and development of sending countries. Examples include the bilateral agreements that Germany has signed with some Central and Eastern European countries.

One final objective is aimed more specifically at strengthening cultural ties between partner countries. During the seminar, we learnt about Australia's Working Holiday Maker programme and its ties with a growing number of countries.

As for *sending countries*, their objectives are to ensure better living conditions and earning capacity for migrant workers, and to promote the acquisition or enhancement of vocational skills and qualifications. Along with remittances, technology transfers and building human capital both foster the development of countries of origin.

Sending countries also see employment-related migration as a way of managing the international mobility of their own citizens, with particular emphasis on the return of skilled workers (*e.g.* South Africa as regards its nurses and doctors).

Finally, sending countries are now placing increasing emphasis on the rights and welfare of their own nationals working abroad, to ensure the best possible conditions for employment-related migration.

Are bilateral labour agreements effective in achieving the above objectives?

The effectiveness of these agreements is not easy to assess when there are so many objectives. To achieve a short-term labour objective, the key to success lies in flexibility. Agreements that are too bureaucratic, complex and costly have every chance of failing. It is important to take account of the salient features of the agreements and the countries concerned, for example those between Germany and Poland. Also of interest are the procedures introduced by the United Kingdom, and in particular those leading to the delivery of a work and residence permit within 24 hours.

For longer-term adjustment, as in the case of workers in the information and communication technology or healthcare sectors, migration alone cannot alleviate labour shortages. Basically, the solution lies in the structural reform of host-country labour markets and training systems. This calls for better human resource management, all the more important to meet the challenges of an ageing population.

To prevent shortages of skilled labour in the OECD area by the year 2030 and maintain high levels of growth, it is time that member countries began thinking about how better to mobilise their untapped labour reserves and ensure that human resources in general acquire the required skills through lifelong learning. This was in fact the theme of the Employment and Labour Ministerial meeting held at the OECD on 29 and 30 September 2003.

Immigration, after all, can only be a supplementary solution. Given the size of the immigration flows required to alter the structural trend towards population ageing, it is unrealistic to believe that immigration alone can offset future labour shortages, not to mention demographic decline. Furthermore, the very size of the flows would pose serious integration problems.

As for objectives such as combating illegal immigration, or improving migration management, the examples cited during the seminar showed that bilateral agreements were not always very effective. In fact it all depends on the type and content of the agreement. In Switzerland, for instance, the agreements allowing seasonal workers to return several times a year for periods of up to nine months have proved to have their limits, and the status of foreign seasonal worker has recently been abolished there.

When there are multiple objectives, making it harder to assess whether agreements are effective, there is bound to be a trade-off. Some objectives may actually conflict. In that case, effectiveness will depend on their respective weighting. For instance, if the aim is to promote rapid labour-market adjustment, there may be security problems, one reason being the lack of information on new arrivals.

Then again, attempts to tackle labour shortages may raise ethical problems such as a brain drain and undermine the objective of promoting economic development in sending countries.

More generally, bilateral agreements, like international trade agreements, may raise the possibility of third countries being excluded. In other words, bilateralism may run counter to multilateralism. It is worth bearing in mind that while world governing bodies such as the World Trade Organization oversee trade, there is no such body to monitor migration.

But regardless of the objectives, the proposal by our International Labour Organization (ILO) colleague merits discussion. The proposal is to promote social dialogue by involving the social partners in drawing up and monitoring migration agreements, to enable all of the stakeholders to benefit.

Are there other ways of achieving these objectives?

Some countries have experimented with approaches other than bilateral agreements. To meet labour market needs, the United-States and Canada, for instance, have given priority to transparency in the regimes governing migration, namely temporary migration - which is for a very specific duration and governed by very precise rules (*i.e.* limited renewal) - and permanent migration, which is also subject to very detailed criteria. Such systems make for better migration flow management and are therefore effective in terms of that objective. They are probably effective too in meeting medium-term needs on the labour market. However, because they require the introduction of new, lengthy procedures, they prove less effective in meeting the short-term needs of the labour market.

Over the longer term and for skilled labour in particular, a comprehensive approach (based on selective policies as in Australia, Canada and New Zealand, for instance, or special visas, as in the United States) is probably more effective than bilateral agreements.

To conclude, the lively discussions that took place on migration (and many other subjects) during the two-day seminar go to show that one size does not fit all. What is effective and acceptable in one country will not necessarily be so in another. Individual adjustments are vital. Again, the purpose of the seminar was to exchange information and in that respect participants learned a great deal from the experiences they shared. We were able, through these helpful discussions, to "clear the ground" and address numerous issues, but did not come up with definitive solutions.

ANNEX 1.A

PRINCIPAL AGREEMENTS SIGNED
BY OECD MEMBER COUNTRIES

Table 1.A.1. **Bilateral labour agreements signed by OECD member countries**[1]

Country	Seasonal employment	Project-based workers	Guest workers	Stagiaire, trainee and apprenti-ceship	Cross-border employ-ment	Working holidaymaker	Others	New agreements under consider-ation
Australia				Switzer-land		Canada Cyprus Denmark (01) Finland (00) France (03) Germany (00) Hong Kong – China (00) Ireland Italy (03) Japan ('80) Korea Malta Netherlands Norway (01) Sweden (01) United Kingdom	Turkey ('67)	WHM:[2] Austria Belgium Chinese Taipei Greece Iceland Malaysia Portugal Singapore Spain Switzerland United States
Austria	Canada		Turkey ('64)	Canada Czech Rep. (01) Hungary ('98) Switzerland	Czech Rep. (01) Hungary ('98)			Australia (WHM) Slovak Republic
Belgium			Italy ('46, '54) Turkey ('64)	Canada Poland ('90) Switzerland				Australia (WHM)
Canada	Antigua and Barbuda Austria Barbados Dominican Rep. Grenada Jamaica Mexico Montserrat St Kitts and Nevis St Lucia St Vincent and the Grenadines Trinidad and Tobago			Armenia Austria Belarus Belgium Czech Republic Finland France Germany Ireland Lithuania Netherlands New Zealand Poland Russia Slovak Republic South Africa Spain Sweden Switzerland United Kingdom United States		Australia France Germany Ireland Japan ('86) Korea Netherlands New Zealand Sweden United Kingdom	Mexico, United States (NAFTA profession-nals)	Italy (WHM)

Country	Seasonal employment	Project-based workers	Guest workers	Stagiaire, trainee and apprenti-ceship	Cross-border employ-ment	Working holidaymaker	Others	New agreements under consider-ation
Czech Republic	Bulgaria ('99) Germany ('91) Poland (02)	Germany ('91)	Bulgaria ('99) Germany ('91) Mongolia ('99) Poland ('92) Russia ('98) Ukraine ('96) Vietnam ('94)	Austria (01) Canada France ('30) Germany ('91) Hungary ('99) Lithuania (00) Luxembourg ('99) Switzerland ('97)	Austria (01)		Germany for the recruitment of house-keepers. Slovak Rep. ('92) for mutual employment without work permits	
Denmark				Switzerland		Australia New Zealand		
Finland		Estonia ('91) Russia ('92)		Canada Netherlands Russia Slovak Rep. ('98) Switzerland United Kingdom ('88)		Australia (00)		
France	Morocco ('63) Poland ('92) Tunisia ('64) Yugoslavia ('65, '86)		Italy ('47) Morocco ('63) Tunisia ('64) Turkey ('64) Spain ('56)	Argentina ('95) Canada ('56) Czech Rep. ('30) Hungary (00) Morocco (01) New Zealand ('83) Poland ('90) Senegal (02) Switzerland ('46) Slovak Rep. (02) Turkey ('50) United States ('88, '92) Yugoslavia ('32)	Italy ('58)	Australia (03) Canada Japan ('99) New Zealand	Algeria ('64 with last amendment in 01)	

Country	Seasonal employment	Project-based workers	Guest workers	Stagiaire, trainee and apprenticeship	Cross-border employment	Working holidaymaker	Others	New agreements under consideration
Germany	Bulgaria (02) Croatia Czech Rep. ('91) Hungary ('92) Poland ('90) Romania ('99) Slovak Rep. ('91) Slovenia	Bosnia-Herzegovina Bulgaria ('91) Croatia ('88) Czech Rep. ('91) Hungary ('89) Latvia ('92) FYROM ('95) Poland ('90) Romania ('90) Slovak Rep. ('91) Slovenia ('88) Turkey ('61) Yugoslavia ('88)	Albania ('91) Bulgaria ('92) Croatia (02) Czech Rep. ('91) Estonia ('95) Hungary ('89) Latvia ('93) Lithuania ('92) Norway ('97) Poland ('79, '90) Romania ('92) Russia ('93) Slovak Rep. ('96) Slovenia ('96) Turkey ('61)	Canada Czech Rep. ('91) New Zealand (00) Poland ('90, students only) Russia Slovak Rep. ('91) Swltzerland	Poland ('90)	Australia (00) Canada Japan (00) New Zealand	Poland ('96) for holiday training For specific recruitment in: construction of wooden houses (Estonia, '02); housekeeping (Poland, Slovak Rep., Hungary, Czech Rep., Slovenia); nurses (Croatia, Slovenia)	
Greece	Albania Bulgaria ('95)							Australia (WHM)
Hungary	Germany ('92) Romania (00) Slovak Rep. ('99)	Germany ('89)	Germany ('90) Norway (until 04) Slovak Rep. ('99)	Austria ('98) Czech Rep. ('99) France (02) Ireland Luxembourg ('96) Netherlands ('97) Romania (00) Switzerland ('95)	Austria ('98)		Germany for the recruitment of house-keepers	
Ireland				Canada Hungary Poland (00)[3] Switzerland		Australia Canada New Zealand		
Italy	Albania ('97) France ('51) Switzerland ('64)[4] Tunisia (00)		Belgium ('46, '54) France ('47) Luxembourg ('57) Netherlands ('48, '60) United Kingdom ('47)	Netherlands ('54) New Zealand Switzerland	France ('58) Slovenia ('91)	Australia (03) New Zealand (01)	Romania for recruitment in catering, IT, healthcare[5]	Canada (WHM) Moldova (framework agreement) Poland (trainees and seasonal agreement)

Country	Seasonal employment	Project-based workers	Guest workers	Stagiaire, trainee and apprenticeship	Cross-border employment	Working holidaymaker	Others	New agreements under consideration
Japan						Australia ('80) Canada ('86) France ('99) Germany (00) Korea ('99) New Zealand ('85) United Kingdom (01)		
Korea						Australia Canada Japan ('99) New Zealand		
Luxembourg			Italy ('57)	Bulgaria (02) Czech Rep. ('99) Hungary ('96) Poland ('96) Romania (01) Slovak Rep. ('98) Switzerland				
Mexico	Canada Spain (02)						Canada, United States (NAFTA professionnals)	
Netherlands	Access of seasonal workers is regulated by the general regime for temporary work permits		Italy ('48, '60) Morocco ('64) Turkey ('64)	Austria Canada Finland Hungary ('97) Italy ('54) Sweden Switzerland		Australia Canada New Zealand		
New Zealand				Canada France ('83) Germany (00) Italy Switzerland		Argentina Canada Chile Denmark France Germany Hong Kong (China) Ireland Italy (01) Japan ('85) Korea Malaysia Netherlands Singapore Sweden (01) United Kingdom		
Norway			Germany ('97) Hungary (until 04) Poland (until 04) [3]	Switzerland		Australia	Philippines (03) for recruitment in healthcare	

Country	Seasonal employment	Project-based workers	Guest workers	Stagiaire, trainee and apprenticeship	Cross-border employment	Working holidaymaker	Others	New agreements under consideration
Poland	Czech Rep. (02) France ('92) Germany ('90) Spain (02)	Germany ('90, '93)	Belarus ('95) Czech Rep. ('92) Germany ('79, '90) Libya ('80) Lithuania ('94) Norway (02)[3] Russia ('94) Slovak Rep. ('92) Spain (02) Ukraine ('94) UK-Jersey (01)[3]	Belgium ('90) Canada France ('91) Germany ('90) Ireland (00)[3] Luxembourg ('96) Spain (02) Switzerland ('93)	Germany ('90)		Germany ('96) for holiday training Germany for recruitment of house-keepers	Italy (trainees, seasonal workers)
Portugal	Bulgaria (02) Switzerland[4]		Bulgaria (02) Cape Verde ('97) Russia (02) Ukraine (02)	Switzerland			Romania (01) for temporary residence in Portugal during job search	Australia (WHM) Moldova (temporary employment) Slovak Rep. (temporary employment)
Slovak Republic	Germany ('91) Hungary ('99) Russia ('95) Ukraine ('97)	Germany ('91) Russia ('95) Ukraine ('97)	Germany ('91) Hungary ('99) Poland ('92) Russia ('95) Ukraine ('97)	Canada Finland ('98) France ('30, 02) Germany ('91) Luxembourg ('98) Switzerland ('95) Vietnam ('94)			Czech Rep. ('92) for mutual employment without work permits Germany for recruitment of house-keepers	Austria Portugal (temporary employment)
Spain	Colombia (01) Dominican Rep. (02) Ecuador (01) Mexico (01) Morocco (01) Poland (02) Romania (02) Switzerland ('61)[4]		Columbia (01) Ecuador (01) France ('56) Morocco (01) Poland (02) Romania (02)	Canada Dominican Rep. (02) Poland (02) Romania (02) Switzerland			Dominican Rep. (02) Colombia (01) Ecuador (01) Morocco (01)	Australia (WHM) Bulgaria
Sweden			Turkey ('67)	Canada Estonia ('90) Latvia Lithuania Netherlands Philippines Switzerland		Australia (01) Canada New Zealand (01)		

Country	Seasonal employment	Project-based workers	Guest workers	Stagiaire, trainee and apprenticeship	Cross-border employment	Working holidaymaker	Others	New agreements under consideration
Switzerland	Italy ('64)[4] Portugal[4] Spain ('61)[4]			Argentina Australia Austria Belgium Bulgaria Canada Czech Rep. Denmark Finland France Germany Hungary Ireland Italy Luxembourg Monaco Morocco Netherlands New Zealand Norway Philippines Poland Portugal Romania Russia Slovak Rep. South Africa Spain Sweden United Kingdom United States	Austria ('73) France ('58) Germany ('70)		Bilateral agreement on the Free Movement of People (only EU nationals)	Australia (WHM)
Turkey			Austria ('64) Belgium ('64) France ('64) Germany ('61) Jordan ('83) Libya ('75) Netherlands ('64) Qatar ('86) Sweden ('67)	France ('50)			Australia ('67)	
United Kingdom			Belgium ('47) Poland (01) with Jersey[3]	Canada Finland ('88) Malta ('92) Switzerland United States ('87)	British Commonwealth countries[6] Japan (01)		For recruitment of nurses in: India; Philippines (02); Spain (00)	
United States				Canada France ('88) Switzerland United Kingdom ('87)			Canada, Mexico (NAFTA professionnals)	Australia (WHM)

Notes to Table 1.A.1:

FYROM: Former Yugoslav Republic of Macedonia.

1. This table does not intend to be exhaustive nor does it indicate the actual status of the agreements, unless otherwise indicated. The digits in parentheses indicate the date of the agreements' signature (for 20th century dates, others 21st century). Many agreements are reciprocal, that is, for the mutual employment of workers. For more details on selected agreements, see Tables 1.A.2 to 1.A.6 of this annex.

2. WHM indicates Working Holidaymaker agreements.

3. Agreed conditions by both sides, but no signed agreement.

4. Seasonal employment permits were abolished in Switzerland as of 2002.

5. Agreements with regional or provincial administrative unit in host country.

6. In addition to the United Kingdom, the British Commonwealth countries include Antigua and Barbuda, Australia, Bahamas, Bangladesh, Barbados, Belize, Bermuda, Botswana, Brunei, Cameroon, Canada, Cayman Islands, Cyprus, Dominican Rep., Fiji, Gambia, Ghana, Grenada, Guyana, Hong Kong (China), India, Jamaica, Kenya, Kiribati, Lesotho, Malawi, Malaysia, Maldives, Malta, Mauritius, Mozambique, Namibia, Nauru, New Zealand, Nigeria, Pakistan, Papua New Guinea, Samoa, St Kitts and Nevis, St Helena, St Lucia, St Vincent and the Grenadines, Seychelles, Sierra Leone, Singapore, Solomon Islands, South Africa, Sri Lanka, Swaziland, Tanzania, Tonga, Trinidad and Tobago, Tuvalu, Uganda, Vanuatu, Zambia, Zimbabwe and other British Dependent Territories (BDTC)/British Overseas Territories (BOTC).

Table 1.A.2. **Recruitment of seasonal workers by OECD countries**

Receiving country	Sending country	Duration (months)	Main sectors	Total number	Description
Austria	Canada	Up to 6	Tourism, agriculture forestry		Bilateral Young Workers Exchange Program limited to graduates and students of colleges and universities of tourism, agriculture and forestry. Annual quota of 50 slots for each country.
Canada	Antigua and Barbuda Austria Barbados Dominican Rep. Grenada Jamaica Mexico Montserrat St Kitts and Nevis St Lucia St Vincent and the Grenadines Trinidad and Tobago	From 6 weeks to 8 months	Agriculture	16 700 (2000)	Bilateral agreement with Commonwealth Caribbean countries and Mexico (SAWP)
Czech Republic	Croatia Bulgaria Kazakhstan	Up to 6	Not specified	Not yet implemented	The arrangements for seasonal labour are part of the bilateral employment agreement for exchange of labour. It includes skilled labour. Annual quotas are set in protocols signed by the parties.
	Poland	Up to 3	All sectors		Bilateral agreement
	Germany	Up to 3	All sectors	1 466 (1999) 1 452 (2000) 1 218 (2001) 1 306 (2002)	Bilateral agreement
	Poland	Up to 3	All sectors		Bilateral agreement

Receiving country	Sending country	Duration (months)	Main sectors	Total number	Description
France	Morocco	Up to 6	Agriculture (90%) hotel and catering	3 946 (2000)	Bilateral agreement
	Poland	Up to 6	Agriculture (90%)	No quota 2 723 (1999) 3 336 (2000) 4 519 (2001) 7 013 (2002)	Bilateral agreement
	Tunisia	Up to 6	Agriculture (90%) hotel and catering	537 (2000)	Bilateral agreement
	Yugoslavia	Up to 6	Agriculture (90%) hotel and catering	54 (2000)	Bilateral agreement
Germany	Bulgaria	Up to 3 in one calendar year	Catering and hotel industry (bars excluded)	332 (1999) 825 (2000) 1 492 (2002)	Arrangements between the employment services of both countries for employment of seasonal workers.
	Croatia	Up to 3 in one calendar year	Agriculture	5 101 (1999) 5 943 (2000) 5 826(2002)	Arrangements between the employment services of both countries for employment of seasonal workers.
	Czech Republic	Up to 3 in one calendar year	Agriculture, forestry, viniculture, entertainment and hotel trade, juke joints, construction	2 157 (1999) 3 126 (2000) 3 036 (2001) 2 958 (2002)	Agreement between the Ministry of Labour and Social Affairs (Czech Rep.) and the Federal Labour Office (Nuremberg) on Procedure of Mediation of Employment in the Germany.
	Hungary	Up to 3 in one calendar year	Agriculture and forestry, catering, vegetable and fruit processing	4 082 (2002)	Bilateral agreements. Worker may participate several times. No quota. No qualification required and no age limits. Annual total varies usually between 4 500 to 5 000.
	Poland	Up to 3 in one calendar year; exhibitions, 9.	Agriculture, forestry, hotels, catering, construction (until 1993), exhibitions	201 681 (1998) 218 403 (1999) 238 160 (2000) 261 133 (2001) 282 830 (2002) Exhibitions: 9 080 (2002)	Declaration signed by both ministries of labour. This also includes recruitment of short-term staff for exhibitions. No quota.

Receiving country	Sending country	Duration (months)	Main sectors	Total number	Description
Germany (cont')	Romania	For gardeners, up to 9; all other workers, up to 3.	Agriculture, services, gardening	7 499 (1999) 11 842 (2000) 20 902 (2002)	Agreement for short-term employment of migrants mainly in seasonal occupations.
	Slovak Republic	Up to 3 in one calendar year	Mainly agriculture	10 332 (2002) 9 559 (2001) 7 694 (2000)	Agreement between the Ministry of Labour, Social Affairs and Family (Slovak Rep.) and the Federal Labour Office (Nuremberg) on the use of German labour offices as employment intermediaries. Employment offers may be for individuals or anonymous. Scope of employment according to the labour market situation. No quota.
	Slovenia	Up to 3 in one calendar year	Agriculture	311 (2000) 302 (2001) 252 (2002)	Arrangements between the employment services of both countries for employment of seasonal workers.
Greece	Albania	3 to 6	Services, agriculture	Not active	
	Bulgaria	3 to 6	Depending on labour market needs	Never implemented	Agreements between both governments on the reciprocal employment of seasonal workers. After the first contract expires, worker cannot sign another contract within 6 months. Offers can be for individuals or anonymous. The agreement had a two-year duration and was never utilised.
Italy	Albania Tunisia	n.d.	Tourism, agriculture	Quota for Albania: 6 000 (for 2001) 3 000 (for 2002) Quota for Tunisia: 2 000 (for 2002)	The employment of seasonal labour is determined by the governments using an annual quota. The quota is also stipulated in the respective bilateral agreements.
Norway	EEA and non-EEA nationals	Up to 3	Agriculture	9 894 (2000) 11 920 (2001)	Not a bilateral agreement. EEA nationals may take up seasonal jobs without a permit. Non-EEA nationals need a work permit. Annual quotas are based on the reported needs of the agricultural sector. 95% of seasonal workers originate from the CEECs (mainly Poland).

Receiving country	Sending country	Duration (months)	Main sectors	Total number	Description
Poland	Spain	9	Agriculture	No labour received	Agreement on the conditions of employment in Poland and Spain.
Portugal	Bulgaria Romania	Specified in each labour contract	Depends on the employers' proposals	Not started yet	Each agreement includes all forms of employment, including seasonal labour and is signed for five years. They regulate the employment of workers in all signatory countries. Entry requirements are specified in each employment proposal submitted by the employer.
Slovak Republic	Hungary	Up to 6	Agriculture	1 244 (2002)	Agreement for Exchange of Labour Annual quota 200
Spain	Bulgaria (new agreement under consideration)	Up to 9	n.d.	No quota. Not started yet	Agreement for the regulation of migration between the two countries. The Ministries of Labour act as intermediaries for labour market demand, which is determined by a joint committee.
	Colombia Ecuador Dominican Rep. Mexico Morocco Poland Romania	Up to 9	Agriculture and other sectors (depending on the employers' proposals)	For Poland: 600 (2001) 1 244 (2002) For Romania: No quota 500 (2002)	Reciprocal bilateral agreements for the regulation of migration between the two signatory countries. The Ministries of Labour act as intermediaries for labour market demand, which is determined by a joint committee. Agreement on the conditions of employment in Poland and Spain and employment of seasonal workers. For Romania, arrangements for seasonal labour are part of the Agreement for Labour Exchange and seasonal workers are obliged to sign an engagement to return at the expiration of their contract.
Switzerland	Seasonal labour permit was abolished in 2002 and replaced with short-term residence and the Bilateral Agreement on the Free Movement of People (the latter for EEA-nationals only).	Less than 12 (short-term residence permit)	Agriculture 13% Hotel, catering 48% Construction 31%	54 900 (2001) 49 300 (2000) 2001 detail: 75% male; 67% aged 35-49. In construction, 60% Portuguese 14% Italians and 9% Germans	

Receiving country	Sending country	Duration (months)	Main sectors	Total number	Description
United Kingdom	Non-EEA nationals	Minimum 5 weeks and maximum 6 months	Agriculture and horticulture	Quota: 18 700(2002) 25 000 (2003) 25 000 (2004) In 2002, Poland 26%, Ukraine 21%, Bulgaria 12%	Applicants must be full-time students and at least 18 years old. Individuals may participate more than once provided they continue to meet conditions and undertake a minimum break of 3 months between periods of participation.

Note: n.d. indicates not defined.

Table 1.A.3. **Guest worker agreements signed by OECD countries**

Receiving country	Sending country	Duration	Annual quota and total number of participants	Description
Czech Republic	Bulgaria	Up to 12 months with possible 12 month extension	2 761(1999) 2 697 (2000) 2 986 (2001) 2 989 (2002)	Bilateral agreement for the mutual employment of citizens. Work permit or trade license required. Agreement targets young, educated skilled labour.
	Mongolia	Up to 12 months with possible 12 month extension	797 (1999) 891 (2000) 1 204 (2001) 1 375 (2002)	Bilateral agreement on mutual employment. Work permit or trade license required.
	Poland	Up to 12 months with unlimited extension	No quota set, but in line with labour market needs. 7 913 (1999) 8 712 (2000) 7 712 (2001) 8 419 (2002)	Mutual employment of labour. Work permit or trade license required. General foreign labour recruitment rules are applied.
	Russia	Up to 12 months with possible 6 month extension (for work permits)	2 701 (1999) 2 858 (2000) 2 777 (2001) 2 597 (2002)	Bilateral agreement on the mutual employment of citizens. Work permit or trade license required.
	Slovak Rep.	Unlimited	No quota 61 320 (1998) 53 154 (1999) 63 567 (2000) 63 555 (2001) 56 558 (2002)	Agreement between the Slovak Republic and the Czech Republic on the mutual employment of citizens. Employment without work permits upon registration with relevant labour office.
	Ukraine	12 months with possible 12 month extension	Annual quota: 30 000 16 646 (1999) 15 753 (2000) 17 473 (2001) 19 958 (2002)	Bilateral agreement on mutual employment. Work permit or trade license required. Agreement was signed for five years and officially terminated in early 2002, which has not reduced the annual flow.
	Vietnam	Up to 12 months with unlimited extension	19 000 (1999) 19 382 (2000) 20 466 (2001) 20 231 (2002)	Bilateral agreement on mutual employment. Work permit or trade license required.
Germany	Poland	12 months with possible 18 month extension	Annual quota: 1000 776 (2002) 830 (2001) 655 (2000)	Agreement on employment of guest workers. Project designed for young workers with a purpose of improving the professional and language skills (on-the-job-training). Skilled workers aged 18-40.
	Romania	12-18 months	Annual quota: 500	Agreement on employment of guest workers. Skilled workers aged 18-35. Several years experience and professional qualification is required.

Receiving country	Sending country	Duration	Annual quota and total number of participants	Description
Hungary	Slovak Rep.		2001 quota: 800 for regular and 200 for seasonal work 2003 quota: 2 000 for regular and 200 for seasonal work. 1 244 (2000)	Agreement between the Slovak Government and Hungarian Government on mutual employment of citizens (for both guest and seasonal workers). Excludes posts in the civil service.
Norway	Hungary	Long-term	Not active	Recruitment of Health care personnel (nurses, radiologists, anaesthesiologists). Agreement signed between the ministries.
	Philippines	Long-term	Project was cancelled due to the lack of interest.	Recruitment of nurses (mainly for elderly care) who have education following American standards.
	Poland	1 to 4 years	44 (2002)	Programme of co-operation on the recruitment of medical personnel is approved and signed at the director's level.
Poland	Belarus Lithuania Russia Ukraine	12-18 months	Not active	Agreement on mutual employment.
	Czech Rep.	n.d.	Not active	Agreement signed between the former Czechoslovakia and Poland on the mutual employment of Czech, Slovak and Polish citizens. General foreign labour recruitment rules are applied.
	Germany	12-18 months	Annual quota: 1 000 No labour received	Agreement on employment of guest workers. Project designed for young workers with a purpose of improving the professional and language skills (on-the-job-training). Recruiting skilled workers aged 18-40 mainly for the hotel and catering sector.
	Libya		400 (1993) 117 (2000) 30 (2001) 7 (2002)	Agreement on employment of Polish workers and their working conditions
	Norway	6-9 months	No labour received	Employment of medical personnel. Entry requirements are the agreed conditions by the two signatories.
	Slovak Rep.	n.d.	No quota set, but in line with labour market needs. 22 (2002)	Agreement signed between the former Czechoslovakia and Poland on the mutual employment of Czech, Slovak and Polish citizens. Individual employment of citizens (excluding civil service) and implementation of temporary student status. General foreign labour recruitment rules apply.
	Spain	more than 12 months	No labour received	Agreement on the conditions of long-term employment in Poland and Spain, mostly in the transportation sector.

Receiving country	Sending country	Duration	Annual quota and total number of participants	Description
Portugal	Bulgaria		Not ratified by the Portuguese Parliament	Agreement on the reciprocal hiring of citizens and Attached Protocol. One agreement includes seasonal, guest workers and project-linked employment. Entry conditions are specified in the employment offer. Agreement aims to facilitate the recruitment of labour and combat illegal trafficking of labour.
	Cape Verde	12 months with possible 2 year extension	About 300 to 400 per year	Portuguese employers may recruit workers in Cape Verde for tasks the internal offer is not able to satisfy. Work is mostly in construction. Employers are responsible for workers' transport between Cape Verde and Portugal.
	Romania		Not ratified by the Portuguese Parliament	Agreement on the temporary stay of Romanian citizens for employment purposes in Portugal. One agreement includes seasonal, guest workers and project-linked employment. Agreement aims to facilitate the recruitment of labour and combat illegal trafficking of labour.
	Russia		Not ratified by the Portuguese Parliament	Agreement on temporary labour migration of Russian citizens to Portugal. Entry conditions specified in the employment offer.
	Ukraine		Not ratified by the Portuguese Parliament	Agreement on the temporary migration of Ukrainian workforce to Portugal. Entry conditions are specified in the employment offer.
Slovak Republic	Czech Rep.	n.d.	2 119 (1998) 2 229 (1999) 2 227 (2000) 2 013 (2001) 2 023 (2002)	Agreement between the Slovak Republic and the Czech Republic on the mutual employment of citizens. Employment without work permits upon registration with relevant labour office.
	Hungary	n.d.	2001 quota: 800 2002 quota: 2 000 63 (2001) 87 (2002)	Agreement between the Slovak Government and Hungarian Government on mutual employment of citizens for seasonal employment and guest workers.
	Poland	n.d.	No quota set, but in line with labour market needs. 619 (1999) 165 (2000) 186 (2001) 119 (2002)	Agreement signed between the former Czechoslovakia and Poland on the mutual employment of Czech, Slovak and Polish citizens. Worker must be at least 18 years old. General foreign labour recruitment rules are applied.

Receiving country	Sending country	Duration	Annual quota and total number of participants	Description
Slovak Republic *(cont.)*	Russia	n.d.	Three quotas: 1200 persons to perform contracts; 150 guest workers; 150 persons for seasonal employment. Total workers: 130 (1999) 121 (2000) 112 (2001) 116 (2002)	Employment of workers posted to perform contracts on the territory of both states and individual and seasonal employment of citizens
	Ukraine		Quota: 200 for individual employment; 300 for seasonal employment; 1 800 for posted workers. Total workers: 516 (1999) 434 (2000) 326 (2001) 297 (2002)	Agreement between the Slovak Government and Ukrainian Government on mutual employment of citizens
Spain	Poland	More than 12 months	n.a.	Agreement on the conditions of long-term employment in Poland and Spain, mostly in the transportation sector.
	Romania	At least 12 months	n.d.	Agreement for exchange of labour between Romania and Spain. The agreement also regulates seasonal labour and short-term migration. It includes provisions obliging the two countries to initiate programmes for voluntary return of migrants. Selection is organised by both sides depending on the job offers.
United Kingdom (Jersey)	Poland	6-9 months		Jersey (UK): short-term employment in co-operation with Jersey Tourism Committee and Jersey Hospitality Association. Medical staff selected.

n.d. indicates not defined.

1. Totals in this column refer to the number of workers from the receiving country officially working in the sending country. For the Czech Republic (receiving country), these figures correspond to the total of working permits and trade licenses issue to foreigners under bilateral agreements.

Table 1.A.4. **Selected list of trainee and trainee agreements signed by OECD countries**

Receiving country	Partner country	Quota	Duration (months)	Annual number of participants (quota utilisation)	Age limits (years)	Description
Austria	Canada		6 months		18-30 (except-ionally 35)	Young workers exchange in field of study (forestry, agriculture, tourism)
	Czech Rep.	Under negotiation	n.a.	Not started yet	Up to 30	Training agreement
	Hungary	300 (1999) 400 (2000) 600 (2001) 900 (2002)	Up to 12 months	Full take-up of quota	Up to 35	Apprenticeship agreement
Belgium	Poland	250	12-18 months	The agreement is not active (1-2 trainees per year)	18-30	Agreement on employment of skilled workers as trainees from Poland
	Slovak Rep.	25	No limit	Not implemented	No limit	Convention between the Czechoslovak Government and Belgium on admission of foreigners intending to improve their language and professional skills
Canada						See partnering countries for selected program details.
Czech Republic	Austria	Under negotiation	n.a.	Not implemented	Up to 30	Exchange of trainees
	Canada	n.a.	1	n.a.	18-30	International youth exchange and tourism – employer specific
	France	100	n.d.	Not implemented	no	Agreement between competent authorities of Czechoslovakia and France with the purpose to facilitate acceptance of trainees
	Germany	1 400	12 with possible 6 month extension	n.a.	18-40	Agreement between the former Czechoslovakia and the former West Germany on the mutual employment of those nationals to improve their vocational and language proficiency. Work permit required regardless of labour market situation.

Receiving country	Partner country	Quota	Duration (months)	Annual number of participants (quota utilisation)	Age limits (years)	Description
Czech Rep. *(cont')*	Hungary	400	Up to 12 months	Not started	n.d.	Apprenticeship agreement
	Lithuania	200	n.a.		n.a.	Exchange of trainees. Agreement has not yet been signed.
	Luxem-bourg	30	12-18 months	n.a.	18-30	Exchange of trainees
Finland	Canada	n.a.	18 months	n.a.	18-30	Canada-Finland Career Development Program. Requires employer-specific and career-related post. Applicant must be a college or university graduate within the past two years.
	Slovak Rep.	No quota	n.d.	5-6 per year	18-30	Agreement between the Ministry of Labour, Social Affairs and Family (Slovak Rep.) and the Centre for International Mobility (Finland) on the exchange of trainees
France	Canada		3-18 months	265 (2002)	18-35	Agreement for the exchange of students looking for training courses, temporary jobs or summer jobs
	Czech Rep.	100	12-18 months	Not implemented	Workers aged 18-35	Agreement between competent authorities of Czechoslovakia and France to facilitate acceptance of trainees (workers)
	Poland	1 000	12-18 months	10.1% (1999) 11.5% (2000) 28.9% (2001) 26.4% (2002)	18-35	Agreement on exchange of trainees
	Slovak Rep.	100	12-18 months	Not implemented	Workers aged 18-35	Agreement on exchange of trainees (workers)
	Hungary Morocco New Zealand		3-18 months	15 (2002) 94 (2002)	18-35	Agreement on exchange of trainees
	United States		3-12 with possible 18 month extension	98 (2002)	18-35	Agreement on the exchange of trainees. Only for employment in the private sector. Minimum of two years of completed higher education.

Receiving country	Partner country	Quota	Duration (months)	Annual number of participants (quota utilisation)	Age limits (years)	Description
Germany	Canada	n.a.	18 months	n.a.	18-30	Canada-Germany Young Worker Exchange Program. Employer must be in specific field of study.
	Czech Rep.	1 400	12 with possible 6 month extension	446 (1999) 649 (2000) 783 (2001) 639 (2002) Utilization ratio generally between 59.5% to 69.1%	18-40	Agreement between the former Czechoslovakia and West Germany on employment of workers to improve their professional and language skills. For persons with basic German language proficiency. In 2002, majority of permits issued in catering/restaurant, nursing and construction fields.
	Poland	No quota	No limit	580 (1999) 585 (2000) 1 334 (2001) 1 285 (2002)	No limit	Declaration signed by both Ministries of Labour on the employment of Polish students
	Poland	No quota	Up to 3 months	200 (2000) 267 (2001) 323 (2003)	No limit	Agreement on working holidays. Mainly in hotels and catering industry
	Slovak Rep.	1000 Pre- 2001 quota: 700	12 with possible 6 month extension	914 (2000) 850 (2001) 848 (2002)	18-40	Agreement between former Czechoslovakia and Germany on employment of workers to improve their professional and language skills. Excludes posts in the civil service.
Hungary	Austria	300 (1999) 400 (2000) 600 (2001) 900 (2002)	Up to 12 months	No Austrian applicants	Up to 35	Apprenticeship agreement
	Czech Rep.	400	12-18 months	not active	n.a.	Apprenticeship agreement
	France	300	12-18 months	8 (2002)	up to 35	Exchange of trainee
	Ireland	n.d.	Maximum 24 weeks	not active	n.d.	Trainee agreement
	Netherlands	no quota	12	not active	at least 18 years	Exchange of nationals for the purpose of training
	Luxembourg	20	12-18 months	2-3 persons	up to 35	Exchange of trainees
	Romania	700	12 months	3	No limit	Apprenticeship and seasonal agreement

Receiving country	Partner country	Quota	Duration (months)	Annual number of participants (quota utilisation)	Age limits (years)	Description
Ireland	Canada	n.a.	12 with possible 12 month extension	n.a.	16-28	International Fund for Ireland. Work must be employer-specific or for "open" employment authorisation, in which case an occupation restriction must be specified if the applicant has not passed the immigration medical. Once the applicant has completed the medical requirements, the term and condition can be removed.
	Poland	No quota	No limit	75 (2000) 74 (2001) 130 (2002)	No limit	Exchange of trainees according to rules accepted by Polish Ministry of Labour and Social Policy (not a bilateral agreement)
Luxem-bourg	Bulgaria	30	12-18 months	Not yet implemented	Up to 35	Exchange of trainees with good language skills, professional education
	Czech Rep. Poland Slovak Rep.	30 30 20	12-18 months	2-3 persons per year in each country	18-30	Exchange of trainees
	Hungary	20	12-18 months	2-3 persons per year	Up to 35	Exchange of trainees
	Romania	35	12-18 (possible 6 month extension)		18-35	
Poland	Belgium	250	12-18 months	No students received	18-30	Agreement on employment of skilled trainees from Belgium
	France	1 000	12-18 months	No students received	18-35	Agreement on exchange of trainees
	Germany	No quota	No limit	No students received	No limit	Declaration signed by both Ministries of Labour on the employment of foreign students
	Luxem-bourg	30	12-18 months	No students received	18-30	Agreement on exchange of skilled trainees

Receiving country	Partner country	Quota	Duration (months)	Annual number of participants (quota utilisation)	Age limits (years)	Description
Poland (cont.)	Spain	50	12-18 months	No students received	n.d.	Agreement on the management and organisation of migration flows in both countries. For the employment of Spanish and Polish trainees (with a purpose of improving the professional and language skills).
	Switzerland	150	12-18 months	No students received	18-35	Agreement on exchange of trainees/students.
Slovak Republic	Belgium	25	No limit	Not implemented	No limit	Convention between the Czechoslovakia and Belgium on admission of foreigners intending to improve their language and professional skills
	Finland	No quota	n.d.	1-2 per year	18-30	Agreement between the Ministry of Labour, Social Affairs and Family (Slovak Rep.) and the Centre for International Mobility (Finland) on the exchange of trainees
	France	100		Not implemented		Agreement between competent authorities of Czechoslovakia and France with the purpose to facilitate acceptance of trainees
	Germany	1000 pre-2001: 700	12 with possible 6 month extension	No trainees received	18-40	Agreement between former Czechoslovakia and Germany on the employment of workers to improve their professional and language skills.
	Luxembourg	20	12-18 months	No trainees received	Up to 35	Exchange of trainees
	Switzerland	100	12-18 months	No trainees received	18-35	Exchange of trainees
	Vietnam	n.a.	n.d.	n.d.	No	Agreement for the training of Vietnamese workers
Spain	Poland	50	12-18 months	102 (2002)	n.d.	Agreement on the management and organisation of migration flows in both countries. For the employment of Spanish and Polish trainees (with a purpose of improving the professional and language skills).
Sweden	Switzerland	No quota	3 months	Not received	Up to 30	Exchange of trainees

Receiving country	Partner country	Quota	Duration (months)	Annual number of participants (quota utilisation)	Age limits (years)	Description
Switzer-land	Argentina Australia Austria Belgium Bulgaria Canada Czech Rep. Denmark Finland France Germany Hungary Ireland Italy Luxemb-ourg Monaco Morocco Nether-lands New Zealand Norway Philippi-nes Poland Portugal Romania Russia Slovak Rep. South Africa Spain Sweden United King-dom United States	50 50 150 100 100 200 100 150 150 500 500 100 200 50 50 20 50 150 20 50 50 150 50 150 200 100 50 50 100 400 200	12-18 months	Total hosted in Switzerland: 800 (1999) 1 100 (2000) 1 300 (2001) For example: - Hungary: 86 (1999) 86 (2000) 100 (2001) 114 (2002) -Czech Rep., usually 2 to 30 persons annually None from the Philippines, Poland, Slovak Rep. and the United Kingdom	Generally 18-30 18-35 for Argentina Bulgaria Czech Republic France Germany Monaco Romania Slovak Republic South Africa United Kingdom United States	Reciprocal agreements on the exchange of trainees. Annual quota set in each agreement and valid for each signatory country. Unutilised units can be transferred to the following year. Agreement with Italy not yet operational.
United States	France	n.a.	3-18 months	319	18-35	Agreement on exchange of trainees. Minimum of two years of completed higher education.

n.a. indicates information was not available to author;. n.d. indicates not defined.

Table 1.A.5. **Agreements on cross-border employment by OECD countries**

Country	Signatories	Quotas	Length of stay	Number of cross-border commuters	Sectors	Aims
Austria	Czech Rep.	Under negotiation	Up to one year	3 992 Czech workers in Austria (March 2003) or 1.86% of the foreign workforce	Services	The agreement is limited to cross-border workers who live in the border region and commute on daily basis. Working permits are required. Exceptionally can allow commuter to work in whole region of Austria not only in border regions. Working permits are issued after testing whether vacancy cannot be filled from domestic labour supply.
	Hungary	1 400	6 month work permits, with possibility of extension	1400 in Austria	60% to 70% in agriculture	Burgenland and Bruck/Leitha districts in Austria and Vas, Gyor, Zala counties in Hungary.
Germany	Poland	No quota	n.d.	n.d. for Germany No labour received in Poland.	Craftsmanship, agriculture, food processing, reparations	Declaration signed by the Ministries of Labour of Poland and Germany on the employment of residents of the border zone (commuting frontier workers, mostly odd jobs).
Switzer-land	EU member countries	No quota	Permit limited to the length of the employment contract if it is for less than 12 months. On presentation of an employment contract lasting at least 12 months, a 5-year cross-border commuter permit is granted.	168 088 (2001), or 7.8% increase on 2000. Details (2001): 66% male 33% aged 20-34 47% aged 35-49 19% aged 50-64 51% French 23% Italian 23% Germans	20% metal/machine 16% trade 8% construction 8% sales representation 8% hotel	Regulated by Bilateral Agreement on Free Movement of People. When the cross-border commuter permit is issued, the commuter must work in the frontier zone and must return home once per week. Commuters may be contracted employees as well as self-employed

Table 1.A.6. **Working holidaymaker schemes in OECD countries**

Host country	Signatories	Quota	Number of participants[1]	Scheme description
Australia (reciprocal)	Canada		6 230 (2002/03)	Scheme is for 12 months and for people aged 18 to 30. Scheme with Belgium is not yet in effect.
	Cyprus		n.a.	
	Denmark		1 091 (2001/02)	Participants in Australia may not be employed for more than 3 months with any one given employer
	Finland		13 (2001/02)	but there is no restriction on the type of employment. In Denmark and Italy
	France		effective 1 Jan. 2004	the work permit allows Australians to work for a maximum of 6 months and
	Germany		3 364 (2001/02); 7 558 (2002/03)	for no more than 3 months with any one given employer. In Finland
	Hong Kong (China)	200 (2002/03) entering Hong Kong (China)	2 412 (2001/02)	you may work for a maximum of three employers
	Ireland		10 799 (2001/02); 11 128 (2002/03)	each for no more than 3 months. Germany only allows 3 months of work. In Ireland
	Italy		effective 1 Jan. 2004	Hong Kong (China) and Norway Australians can work for no more
	Japan		9 711 (2002/03)	than three months with any given employer/
	Korea		4 656 (2001/02)	
	Malta		5 869 (2001/02)	The first year of the scheme in Italy will be limited to 1 500 Australians.
	Netherlands		5 729 (2001/02); 5 858 (2002/03)	
	Norway		428 (2001/02)	
	Sweden		77 (2001/02)	
	United Kingdom		40 968 (2001/02); 39 721 (2002/03)	
Canada (reciprocal)	Australia France Germany Ireland Japan Korea Netherlands New Zealand Sweden United Kingdom			Scheme is for 12 months and for people aged 18 to 30 except for Germany (3-6 months) Ireland (must also be post-secondary students) Korea (up to 25 only) and Sweden (must also be post-secondary students). Some agreements are employer-specific (Germany and Ireland).
Japan (reciprocal)	Australia France Germany Korea New Zealand United Kingdom			Scheme is for an initial stay of up to 6 months (one year for the United Kingdom) and for people aged 18 to 30 (up to 25 in principle for the United Kingdom). Participants can work in any kind of job part-time or full-time.

Host country	Signatories	Quota	Number of participants[1]	Scheme description
New Zealand (reciprocal)	Argentina	300; 300		Scheme is for a maximum of one year and for people aged 18 to 30. Total cap on working holidaymakers entering New Zealand is 20 000.
	Canada	800; 400		
	Chile	200; 200		
	Denmark	200; 200		
	France	500; 200		
	Germany	1 000; no cap		
	Hong Kong (China)	200; 200		
	Ireland	2 000; 1 000		
	Italy	250; 250		
	Japan	No cap; no cap		
	Korea	800;200		
	Malaysia	100; 100		
	Netherlands	500; no cap		
	Singapore	200; 200		
	Sweden	300; no cap		
	United Kingdom	9 000; no cap		
United Kingdom[2]	British Common-wealth (53 countries)	None		The scheme is for a maximum of two years and for people aged 17 to 30. Employment is possible in any sector on a full time basis for the duration of the stay (no part-time requirement).
	Main nationalities: Australia		17 000 (2000)	
	Canada		3 770 (2000)	
	New Zealand		6 350 (2000)	
	South Africa		9 570 (2000)	

1. For New Zealand, the first quota number is for nationals entering New Zealand, the second is the quota for New Zealanders in the partner country.

2. The UK scheme description reflects changes made in June 2003.

ANNEX 2.A

PROGRAMME OF THE SEMINAR ON BILATERAL LABOUR AGREEMENTS AND OTHER FORMS OF RECRUITMENT OF FOREIGN WORKERS

Seminar jointly organised by the OECD and the Swiss Federal Office of Immigration, Integration and Emigration (IMES)
Montreux, 19-20 June 2003

Thursday 19 June 2003

Opening Session
Statements by :
Mr. Dieter Grossen, Deputy Director, Federal Office for Immigration, Integration and Emigration, IMES, Switzerland
Mrs. Martine Durand, Deputy Director, Directorate for Employment, Labour and Social Affairs, DELSA/OECD

First Session: Overview of Bilateral Labour Agreements and Other Forms of Recruitment of Foreign Workers
Chair : Elizabeth Ruddick (Citizenship and Immigration Canada) and Dieter Grossen, IMES, Switzerland

- The scope and methodology of the OECD Study on Bilateral Labour Agreements and Other Forms of Recruitment of Foreign Workers

  Daniela Bobeva, Director, International Relations and EU Integration, Bulgarian National Bank

- Round table on the characteristics and challenges of bilateral agreements on seasonal and temporary workers, through examples from Switzerland, France, Germany and Poland.

- Round table on the characteristics and challenges of other forms of recruitment of foreign workers, temporary and permanent, through examples from the United Kingdom, Ireland, the United States and Australia

- Round table on « newcomers » through examples from the Czech Republic, Romania, Italy and Spain

Second Session: Recruitment of Foreign Workers and Evaluation of Policies in Practice

Chair: Dominique Labroue, Deputy Director, Directorate for Population and Migration, Paris, and Dagmar Feldgen, Ministry of Economy and Labour, Berlin

- Round table on the expectations of government authorities and employers in the area of new technologies and healthcare personnel through examples from Germany, Hungary, the United States, the United Kingdom and Switzerland

- Round table on the viewpoint of the social partners through examples from Poland, Bulgaria and Switzerland

General debate on the ways of reconciling the expectations of the different partners through examples from Canada, Romania and Switzerland

Friday 20 June 2003

Third Session: Labour Recruitment and Co-operation for Development

Chair : Roger Kramer, Director, US Department of Labor, Washington, and Antonio Maceda Garcia, General Director for Migration Movements, Madrid

- Presentation of the main results of the OECD study on the evaluation of and the prospects for foreign labour recruitment by Daniela Bobeva and Jean-Pierre Garson, OECD.

General debate on the challenges and limits to the negotiation of future bilateral labour agreements

- Labour migration and co-operation for development : what can be learned from several examples of partnerships in place at international and regional level (France, Germany, Spain, Italy, Romania, Bulgaria, Morocco, the Philippines and Ecuador)

Summary of Debates and Recommendations
Martine Durand, Deputy Director, Directorate for Employment, Labour and Social Affairs, DELSA/OECD.

Closing Session
Closing address by Mrs. Ruth Metzler-Arnold, Federal Counsellor, Head of the Federal Department of Justice and Police, Switzerland.